JO SWINSON
EQUAL POWER

JO SWINSON
EQUAL POWER

AND HOW YOU CAN MAKE IT HAPPEN

Atlantic Books
London

First published in Great Britain in 2018 by Atlantic Books,
an imprint of Atlantic Books Ltd.

Copyright © Jo Swinson, 2018

The moral right of Jo Swinson to be identified as the author of this work
has been asserted by her in accordance with the Copyright, Designs and
Patents Act of 1988.

10 9 8 7 6 5 4 3 2 1

A CIP catalogue record for this book is available from the British Library.

The extract from *Desert Flower* by Waris Dirie (Virago, 2001) is reproduced
by kind permission of Virago, an imprint of Little, Brown Book Group.

Every effort has been made to trace or contact all copyright holders. The
publishers will be pleased to make good any omissions or rectify any
mistakes brought to their attention at the earliest opportunity.

Hardback ISBN 978 1 78649 187 9
E-book ISBN 978 1 78649 188 6
Printed in Great Britain by Bell & Bain Ltd, Glasgow

Atlantic Books
An Imprint of Atlantic Books Ltd
Ormond House
26–27 Boswell Street
London
WC1N 3JZ

www.atlantic-books.co.uk

For Dad, who taught me the power of asking questions
For Mum, who showed me the strength that lies within

Contents

Introduction

You'd have thought I'd have figured it out before. After all, I had been a Member of Parliament for a decade, and Minister for Women for more than two years. But every time I made a comment on gender equality, only to find my words twisted wildly out of context by newspaper stories the next day, I assumed that it was my fault, that somehow I'd got it wrong. I hadn't been careful enough with my choice of language, or my meaning must have been unclear. Then it finally dawned that this media response was an inevitable part of the same endemic problem.

Gender inequality is everywhere. It is ingrained throughout society, in each and every one of us. We are all sexist, and so are our institutions and power structures. That's why attempts to challenge it are often met with such ridicule and resistance. There is no perfect form of words to express ideas of gender equality that will not be deliberately misunderstood by those who feel threatened by the prospect. So there's no point worrying about the shrieks of outrage from outlets that are committed to preserving the status quo of power inequality – where power is hoarded and concentrated in the hands of rich white men.

(*Daily Mail*, eat your heart out, I can't wait for your hot take on *Equal Power*.)

What I have learned about gender power in society is what I want to share with you in this book. Most of all, I want you to feel encouraged, empowered and emboldened to take action that will challenge gender inequality. Each chapter includes lots of ideas for things you can do, from having a conversation differently to campaigning for major change. When something resonates, or you come across something you'd like to do, please jot it down, and make a promise to yourself to try it out. We're all part of the problem to varying degrees – but equally, we can all be part of the solution.

Invisible, Unintentional, Universal

As a minister with a significant portfolio in the Department for Business, Innovation and Skills spanning corporate governance, employment law, competition policy, consumer affairs and the Post Office, my responsibility for Women and Equalities had to be fitted into about a fifth of my ministerial time (and this position had been tellingly forgotten in the 2012 reshuffle, so was not allocated to me until several days later). I'd initially viewed the equalities portfolio much like my other areas of responsibility, yet it was the most intractable and biggest of problems to address – and not only because of the difficulties of winning battles against Conservative members of the coalition government. The Department for Business had a budget of £26 billion, and 800 civil servants in one building alone, with thousands more across partner agencies. The Government Equalities Office had less than £20 million, and only narrowly avoided a further £6 million cut when I enlisted help from the Chief Secretary to the Treasury, my Liberal Democrat colleague Danny Alexander. Its 100 staff were cut to 50, and it featured low down in the official government pecking order.

But even with far greater resources, government alone is not going to solve the problem of gender inequality, because it is often invisible, unintentional and universal.

Celebrating the milestones in equality for women is important – such as the centenary of the first UK women achieving the right to vote in elections in 1918. But benchmarking against history can lead us into a false comfort about progress, instead of seeing the huge gulf that still exists and focusing on what we need to do to close it. A century on from women in the UK winning the right to vote, nowhere in the world has gender equality been achieved.

When I was 13, my school organised a day-long conference called 'You Can Do Anything' for all the girls in my year group. People who worked in a range of different jobs came and spoke about what they did and answered questions from the teenage audience – a firefighter, a scientist, a police officer, a salesperson, a council worker. This careers event was timed to broaden our horizons and inform our looming subject choices. While in subsequent years it was open to both boys and girls, it was clear that even in the early 1990s, people were trying to figure out why women were largely missing from some careers and what they could do to change it.

If you'd asked me, I'd have said I thought I could do anything. At the time I wanted to be an author; later on, inspired by Young Enterprise, I decided I wanted to go into business. My grandfather always said he thought I would be a politician. Throughout my

1980s childhood, it didn't cross my mind that it was unusual for a woman to be prime minister – the very act of being the first woman to lead the UK government is one of Margaret Thatcher's most powerful legacies, and it is too often dismissed in an understandable rage about the policies she advanced. Whatever you think of Theresa May's politics and judgement, girls growing up today take as read that a woman can run the country. But while symbolism and role models matter, even with a woman at the top, the corridors of power are stuffed with men.

When I arrived in Parliament as its youngest member in 2005, a fresh-faced 25-year-old full of anticipation, I'd have told you I didn't experience sexism. I expected the world to treat me on the same basis it would a man, and on the face of it, in the main, it appeared to do so. I didn't see the covert closed circles of men making the decisions, and they didn't see – or think it mattered – that they were all predominantly white men. When my husband Duncan was elected as an MP in 2010, the comparison between the experience of a man and of a woman as an MP was impossible to avoid. The lived experience of Parliament, of media scrutiny, the instinctive approach to situations, the acceptance into the club – all differed greatly.

The experiences of men and women in our society are different in countless ways, and as we don't walk in one another's shoes, these differences are often invisible.

Imagine that our society is a forest. Everyone is forging their own particular path. Gender inequality is pervasive: discriminatory laws and rules, sexist behaviour and incidents, gendered language and stereotypes, all form barriers across those varying paths to different degrees.

Introduction

A mildly sexist joke might be just a gossamer thread or a fern falling down, easy for most to brush off, but when meshed with thousands of other tiny injustices it becomes part of a strong web that is harder to push through. Some will make it, then find themselves covered in sticky cobwebs and scratchy briars that linger for miles. A law banning women from travelling or working without a man's permission, however, might be like an array of thick steel cables – a significant constraint and very hard to break.

Some of these roadblocks have been there for centuries, and at first glance it can be hard to tell which ones are so entrenched they have fossilised into impenetrable stone, and which have instead become a brittle facade and will fall away with a well-aimed kick.

All the while we make our way through the forest, we are spinning our own threads and webs of comments, assumptions and behaviours that can by turns constrain us, or float across and become fixed obstacles in the path of others. New barriers are produced constantly, whether the unintentional by-product of conversations and experiences, or in some cases a deliberate effort to preserve the status quo. The media outlets of some powerful rich white men create webs on an industrial scale, with publications like the *Sun* or the mainstream porn industry churning out their coils of misogyny and catapulting them far and wide.

The thick cords of sexual assault and violence against women are often darkly visible from miles away, and unite forest dwellers from all corners in their public condemnation. But these same cords can be translucent, and people often don't see those blocked by violence and sexual harassment when it is close to home.

The bindings of the balance of domestic responsibilities or of the pressure of body image blend into the background as part of the normal landscape, a permanent and apparently natural feature of the forest canopy. A man taking parental leave to care for his child is met with signs telling him he has clearly wandered down the wrong path and should turn back. Often the interlocking meshes of political under-representation and economic imbalances are barely seen from a distance, or can only be seen in a certain light, from a certain perspective. Young women beginning their journey may be pleasantly surprised by the relatively open track in front of them, and dismiss the warnings of older women about what lies ahead, assuming that the paths have been cleared since their mothers' day. Men may look across and imagine that women are facing a similar path to them, not seeing the myriad additional hurdles that women have to overcome to keep making progress.

Every now and again, a woman emerges in a clearing on higher ground – a position of power where everyone in the rest of the forest can see her. People look and point and say it proves that women can make it through the forest, quietly forgetting that the number of men in these clearings is so much greater. Some notice that these women are often covered from head to toe in a filthy gunge of cobweb, faces scarred and scratched from fighting through the thicket, and that as they reach this higher ground, from different corners of the forest comes a targeted assault of character assassination, sexualised abuse and patronising nonsense. These women brazen it out, holding their ground with grace and outward serenity. But plenty of women see this spectacle, shake their head and conclude: 'No way am I doing THAT.'

In addition to obstacles created by gender stereotypes, there are a wide range of forces that hinder or propel different people through the forest, such as race, religion, disability, income, nationality, sexual orientation and age.

Socio-economic, racial and other power imbalances are interwoven with the issue of gender. This story can only be told by recognising those interplays, dubbed 'intersectionality' by Kimberlé Crenshaw back in the 1980s, and still not widely enough understood.[1] Those imbalances are also topics worthy of full exploration in their own right, and as others have written more eloquently about them than I could, I encourage you to read their writings, too.

Plenty of people feel uncomfortable with the rigidity of gender norms, even those who are cisgender, or 'cis' – that is, they identify with the same gender as when they were born. There are many who do not define themselves as either a man or a woman, often describing themselves as gender-fluid or non-binary. Trans people identify with a different gender to the one they were assigned at birth. It is hugely important that trans and non-binary people are able to live freely without having to pretend to be someone they are not. Fighting prejudice against trans people is an important part of promoting gender equality. Indeed, restrictive and tightly defined gender roles in society are a problem for men, women and gender-fluid people alike, whether they are cis or trans.

The Power to Change

At the heart of this book is the issue of power, where it lies in our society and to what ends it is used. As a liberal, I distrust concentrations of power, whether in the hands of the state, large corporations, groups or individuals. A world of Equal Power is one where each individual is valued and can make their own genuine choices, free of fear and the constraints imposed by their gender. It is *not* a world of conformity where everyone has to be the same.

All sorts of things can confer power on people or institutions, depending on the circumstances: financial assets, fame, access to information, physical strength, property ownership, status within society or an organisation, political office, or control of media outlets. While different people will feel powerful or not depending on individual circumstances and situations, the gender imbalance in these centres of power is clearly weighted in favour of men as a group. That power imbalance is the focus of this book.

I'm a thirty-something, cis, able-bodied, middle-class, straight, white woman who happens to be a mother, an MP, Scottish, British, European, a liberal, a humanist and a feminist. All of these things have shaped my experiences and my path. Some of these are choices, some of these are innate. Some give me privilege and make it easier for me to navigate the world, others make it harder. We all tread our own path through the forest.

Instead of despairing at the state of the world, let's roll up our sleeves and change it. If we want a world where every new baby arriving in it has the same opportunity to thrive, then we all need to do what we can to clear the forest paths. Those with the easiest routes have the most responsibility, and often the greatest resources, but everyone can and should do their bit.

So this isn't just a book, it's a call to arms. You haven't just picked up some reading material for the commute, you're holding an action plan. The power I'm describing doesn't only lie with others – you yourself have the power to make a difference. So let's do it. Equal Power, here we come . . .

Jo Swinson
October 2017

1

POLITICS:
A Woman's Place
is in the House
of Commons

Gladys Eagar was born in 1913 in north London, the daughter of a print worker and a cleaner. Ninety-five years later, she visited the Houses of Parliament to watch the pomp and splendour of the State Opening. It was a wonderful day. She put on her favourite dress, bought a few years earlier for her grandson's wedding. Her middle son, Peter, picked her up from the maisonette where she lived in Winchmore Hill. She'd been there since 1947; her husband, David, worked for the gas board, and the flat came with the job. Even long after he'd retired, they continued living there in the home where they had raised their three sons. It was above a gas showroom, which later became an office furniture shop, and a door on the side street opened onto the steep staircase up to the living areas on the first floor. David walked with a limp which worsened with age, so they'd had a stairlift installed. When he died earlier that year, she'd decided to have the stairlift removed. Every day Gladys ventured out along the Broadway to chat to the shopkeepers and buy provisions, climbing the stairs and managing an independence of life that most of us will only be able to wish for in our nineties.

That morning, Peter helped her into the waiting taxi and they began the journey towards Westminster. The streets nearby were heavy with police and iron security barriers, and they were stopped by a cordon on the Embankment, some considerable distance from the entrance to Parliament. Approaching a nearby police van, Peter explained to the officer that he was taking Gladys to watch the State Opening, and asked whether there was anywhere closer that the taxi could drop them. The kindly officer encouraged them to jump in the van, and she helpfully drove them both along the road right up to the door of the House of Lords.

Gladys had always been a royalist, and a huge admirer of the Queen, and she was in awe of the sense of occasion. Her seat was in the Royal Gallery of the House of Lords, and she and the other invited guests there were shepherded into blocks of raised seating. She was a tiny woman - once 4'11" but the ageing process had concentrated her into a 4'9" stature. Struggling to see the events unfolding over the heads of those in front, she swapped with a taller gentleman so she could sit at the end of the row, with a perfect, unobstructed view down the gangway. At the allocated time, everything done with military precision, Her Majesty the Queen arrived in the royal coach, her crown and dress glittering, and made her way through Parliament. As she processed through the Royal Gallery, Gladys looked on with joy.

The span of Gladys's life had seen huge change. When she was born, women were unable to vote. Her early years saw the devastation of the First World War, and one million more women entering the labour market,[1] many stepping up to do the jobs left by men who were fighting on the front line. The suffrage movement gained ground, and in 1918 women won the right to vote with some restrictions, enfranchising about 40 per cent of women.[2] The first woman MP, Nancy Astor, sat in the House of Commons a year later, although it would take almost four decades for women to be allowed to sit in the House of Lords (1958). The first woman minister was Margaret Bondfield, appointed in 1924, and she became the first female Cabinet minister in 1929, shortly after women gained the right to vote on the same terms as men (1928).[3]

By the time of the Second World War, Gladys had married and become a mother, nursing her infant son and cradling him in shelters as London was bombarded from the air during the Blitz, all on her own while her husband David was working away tending injured RAF pilots in a special burns unit. Again, the role of women in the war effort was a catalyst for wider social change, and increasing numbers of women entered the labour market, even after marriage. Gladys worked as a dinner lady for 'pin money', but the family model was still very much the husband as breadwinner. By the time her sons married and started their own families in the 1960s and early '70s, women's role in the workplace wasn't seen in quite such limiting and patronising terms. Her daughters-in-law took up professional roles – one as a nurse, another as a teacher. In politics by this time, a total of seven women had become Cabinet ministers, though women were still very much the exception. Parliament was more than 95 per cent male. When the Conservative Party elected Margaret Thatcher as leader in 1975, Gladys had four grandsons and two granddaughters. Four years later, Thatcher became the UK's first ever woman prime minister, and a few months after that, Gladys's youngest grandchild was born. Another little girl, Joanne. Me. Twenty-five years later, I was elected to Parliament.

In my grandmother's 101 years, huge strides were undoubtedly made towards gender equality in our politics, and many glass ceilings were smashed. Yet I remember what she told me after her visit to the State Opening of Parliament. She said she had 'such a wonderful time, it's like things used to be' – the unfailing politeness and decorum, doors held open, people quick to offer assistance out of deference for age. I love that she had such an amazing day, and that the brilliant people who work in Parliament made it so special for her. But her remarks contained a wider truth that goes beyond courtesy and ceremony. There's no doubt about it, Parliament and our political system is too much 'how things used to be' in all sorts of areas where it should have moved with the times.

Gladys sadly died in 2015, but there are still people alive today who remember a time when women were not even allowed to vote in Britain. That is how scarily recent such a grave political injustice is – and indeed in many other countries it took much longer to rectify. Women in Switzerland were only allowed to vote in 1971.[4] In 2015 women in Saudi Arabia voted for the first time in local elections.[5, 6]

There is a real danger that we fall into the trap of comparing now to days gone by and concluding that because things are better, things are fine. In the UK, women MPs comprise roughly one-third of the House of Commons. We have our second woman prime minister in Theresa May, Nicola Sturgeon serving as Scotland's First Minister, and the most powerful politician in Europe is German Chancellor Angela Merkel. But this is far from political equality, and these historic achievements can mask continuing underlying problems and a power imbalance in politics. Just as Barack Obama's presidency did not mean the end of racism in the US, individual women getting to the top of politics does not mean that political power is shared equally between men and women.

Welcome to Parliament

Wandering the corridors of the Houses of Parliament as a new MP at the age of 25, I was deeply aware of having arrived at a historic institution. The building itself feels like a maze, full of doorways tucked away and secret staircases that seem to move, Hogwarts-style. The grandeur and dated splendour is both beautiful and dominating - it took me a long time to feel like I fitted into these surroundings. People were friendly, but with a firmness for tradition that could make you feel like an alien in your own workplace. I remember my friend Jenny Willott, also newly elected, telling me that she had been gently but pointedly told off by one of the doorkeepers. She had, apparently, done two things wrong. The first was to go into the House of Commons chamber wearing a coat. The second had been removing the coat while in the chamber. At times, it felt like you couldn't win.

Over time I got used to the weirdness of the institution, and found my voice and place within it. It took me longer to study and start to understand how political power ebbed and flowed, however. I think I expected that power came with positions – for example as an elected MP, or a government minister. The truth is much more complex, so let me tell you what I have learned about the nuances of political power.

I hadn't fully recognised, even as an opposition MP, all the constraints that ministers were working under: legal advice, government procedures, the need to secure collective agreement, party management. I naively assumed individual ministers could just snap their fingers and make a decision to accept an amendment to a bill they were taking through Parliament.

There are many places political power lies. Party leaders, of course – though there are more checks than you'd think on their ability to manoeuvre. Then there's the machinery of government, including ministers, civil servants, 'private offices' and special political advisers (SPADs). Informal cosy coteries surround political leaders and have their ear. The government schedulers, who decide which bills receive precious parliamentary time, enjoy their upper hand with a mixture of high principle, low politics and smugness – and woe betide anyone who suggests that the provisional timetable should be revealed even within government, let alone to others in Parliament. Party whips still jealously guard their power and the mystery over decisions on permitted absence from votes.

Maverick MPs can at times hold the whole proceedings to ransom until ridiculous hours by making lengthy speeches. Rebellious MPs can hold significant power, but if they are disorganised or become serial rebels that power fades, unless the government has an ultra-slim majority, as this current Parliament now demonstrates. Sections of the media that can command large audiences hold significant sway, with their ability to splash away reputations and strangle new policies at birth, sometimes with a casual regard for the facts. The power of the wider party machinery varies between parties, but includes staff in key positions, committee structures, conferences, elected representatives in different bodies, and sometimes external affiliated organisations. And ultimately, of course, the voters have power: once every few years rocking up to a local primary school or church hall, and making a mark with a stubby pencil on a piece of paper to sum up all their hopes, fears and ideas.

With the exception of the voters, every other power base within the political system remains overwhelmingly dominated by men.

It wasn't until 2017 that the total number of women MPs ever elected to the House of Commons finally overtook the number of men elected as MPs in a single general election.[7] We have never had a woman as Chancellor or Defence Secretary. The reshuffle after the 2017 election left five government departments with entirely male ministerial teams, including the Foreign Office and the Ministry of Justice.[8] Gender equality at the top of the civil service is going backwards – just three of the top sixteen posts are held by women, down from eight in 2011.[9] Pick any political party you like – with the exception of the Women's Equality Party – and go to their conference: you'll see man after man taking to the stage. Just a third of councillors in England are women,[10] with even fewer in Wales (28 per cent)[11] and Scotland (24 per cent).[12]

Only 15 countries around the world are led by a woman, which is fewer than a tenth of the 193 countries in the United Nations.[13]

Governments at national and local levels wield huge influence over people's everyday lives, making decisions on everything from health services to national security, taxation to transport, employment to education. The Houses of Parliament, the Scottish Parliament, the Assemblies in Wales, Northern Ireland and London, and councils up and down the country hold the people wielding the executive power to account. If these bodies do not reflect the society they serve, then they lack important voices and perspectives, and their debates and decisions are the poorer for it.

So far, so what? I've told you things you knew, or suspected at least. The interesting conversation is what is driving this power inequality between men and women in our political systems, and what we can do about it.

The barriers to greater participation in politics by women have often been described as 'the 4 Cs': cash, caring, confidence and culture. All of these do play a role, but I'd like to add a fifth 'C' – the closed club.

Cash

Politics can be pricey. Most people involved in politics are volunteers, and that includes political candidates. Travel, accommodation and registration fees to attend party conferences can easily run into hundreds of pounds each year. On top of that there are often training and campaign events or by-elections to go to, and party fundraisers with their endless raffles, requests for auction prizes, and sometimes even an expectation that candidates themselves should be able to write a fat cheque to help fund the campaign. But the biggest financial impact is no doubt lost earnings. Few successful candidates work in another job during the six-week election campaign, and many spend much longer than six weeks full-time as a candidate, without earning other income. One survey put the cost of a winning candidacy, taking all these factors into account, at over £40,000.[14] The nature of the five-year political cycle encourages people to throw everything at their bid to win; unlike most job applications, if you don't make it this time, you typically have to wait five years for the next chance. And, of course, there is no guarantee of success – I've known people remortgage their house and get into significant debt through a campaign, only to lose and find themselves exhausted, dejected and in severe financial hardship. This certainly affects men as well as women. But when men earn 19 per cent more than women on average in the UK, the financial barrier to politics is even higher for women. The Conservative Party is attempting to square that circle with bursaries for candidates who are less-well off,[15] and the Women's Equality Party offers candidates funding to help with childcare and other costs.[16]

It's not just personal finances, however – the campaign has to be paid for, too. Fundraising often falls largely on the candidate's shoulders: as the public face of the campaign, you're asking people to buy into you as an individual, as well as the party. Over the course of 18 months or more, a parliamentary campaign can cost tens of thousands of pounds when you factor in staff, office costs, printing, postage and telephoning – and if you don't have a large team of volunteers to help with delivering leaflets, stuffing envelopes and making calls then the cost can easily be much higher. I remember going on a training course about fundraising where one of the tips was to 'think about your contacts, your friends, your family, your network – who would be able to write a cheque for £1,000?'. Let's just say as a twenty-something, my list was devastatingly short. But this is even more of a barrier for people from lower-income backgrounds, and the socio-economic diversity in Parliament is worryingly going backwards.[17] Anyone who has operated in the senior echelons of business and finance has an inbuilt advantage here – and they are disproportionately men. It's like power squared. Those with financial power are better able to access political power.

Stricter spending limits on campaigning – not just at election time, but throughout the electoral cycle, would help solve this problem, as would limits on how much any one individual or company can donate. Cross-party talks on limiting political spending and donations have always got stuck in a stalemate because no party wants to lose the existing advantages they have – the Conservatives from big-business donations and Labour from the trade unions.[18]

There was an Access to Elected Office Fund established in 2011 to support candidates with disabilities to meet the additional costs they incurred.[19] It is deeply regrettable that this fund was mothballed after 2015, with no current sign that the government intends to revive it. There is also some £9 million of public money given to political parties for policy development and the work they do holding the government to account.[20] (The government of course has the extensive resources of the civil service at its disposal for policy research.)[21] It is possible that this existing state funding could be tied to parties achieving some basic diversity targets, giving an additional impetus for them to improve the situation.

Public funding for political parties is never popular, least of all in post-2008 economic austerity, but an effective democracy costs money to run. Without using these levers and changing the finances, it will be much harder to draw power away from the wealthy in our politics, and the gender imbalance will be tougher to tackle.

Caring

Running for office while holding down a job is challenging enough, but when you add caring responsibilities into the mix, it often becomes impossible. The pattern amongst my Lib Dem colleagues was that women were either elected young, like myself, with no children, or when their children were teenagers or had left home. This was not the case for the men, many of whom were first elected when their children were very small.

Across Parliament there is a marked difference between the men and women MPs and how likely they are to be parents. Nearly three-quarters of the men are, and just over half of the women,[22] yet in the general population around four in five women have children. Being a parent doesn't make an individual better or worse at the job, though shockingly some try to score political points on the 'childless' status of their opponent – the brief 2016 Conservative leadership contest saw Andrea Leadsom suggest she had more of a stake in the future than Theresa May, because she has children and May does not.[23] Interestingly, the parenting status of male politicians is much less likely to come under scrutiny. Labour Cabinet minister Ruth Kelly seemed to acquire a permanent prefix in newspaper articles – 'mother-of-four Ruth Kelly'– but for the men it is much rarer that their role as a father is mentioned – generally at exceptional times like the birth, or tragically the death, of a child.

Looking at Parliament as a whole, however, a lack of parents in politics does matter. Firstly, because parents are under-represented we are missing out on that perspective in debates, just as is the case with other under-represented groups. Secondly, the gender discrepancy means the parent-gap compounds the existing lack of women in politics: those parents who are missing from politics are mainly mothers.

Not many MPs are elected in their twenties. At any given time, of the 650 MPs only a handful are under 30. There's a fair bit of media snark about young MPs: the patronising assumptions that they've 'never done a proper job', and the infantilising title 'Baby of the House' – you can imagine how much I loved that! As a young woman, it was a double whammy. I was experiencing a 'meteoric rise' when tipped to join government two years later than other MPs elected at the same time as me. Newspapers would emphasise that I was a 'junior' minister without applying the same descriptor to older male colleagues at the same level. Yet, if you look over time, many of our country's greatest and most prominent politicians have been elected young: Charles Kennedy at 23, David Steel at 26, Lloyd George at 27, Roy Jenkins at 28, Ken Clarke at 29, Tony Blair at 30, Harriet Harman at 32, Gordon Brown at 32, Margaret Thatcher at 33, Shirley Williams at 34, and even Winston Churchill at 25. So perhaps we should be a little less dismissive of young MPs. Surely it would be better to encourage young people of all genders to become politically active, and celebrate their public service when they do.

Lots of MPs are first elected in their thirties and early forties, often after fighting a couple of elections and building up constituency support, or earning their spurs in an unwinnable seat before being chosen for one with a better prospect of success. This coincides with the point that many women are aware that if they want children but haven't yet done so, they'd better get their skates on. I have lost count of the number of fabulous women candidates who ran brilliant campaigns in their twenties and then felt they were not in a position to fight the next election due to starting a family. Of course, you can stand and get elected while pregnant – as Harriet Harman did in 1983, Ruth Kelly in 1997, Kitty Ussher and Natascha Engel in 2005, Jenny Willott in 2010, and Lisa Nandy and Rachel Reeves in 2015. But it's not without its practical challenges, and not all women will want to combine pregnancy with electioneering.

It doesn't necessarily get easier after the birth. Caring for a newborn is exhausting, and breastfeeding requires a similar amount of energy as running ten kilometres every day, plus in the early weeks the frequency of feeds can make it well-nigh impossible to get anything else done. But as an MP with a fair degree of autonomy and flexibility in how you do the job, this is arguably much more straightforward to manage than as a candidate or in many other roles.

Combining politics and becoming a mother can seem a daunting prospect. It is also tricky to plan. There is uncertainty about when you'll conceive, and uncertainty about the electoral timetable. That was even worse before the Fixed-term Parliaments Act, which apparently removed the ability of the prime minister to call an election whenever they liked – though 2017 showed that surprise elections are still possible.

But the biggest hurdle isn't actually the year or so covering the physical experience of pregnancy, birth and early bonding. It's the expectation, often shared by men and women alike, that women take the lion's share of the responsibility for that child for the years and years that follow. Men don't tend to consider combining politics and being a father a daunting prospect, any more than they plan their career around the best time to become a dad. And the same holds true for caring for elderly relatives, too. How often is it the daughter that visits her aged parents daily, organises care services and provides the emotional support?

'Emotional labour' is a term coined to describe the social glue that women tend to provide in families and friendship groups. From organising birthday presents to arranging social gatherings, remembering what day to pack the school gym kit to sorting out the playdates, it's the business of taking responsibility for making relationships and home life work. In political terms, this is often undertaken by the 'constituency wife'.

In the days where it was expected that women would not have a paid job, constituency associations expected something of a two-for-one deal. They would interview the male candidates, and also put them through their paces at a social event, at which they could also meet and 'assess' the wife. What an awful concept. While hubby was away in Parliament, she might even stand in for him at some local events – perhaps visit the local hospice or contribute a pot of homemade jam to the church fete.

In practical terms, though, I know how invaluable a constituency wife would be. As an MP you spend Monday to Thursday away from home, and often work 70 hours a week. When you're back in your constituency, your diary is packed, fitting all the advice surgeries, meetings with constituency staff, visits to schools, businesses and local groups, fundraising, correspondence and knocking on doors into the Friday-to-Sunday block. The nuts and bolts of looking after a house, making sure there's milk in the fridge, that the washing is done and the plants are kept alive is not easy to squeeze in.

At this point I feel I must pay tribute to my mum, who has been a tower of support and practical help for me every step of the way since I was first selected as a candidate in 2002. From the rainy Saturdays we spent delivering thousands of leaflets together in Bishopbriggs (followed by a takeaway in front of Strictly), to going round to my flat to replace the buckets when I had a leaky roof and was 400 miles away, I couldn't have done it without her.

Changing patterns in the workplace mean fewer MPs now have a stay-at-home spouse, yet this has coincided with increased expectations of MPs. Gone (thankfully) are the days when an MP only made a visit to his constituency annually. MPs are now rightly expected to be visible and active within their patch, and it is positive that more people now contact their Member of Parliament – evidenced by a significant increase in correspondence levels to MPs. Voters expect more. But this means it is no wonder that money plays an even larger role. In this scenario, the people more likely to be successful as candidates are those who can personally dedicate unreasonable amounts of time and money to the campaign.

We therefore have a system where it is unusual for women MPs to be elected at an age at which they could later choose to start a family, yet the demands of candidacy are often incompatible for those with family responsibilities who are caring for small children or elderly relatives – usually women.

We need to get over ageism and encourage young people into politics, and banish the phrase 'you've got plenty of time', so often used to calm the ambition of youth. Similarly, we need to judge potential candidates on their skills and abilities, not just on how free their diary is. We should also look seriously at and pilot innovations such as job-sharing, to open up the role to people who don't have 70 hours a week to commit. Then we need to take collective responsibility for the politics we have created. Even if you don't want to stand for election, there are lots of things you could do to make it easier for others who *are* standing, whether you belong to a party or not. A few hours a month knocking on doors, delivering leaflets, making phone calls, volunteering in a party campaign office or even doing some childcare can make a real difference. The healthier local political organisations are, the more a candidate can focus on the role of leading the campaign, rather than having to be the fundraiser-in-chief, recruiter-in-chief and deliver 300 leaflets before breakfast, too. All of which makes it more manageable to combine political candidacy with other responsibilities.

Confidence

Putting your head above the parapet, making your point forcefully, stepping forward and saying firmly 'I think I'm the best person to do this' – these ingredients of politics do not chime with the subliminal, and often explicit, messages our society gives girls about how to be 'feminine', 'ladylike' and generally win praise. In fact, women who stand for office and are perceived or portrayed to be seeking power are penalised, while men are not.[24] It's not therefore surprising that confidence is a key factor in the under-representation of women in politics.

My own political journey owes a huge amount to the people who encouraged me at every step along the way, from my English teacher Mrs Reid, who nurtured my interest in debating at school, to countless individuals within the Liberal Democrats who kept pressing me to take my next step. A key moment was a campaign training event I went on called Activate. It was a quirk of fate that I went to it at all. I nearly didn't go.

I had just finished my first year as an undergraduate at the London School of Economics, and was looking forward to summer adventures, possibly a trip to Paris with my boyfriend. Then he ended the relationship. Glumly mooching about one morning soon afterwards, my 18-year-old self opened a letter from the Lib Dems; I'd joined the party at Freshers' Fair. This letter was an invitation to Activate, a residential weekend in the Peak District, to learn all about political campaigning. They had subsidised it, so it was only a tenner. Throwing caution to the wind, I figured it was time to stop mooching and meet some new people – what was the worst that could happen?

The weekend was brilliant: a great introduction to how the

party worked, what was involved in campaigning, and how I could get further involved. Perhaps most importantly, it gave me a network of about 20 other young people at a similar stage, so it wasn't like taking a step into the dark alone. A few of us decided to go to the party conference that autumn, which would be so much easier because we'd know at least a few people. My participation snowballed from there – being elected to the national committee of the Liberal Democrat Youth and Students organisation (LDYS), becoming a party trainer and then vice chair of my local party.

Even so, I still needed to build my confidence. I remember my early party conferences, and going to fringe meetings where a few dozen people would gather to hear from a panel on a specific issue and then ask them questions. Just raising my hand to ask a question prompted all sorts of soul-searching – *what exact words would I say, what if people thought the question was stupid, maybe I should just let other people do the talking* . . . Typically, I'd spend most of the session crafting a question, then eventually pluck up the courage to raise my hand, at which point it would be too late to be noticed by the chair and I'd feel frustrated and be kicking myself. The same thing happened when, as a student, I applied to be in the *Question Time* audience. A regular viewer, I was a bit in awe of even being there seeing it all happen: production staff rushing around, huge wheeled cameras being manoeuvred into position, and sensing the ripple of excitement in the audience as the warm-up act was replaced by David Dimbleby and the show was about to start. Again, I spent half of the recording worrying about whether I should put up my hand, and the other half frustrated that I wasn't called on to ask my question.

Later, I decided to set myself little targets when I went to political events, to force myself to speak up. I'd look at the agenda, decide what debates or meetings I'd be attending, and think a bit in advance about the types of issues I might talk about. In 1999, a little over a year after Activate, I made my first speech to a party conference aged 19. At every conference after that, I looked for the right opportunity to have my say. Years later I did the same in the House of Commons. In such a strange and imposing place, I was determined to be confident and comfortable in the environment, so I endeavoured not to let a week go by without making some kind of intervention, asking a question or giving a speech. Asking my first Prime Minister's Question terrified me. To this day I recall the exact words I used[25] – so ingrained they had become by endless practice, pacing up and down the House of Commons' Terrace – as well as the sweaty palms and my pulse racing so fast I felt sure people sitting next to me must be able to hear my heart thumping. But the next time was a little bit less terrifying, the time after a bit less still. Asking a PMQ still makes me nervous – I don't think that ever goes away – but there is no doubt that practice is one of the best ways I've found to deal with nerves.

It was the chair of LDYS, Polly Martin, who first encouraged me to apply to become a parliamentary candidate. She said I'd be good at it, and learn a lot from doing so. I didn't want to be an MP, but I figured it would be an interesting experience and a good talking point in the future – and of course there would be a wide range of seats where I could stand with no danger of winning. I was 20, not yet old enough to stand for Parliament (back then you had to be 21, though it was lowered to 18 a few years later), but I went through the process to become an 'approved candidate', which consisted of an application form, an interview, and a series of tasks like making a short speech, role-playing listening to a constituent in an advice surgery and a group discussion exercise. Once I was on the candidates list, I was allowed to apply for seats on the basis that my 21st birthday was in February, before the expected date of the election in May 2001. As I was working in Hull for the local radio station Viking FM, I decided to try to become the Liberal Democrat candidate for the constituency of Hull East, where the sitting MP was Deputy Prime Minister John Prescott.

We didn't have many Lib Dem members in the constituency, and even fewer attended the hustings to select the candidate. I was chosen, beating the other contender, Angie Wastling, by eight votes to six. Our campaign was run on a shoestring, with one basic black-and-white A4 leaflet, a couple of public meetings and a few press releases sent to the *Hull Daily Mail*. We knew we couldn't win Hull East at that election, so most of my time was spent campaigning in the nearby constituency of Haltemprice and Howden, where I lived and was vice-chair of the local party association. It was a bit of a long shot, as the Conservative MP David Davis had a majority of 7,500, but we ran a strong campaign which cut his majority to under 2,000.

I learned a bit about power on election night. I'd psyched myself up for the declaration of the result, which could be televised to millions. I'd planned the short speech I would give after John Prescott (in safe Labour Hull on the eve of a second Labour landslide – the winner was never in doubt). But unlike all the footage I'd seen on election-night TV coverage, with all the candidates lined up on a stage while the returning officer reads out the votes, I found that wasn't the way it was done in Hull. Only John Prescott and his wife Pauline were allowed up on the stage in this Labour stronghold. So after the excitement of achieving a 6 per cent swing to the Lib Dems, and beating the Tories to take second place,[26] the actual announcement felt like a bit of an anticlimax.

Nonetheless, I had caught the bug. At the same time, I was becoming more disillusioned about my job and the company I worked for. The important charity work we did in the local community only seemed to matter to the central management in how much publicity it would get us. I concluded that to be happy at work I would need to find a company whose values I shared. Then another idea started to take root in my mind. After finding my experience on the campaign trail fighting for my beliefs much more fulfilling than my job, I started to muse on whether I might stop treating politics as a hobby, and instead try to stand somewhere I had a chance of winning.

That summer I spent lots of time thinking why there were so few women MPs. For the Lib Dems, 2001 had been our best election yet, winning 52 MPs – but just five were women: Jenny Tonge, Sandra Gidley, Sue Doughty, Annette Brooke and Patsy Calton. It was a frankly appalling record. Discussion raged on our online forums: What was the problem? Was it sexist local parties, too few women coming forward to be candidates, or something else?

One viewpoint maintained that this was sexism – men being chosen over women due to sexist attitudes – and the only solution to this would be all-women shortlists. Labour had already implemented this, and it saw them elect more than 100 women MPs in 1997. Yet in the online posts analysing data from our Candidates' Office, a stubbornly persistent percentage was everywhere – 23 per cent of our list of approved candidates were women, 23 per cent of our selected candidates were women, 23 per cent of people applying to be candidates in the first place were women. There were some variations – for example, 28 per cent of our target-seat candidates were women, but none of our candidates were women in seats where we had MPs standing down. Most tellingly, the actual chances of getting selected in target seats overall were the same for individual men and women, but there were overwhelmingly more men at all stages, which was giving us our skewed result.

Convinced that this was a pipeline problem rather than one of sexism in the selection process, a group of us developed an alternative plan. We needed to address the imbalance in candidates coming forward by proactively talent-spotting, and encouraging and supporting women to become more involved at all levels, including candidacy. We needed nothing short of a major campaign in the party, treating this problem like a critical by-election we simply had to win. It would require funding, serious commitment and resources. Real change at the grassroots was and is a better solution than cosmetic change among our group of MPs.

The decision would be made at a high-profile party conference debate, which pitted the all-women shortlists option against our alternative approach. I summed up our proposals in a speech at the end of a fiercely argued debate: the conference hall packed with hundreds of delegates was easily the biggest audience I'd ever addressed, which was a daunting prospect. Learning that I would have to follow my heroine Shirley Williams – but speaking on the opposite side of the debate – did nothing to ease my nerves.

We were in Bournemouth, where the conference centre is on the seafront by a steep hill, and my stress was so intense that I remember running up and down that hill in my suit to try to burn off my excess nervous energy. I felt so passionately about the issue – both that we should get more women into powerful positions across our party, and that we should do it by tackling the problem at the source rather than by a tokenistic gesture to place a few more women in winnable seats. Passion can help a political cause, but I was genuinely worried that for me it would spill over into that horrible sensation where your throat tightens and speaking becomes impossible. A squeezed voice catching on the brink of tears was not the rousing oratory I had in mind!

This moment helped me realise the power we all have to boost the confidence of others. Preparing for a television interview before the debate, fear must have shown on my face. I'll never forget the kindness of the journalist Zeinab Badawi, who placed her hands on mine and just said calmly, 'You're going to be okay.' That reassurance meant a huge amount to me.

Four years later, my challenge was different but the fear was the same, as I got ready for my first appearance on BBC *Question Time* as a new MP. Then it was Labour MP Douglas Alexander with the cheery encouragement: 'Don't worry, you'll be fine. I'm the government minister, they'll be shooting at me.'

Seven years after that, it was my first ministerial questions in the House of Commons. I felt nauseous as I approached the chamber, empty and quiet before the day's session began. I saw

Conservative MP Matthew Hancock, another new minister at the Department for Business, Innovation and Skills (BIS), and asked him how he felt. 'Honoured' was his strident response. Not quite the shared camaraderie I was seeking. From unlikely quarters, the reassurance did come, though. Michael Fallon was also a new minister at BIS, but had previously served as a minister in the 1990s – an archetypal Conservative who I didn't expect to bond with. Seeing that I looked rather nervous, he quietly confided that he was too. 'But you've done this before!' I said. He replied that it was 20 years ago, and anyway, the fear never goes away and nor should it.

We all have this power at our disposal, to see when others – even our competitors or opponents – are approaching a difficult challenge and an extra boost will help; at the right moment it might be as little as a smile or a kind word at that human level that can make all the difference.

Back to 2001, and the all-women shortlists debate. My speech was well received and we 'won'. The Liberal Democrats rejected all-women shortlists and instead set up the Gender Balance Task Force, now the Campaign for Gender Balance. I got stuck in, identifying and cajoling women to recognise that they could do more – to make a speech at conference, lead a campaign team and aspire to elected office. I still have the little Filofax I kept, with handwritten notes on the dozens of women I was encouraging, to keep track of what stage they were at in the process, how I could support them best and when I should make contact again.

Later, I took on chairing the Campaign for Gender Balance, and tried to engage my fellow Lib Dem MPs in the talent-spotting task. It was a dispiriting experience. Given the widespread rejection among many of them of the all-women shortlists option as 'illiberal', I had expected more enthusiasm for making the alternative work. Yet when I circulated a list of how many approved women candidates were in each of their constituencies (in most cases, none), with a request for them to write down the names of women in their area who would make good candidates for the Campaign for Gender Balance to approach, encourage and support, fewer than a third of my fellow Lib Dem MPs even responded.

In subsequent contests to become party leader, my MP colleagues who were standing for that role told me at the time how important gender balance was to them – yet actions speak louder than words. MPs are in an ideal position to encourage talented people from under-represented groups to become candidates, as they come into contact with committed community activists and successful people in their area all the time. Despite the warm words when they wanted my vote, many of them didn't promote diversity in their own backyards. Time after time, when candidates were selected for winnable seats close to theirs – or indeed when they themselves stood down – the shortlists were exclusively male, because no women had applied.[27] As a proud Liberal Democrat this depresses me, but I am determined to change it. Putting my cards on the table about the past challenges is an important part of that, because we need to prick the bubble of complacency that exists in some quarters, where people assume that because we are a liberal party, promoting equality is in our DNA.

Wrong.

Like any other part of society, gender inequality is embedded in the Liberal Democrats, and it needs to be challenged proactively.

There is a brilliant organisation called 50:50 Parliament whose aim is pretty self-explanatory. One of their campaigns is #AskHerToStand[28] – and anyone can take part. All you need to do is identify a woman you know who would be great at representing her community and speaking out on issues she cares about, and literally ask her to stand. Whether as a councillor, MP, MSP or Assembly Member, your encouragement can help give someone else confidence. The lovely thing about it is that even if she doesn't want to stand (or doesn't want to yet), she will still get a boost from the conversation.

Inevitably, in a chapter about why we don't yet have equality in Parliament, I am sharing details about the negative consequences of having so few women MPs. But let me explain, too, why I love my job as an MP – and why if you're a woman who has never considered standing for elected office, it may well be for you.

Being an elected politician – whether at local or national level – can be incredibly rewarding. A big part of the job is about helping individuals in your area, whether with specific problems they are facing or ideas they have for change. You can really make a difference to people's lives. You also have the huge privilege of getting up in the morning and going to work to try to implement the things you believe in. While there are constraints on your time, such as fixed meetings or votes, another positive is that you have a lot of autonomy regarding how you structure your day. Ultimately, you are accountable to the people who elect you, and they typically don't know or mind whether you are getting things done for them at 6 a.m., 2 p.m. or 10 p.m.

Lots of women have said to me that they don't think they'd be a good politician because they don't like speaking in public.

My answer is twofold. Firstly, speeches are actually a tiny part of the job. Most of your time is spent listening to people, working out how to get things done, and building alliances with others to achieve shared goals. Being able to develop a rapport and empathise with people is a much more useful skillset for politicians than delivering a rabble-rousing speech.

Secondly, potential candidates often rule themselves out when they benchmark against politicians they see on the TV who have been doing it for years. Everyone learns politics on the job, there is no prerequisite course or exam you need to sit. The only qualification to be a successful politician is that you have to care. You have to care about people and their lives, whether that's local concerns like the lack of a pedestrian crossing on a dangerous road, big national issues like making taxes fairer, international challenges like tackling climate change – or any number of other issues that get you fired up. Everything else can be learned – writing a press release, making a speech to a residents' association, scrutinising potential laws, launching a campaign or running a constituency advice surgery.

If you're even half-thinking about standing for election, then I urge you just to take the next step in your journey, whether it's joining a party, emailing a party official to arrange to meet and find out more, or going along to a training event run by a political party or a non-partisan organisation like the Parliament Project.[29]

Culture

The Christmas after I was elected in 2005, one of the books under the tree for me was *Women in Parliament: The New Suffragettes*, by Boni Sones and Margaret Moran. They had interviewed dozens of women MPs about their time in Parliament over the years, and I found it shocking reading. In 1997, it had been a watershed year for women in the House of Commons. Labour's use of all-women shortlists, combined with their landslide election victory that year, had boosted the number of women MPs to 120 – far beyond the previous record of 60.[30] In Sones and Moran's book I read about the experiences of women who, just eight years before I became an MP, had endured the indignity of men on the opposing side making 'melon' gestures with their hands on their chests when a woman MP stood up to speak. The House of Commons I knew was shouty and brutish and braying, but I couldn't imagine that kind of thing happening. The truth was, the arrival of so many women MPs had started to change the culture, so what some dinosaur MPs thought was okay in 1997 was not happening by 2005.

To get a more far-reaching perspective on how things had changed for women in politics, I invited my political heroine Shirley Williams to lunch. Shirley retired from the House of Lords in 2016, after more than 50 years in front-line politics. Elected as a Labour MP aged 34 in 1964, she served as a minister for eight years (in Cabinet for five years), and was one of the 'Gang of Four' Labour figures who broke away to form the Social Democratic Party (SDP) in 1981. She was an SDP MP from 1981 to 1983, finally becoming a Liberal Democrat when the SDP and Liberals merged in 1988, and was an active member of the House of Lords from 1993 to 2016, including as leader of the Liberal Democrats in the Lords from 2001 to 2004.[31]

We ate in The Adjournment, one of Parliament's more modern restaurants, at one end of the glass atrium of Portcullis House, which is home to offices for hundreds of MPs. Over steak, a burger and a delicious glass of Merlot (at Shirley's encouragement), we discussed the changes for women in politics over a half-century. Shirley told me how when she first stood for Parliament, in Harwich at the age of 23, her Tory opponent referred to her as the 'schoolgirl candidate' and patronised her 'in every possible way'. She explained how few unmarried women stood for election – as if to be taken seriously you first had to 'pass the test of being marriageable', and how it was practically unheard of for women with children to be MPs. When Shirley was elected, her daughter Rebecca was three years old, and she found the press were always looking for ways to describe how in being a mother and an MP you were 'selling your child short'.

I was stunned when Shirley recounted the national seamen's strike of 1966, when she was a minister in the Labour Department. The Minister of Labour, Ray Gunter, was in hospital recovering from a heart attack and she was the only other minister in the department, so she reported to Cabinet as the crisis unfolded, and a national state of emergency was declared.[32] The Labour Department's most senior civil servant, the Permanent Secretary, was passionately opposed to the idea of women ministers, and refused to speak to Shirley directly as she was 'too junior'. This led to the ridiculous spectacle of a civil servant scurrying between the offices of the minister and the Permanent Secretary with written messages, just to 'save' the dinosaur mandarin from the indignity of having to speak to – and, presumably worse, take direction from – a woman.

Then there was the occasion she was running back from a meeting to vote in the House of Commons, and, pressed for time, she asked the MP Sir Bernard Braine, a 'fine, old-fashioned knight of the shires', what subject they were voting on. He said to her, 'Don't you bother your pretty little head about it, it'll only upset you,' and actually patted her on the head for good measure. Shirley seemed almost amused that I was surprised at that incident, which does show that our political culture has made some progress. Today, the subtext of some comments might be 'don't bother your pretty little head about it', but it is disguised in different language. Thankfully, the blatant, in-your-face sexism is more a thing of the past.

Shirley spoke warmly about the male champions of her political career, too. There was the local party chairman in Harwich, where she first stood for election, who was 'furious about people treating women as a lesser breed'. He deliberately stood in the selection contest against Shirley to put off other applicants, and then withdrew at the last minute so that she could be chosen. The Minister of Health Kenneth Robertson championed Shirley by appointing her as his parliamentary aide two days after she was elected as an MP. He made a point of taking her to all the important meetings, saying, 'I want you to learn what it's like to be a minister.' And she did: just two years later she was appointed as a minister in the Department of Labour. Shirley is a huge inspiration, having broken down barriers throughout her career and succeeded at the highest levels of politics, standing her ground on matters of principle with a warmth and wisdom that I have not seen matched. Shirley, I salute you.

The position of women in politics changed greatly over the course of Shirley's political career. Looked at through the lens of history, the House of Commons today is not explicitly sexist, though there were plenty of times where I felt very aware of being a young woman and treated almost as a novelty.

Asking a question about the minimum wage for 16- and 17-year-olds drew a jibe from a minister about whether I was one of them. Making a point about local government finance and the disaster of the poll tax prompted a Conservative MP to question whether I could know what I was talking about because of my age. I responded that I may only have been about ten at the time, but the fact that it imprinted itself on my mind is a sign of just how badly the Tories had got it wrong. He did at least have the grace to admit he had been 'ungallant' – probably the first and only time I've heard someone use that word in conversation.

I lost count of the times at events when I was asked who I worked for, and I enjoyed the look of puzzlement followed by the penny dropping when I said, 'The people of East Dunbartonshire.' Even as a minister it didn't stop. When I introduced a new law to create a Groceries Code Adjudicator – a supermarket watchdog to ensure suppliers were treated fairly – I had to decide who to appoint to that role. A senior official from the Office of Public Appointments came to my office to discuss the recruitment process and final candidates. He found me looking through some papers on my desk, and struck up conversation. As we spoke, it became clear he thought I was the secretary, not the minister, and when my actual secretary walked in and he realised his mistake, his face was a picture.

I also experienced the kind of excessive chivalry that serves to remind you that you are something of an anomaly, but is harder to object to. Holding doors open for people is a courteous thing to do, whether they are a man or a woman. Only doing it for women is a bit last century, especially if you're making a big deal out of it. But, ho hum, no harm done, I used to think, smiling gratefully and recognising that this was intended as a kind gesture and to show respect for women. One time, however, a male MP had reached the door of the voting lobby significantly ahead of me, yet was loitering just so he could chivalrously let me go first through the door. This was a man who I knew had cheated on his wife while she was being treated for cancer, before running off with the other woman. On that occasion, I just snapped at him to go through the damn door.

I recall a meeting with a Conservative minister, later promoted to Cabinet, to discuss a policy disagreement between us and try to forge a way through – a common occurrence in coalition government. What was uncommon was when I entered the room and went to shake his hand, he leaned in and deliberately planted a kiss on my cheek. Now, I'm generally a big fan of kissing. It's a lovely way to show affection to friends, family and close colleagues. I did not count this man in any of those categories, and would rather not have kissed him in greeting even on a social occasion. But this was a formal business meeting, and it was entirely inappropriate. We had serious issues to discuss, affecting thousands of people's lives. I was too stunned to say anything, and focused instead on winning the policy battle, which we ultimately did.

One ministerial colleague told me that she was careful in meetings with a particular minister, as he always seemed to be looking for an excuse to touch her. Her solution was to ensure they were seated on opposite sides of the table.

Unwelcome touching and kissing, hands on shoulders – some will say this isn't important, that it's mountains out of molehills, all a fuss about nothing. But it does matter. It sets the tone, it marks women out as different and it is the tip of the iceberg in a political culture that does not treat women as equals.

As a student attending party conferences, I learned about the MP who liked to spend his time in the bars chatting to young women and not very discreetly looking down their tops. When I was a young MP, two friends confided in me about a worrying encounter where they had both been touched against their will by the party's powerful Chief Executive, Lord Chris Rennard. I was appalled, and my concerns escalated when I spoke to other women who told me they had experienced similar unwelcome advances. There was a clear pattern of behaviour, often taking place at party training events or conferences: the women told me Lord Rennard had touched them inappropriately, and in some cases had proposed going back to his hotel room. The women's reactions ranged from people who had been pretty shaken by it, to those who had personally brushed it off but were concerned about it happening to others. I understood my friends' wishes at that time not to have to relive their experiences publicly, but we agreed the behaviour simply had to stop. Yet the party had no proper processes for dealing with sexual harassment by such a senior figure.

So I spoke to the Chief Whip. I spoke to the leader's aide. I spoke to the leader's chief of staff. All the time I respected my friends' confidentiality, and described what had happened without their names – while emphasising that I had personally heard several different women tell me this had happened to them, so I was absolutely convinced there was a worrying pattern and a serious problem.

Eventually, it was agreed that Danny Alexander, the leader's chief of staff, would speak to Lord Rennard, to tell him of these reports and impress on him that such behaviour was simply unacceptable and had to stop.

I wanted to reassure the women about what action had been taken, so I asked Danny how the conversation had gone. It hadn't happened yet. So I made a note in my Filofax to ask again the following week. And again. And again. And eventually I asked and the conversation had actually taken place. Rennard had denied everything, naturally, but at least the message had been clearly delivered. I reported back to my friends and the other women, and made it very clear that if they heard of any repetition, to let me know immediately. To my knowledge, thankfully it never happened again, and Rennard stood down from his job as Chief Executive a few months later. But the damage had already been done, and the party's response to the whole episode was entirely inadequate.

I've reflected long and hard about my actions a decade ago. Did I do enough? My fear is that I did not. At the time I thought I had done everything I possibly could, trying to support my friends while getting the party to act on the problem, in what felt like a lonely mission. It taught me that no single individual in any organisation should be allowed to hoard as much power as Lord Rennard did within the Lib Dems; no one wanted to challenge him, and even to this day he has not admitted what he did was wrong nor has he properly apologised to the women. Instead he cites the police decision not to prosecute and a selective quote from an internal report to proclaim his 'innocence'. Had one of the key people involved, who has never gone public with her experience (as is her right), been prepared to testify, the police decision on prosecution may well have been different. And regardless of the question of criminality, I am in no doubt that such behaviour breaches the acceptable and professional standards expected of any chief executive or parliamentarian. It is hugely frustrating that, at that time, the party's own internal complaints procedures meant that complaints had to be judged according to the criminal standard of proof ('beyond all reasonable doubt') rather than the balance of probabilities ('more likely than not to have occurred') which is used in many professional disciplinary contexts.

There is one thing I would definitely do differently now. I appreciate all the understandable reasons why women do not wish to speak out about sexual harassment: not wanting to relive the horrible experience, misplaced feelings of shame, fear of being judged, concern about what it might mean for their future career, and additionally, in high-profile circumstances like this, worry about media attention (the women in this story endured horrendous hounding by the media, some of which can only be described as stalking – one had to take time off work, go and stay with a friend and change her phone number). In 2007, as my friends listed these concerns, I empathised, and did not push them hard for a written complaint. I did not have confidence that their names being attached to the reports would be anything other than a miserable experience, to compound what had already happened. Since then, my party has thoroughly overhauled its complaint processes, and we employ a pastoral care officer whose job it is to ensure the process is sensitive to people's needs. My strong advice now would be to make a formal written complaint.

That Lord Rennard remains in the party, showing no remorse or contrition, while many of the women involved have left, fills me with sadness and anger. When I hear suggestions that the women who spoke out should not be believed, or that they were somehow manipulated, it makes my blood boil. I remain deeply frustrated that a party appeals process found they had no grounds to dismiss him from the party. It just feels wrong, and I do not want Lord Rennard to continue as a member of the party. As far as I am concerned, he is not welcome.

Sexual harassment is, of course, a big problem more widely in the political environment, and beyond. It exists right across the different parties and institutions involved. One investigation found that a third of staffers in Parliament had personally experienced sexual harassment, with both men and women reporting predatory behaviour from MPs.[33] When respected journalist Isabel Hardman called out a sexist MP who proclaimed to her, 'I want to talk to the totty!', various women journalists shared their own stories of being felt up and propositioned in the course of doing their jobs reporting on Parliament.[34]

The alcohol-fuelled culture in politics – and especially Parliament – is unhelpful, as are the informal mechanisms for recruitment and promotion, and the lack of proper policies on workplace bullying and harassment, which make it harder for people to challenge inappropriate and unacceptable behaviour. In parts of the political system, there is also a generational gulf, with some senior politicians wondering what all of the fuss is about.

On a positive note, the culture as regards sexual harassment in politics is changing. The casual groping of junior staff and volunteers that passed without comment decades ago is increasingly called out and challenged today.

Part of this is down to politics becoming more professional. Changes to the timings of House of Commons debates mean that voting is now generally over by 7.30 p.m. – except on Mondays, when MPs are travelling to Westminster from all corners of the United Kingdom and so there is a later start and a 10.30 p.m. finish. Doing more of the business in office hours makes the institution seem more like a place of serious work, and less like a gentleman's drinking club.

But there's still a long way to go. So what can we do? With so many factors driving male dominance of politics, we need a wide range of solutions. Professor Sarah Childs is an expert in gender and politics, and in 2016 she published an authoritative report on how the UK Parliament can improve its record on gender representation.[35] The result of a year's intensive work in Parliament listening to MPs and staff, her 43 recommendations were wide-ranging. They included the imperative of counting: better monitoring data about participation in debates, membership of committees, the mix of experts consulted by committees, and candidates in winnable seats.

There were a host of proposals for practical change. Some were very simple, such as the updating of the dress code so it doesn't only relate to men, or the redesign of security passes with more visible photos and names to prevent the frequent 'are you allowed to be here?' questioning of women, young people and people of colour who work in Parliament. Or getting rid of the barmy procedure for reserving a seat in the House of Commons, which is at best an inefficient use of time, and for those who have caring responsibilities that mean they are dropping their child at nursery or school, or helping an elderly relative before their carer arrives, can be impossible.

Other suggestions were more complex but crucial: better predictability of voting times and the parliamentary calendar so people can plan the rest of their lives around their work in the Commons; creating formal policies around maternity, paternity, adoption and caring leave; and the provision of an on-site crèche to complement the nursery. Some addressed the cultural barriers, from ensuring that artwork around Parliament reflects diversity rather than just statues and paintings of white men, to trialling different architectural layouts and debate formats. Some of the recommendations have already been implemented, and others, like the crèche, are being piloted or planned.

My favourite suggestion was that the security passes for journalists covering Westminster politics should be allocated so that no less than 40 per cent should be given to men, and crucially no less than 40 per cent to women – though the House of Commons has not yet agreed to implement that particular recommendation. The 'lobby' of political journalists is astonishingly male, even more so than the group of elected representatives they cover. Speaking to women journalists, perhaps most worrying is that the proportion doesn't seem to have shifted over the last decade or so.[36] And back in the editors' offices, it is huddles of men who are making the major decisions: the story leads, the headlines, the photos – scantily clad women where possible, of course.

The media coverage of Professor Childs's report brilliantly made the case for why this recommendation is so important, and why we need many more women in the media covering politics. The headlines screamed 'BREASTFEEDING COULD BE ALLOWED IN COMMONS' and most articles barely mentioned the rest of the recommendations.[37] The word 'breast' was mentioned just twice in the 20,000-word report – on page 21 in a subsection under recommendation 12 about parental leave. While the report did suggest that lifting the ban on infants accompanying their MP parents into committee rooms or the main chamber would be helpful, it also noted that in practice this would be likely to be used rarely. Yet the journalistic response was little more than a puerile chuckle: 'They mentioned boobs – lol!' It is frustratingly common for the media to twist equality arguments into sensationalist, controversial clickbait, serving both to ignore the serious points being made and to paint the overall approach as ridiculous. The media's power to frame the debate is substantial, and means the public discourse of our politics is currently viewed through the lens of white middle-aged men. We're missing out on a richness of perspective.

Closed Club

Many rail against the 'professionalisation' of politics, as if being unprofessional is better. As in many industries, proper procedures and assessments for recruitment and promotion are helpful to equality. They might seem rather boring compared with the alternative of plotting with your mates in comfy leather armchairs while you work your way through a bottle of Famous Grouse, but better decisions get made. The sceptics say that politics is just different, and it won't change – appointing key allies as advisers is essential due to the trust needed in the intense power dynamics at play. Unsurprisingly, this means people appoint others who are much like themselves. The House of Commons is already hideously unrepresentative when it comes to gender, race, disability, socio-economic background and so on.[38] The old boys' club reinforces and multiplies that disparity.

Reshuffles always prompt a flurry of excitement in political circles. In a political equivalent of fantasy football, commentators and pundits delight in predicting who might get what job, and I am not immune to the fun to be had. My husband Duncan (also a Lib Dem MP from 2010 to 2015) and I have whiled away many a happy hour hiking through beautiful scenery in the Highlands, the Lake District and the West Country while puzzling out who could take on the various policy briefs – in our own party, and also looking across to Labour and the Conservatives.

But it is actually a serious test of effective leadership for the person making the final call. Balancing different strengths within a team, political and policy experience, the need for diversity of perspectives, anticipated controversies and constituency considerations is a fascinating Rubik's cube – and sometimes leaders get so far and then resort to peeling off the coloured stickers and swapping them to try to make the last bit work, with square pegs in round holes. Many political leaders say they hate reshuffles. The reality is that alongside the factors listed above, there are huge egos and power dynamics at work. With no formality at all around the process, it is entirely in the leader's gift. So it can be hard for them to resist the requests of their mates – or sometimes strong political rivals – in creating their team. A leader in a weak position has less room for manoeuvre:

can they afford to make powerful enemies? Those with power in politics are still predominantly men, and so this reinforces that imbalance. They go in, they play hardball, or they refuse to play ball at all. It took several reshuffles in my first Parliament to understand what you have to do. You have to take the initiative and go in to see the leader and make a strong case for what you want. You have to pick the timing, too – reshuffles are not done according to a schedule, and leaders will always say they aren't even thinking about them yet. Go in too early and you risk being forgotten by the time of the decision, too late and it's all been effectively decided.

To break out of this cycle of 'jobs for the vocal and powerful boys' takes strong leadership, not happy accident. It can be helped by prior commitments, made outside of the febrile reshuffle period, that a leader can then point to and in some ways use as a shield from powerful interests. David Cameron's promise that a third of his Cabinet would be women[39] by the end of the 2010–2015 Parliament served as much to give him the space to drive change as to win any political kudos for equality. He didn't hit the target, it's worth noting, although a third of Conservative Cabinet ministers were women. But the eight people who served as full Liberal Democrat Cabinet ministers at different stages of the Parliament were all men.

Making decisions about who to promote or fire, who should lead on a new project and what the key messages will be, based on instinct and anecdote rather than a detailed analysis and robust process is a recipe for disaster – and even more so if those in the room are a fairly homogenous group. Why should you be surprised if most of the names who are suggested for opportunities are white men of a certain age, if the people you're asking for advice are all white men of a certain age? It's not about their ethnicity, or their gender, they'll say; *I just want the best person for the job* – and the available people just happen to be disproportionately white men. *She's not quite ready yet, or she wouldn't be interested* . . . It's lazy thinking, but very common.

This old-boys-multiplier effect is powerful, and to guard against it requires a proactive approach to seeking out talent and demanding diversity in the suggested names. It's about embedding a culture of valuing different perspectives and building mixed teams so there is a wide pool of talent to choose from, and so, importantly, people have the chance to get crucial experience that will set them up for future opportunities – like Shirley Williams observing meetings as a parliamentary aide, making her a safe and obvious choice to be promoted to become a minister herself.

Leadership is a vital component in the art of politics: identifying the strategic vision and choosing a path to achieve it. But we should not glorify an individual leader and expect them magically to have all the answers. Leadership is also about building the right team, with a mix of skills and qualities, and inspiring them to act.

Sheryl Sandberg's brilliant book *Lean In*[40] has a chapter titled 'Sit at the Table', the message of which was as needed around the Lib Dem table as any other party or organisation. Political meetings in the deputy prime minister's office were often around a big table that didn't quite have enough chairs for everyone, so some comfy sofas and armchairs were used as a kind of overflow. Inevitably, although people could interject from there, the main power dynamic was round the table. If all the seats at the table were taken, and later someone senior came into the room (e.g. a minister coming from another meeting), someone at the table would vacate their seat. The few women in the meetings did so disproportionately often.

Physical space and location matters. Ideally, find somewhere to meet that can accommodate everyone, but if that's not possible, I think the advice for women to 'sit at the table' is spot on. Those convening a meeting should also look out for and address situations where women (and their voices) are marginalised in the architecture of the room.

The informal, secret-squirrel approach to much political decision-making concentrates power in the hands of those 'in the circle', disproportionately men. Women may not be deliberately excluded, but often somehow are not invited into the room when the decisions are made. One of the funniest and most blatant examples of this I have heard was from the former Finnish MP Johanna Sumuvuori. The Finnish Parliament, in true Scandinavian style, has saunas for MPs and staff, with separate saunas for men and women. Johanna explained how her male colleagues on the Finance Committee would joke that they'd already made all the decisions in the men's sauna before they arrived at the actual Committee. Behind the joke, there was an element of truth – the 'Sauna Committee' is a memorable and specific example of something that happens widely in politics, and whether it's called a 'kitchen cabinet' or a 'sofa government', it's about the decision-making power being hoarded by a small clique which is often less representative than the group it is a subset of. Leaders should recognise that formal structures and processes are more transparent and accessible than their Sauna Committee equivalents. While leaders will always have trusted advisers, they should take care to avoid compounding existing inequalities of power when they choose who will have their ear. Seeking counsel from a diverse group of individuals is one way to stay attuned to power imbalances and appreciate different perspectives.

Pressure from individual members of the public can help drive the right behaviour from our political leaders. One of the easiest ways to do this is astonishingly simple: count.

Count

Counting is the first step to accountability. It can show things that we might otherwise miss. Political power can't be measured purely by numbers of MPs or ministers, but it's a useful proxy. As well as knowing how many candidates or councillors or MPs are men or women, we should extend this counting, sometimes formally and sometimes informally, to other political situations. How many men and women attend a hustings meeting, how many ask questions, how many are on the decision-making committees, how many are party conference speakers, how many are journalists covering politics?

Even when progress has been made, we need to avoid benchmarking against the previous appalling level of representation and coming to the false conclusion that now we have a smattering of women around the place it's all fine, thank you very much.

Equality is 50 per cent of the House of Commons, not 32 per cent. Of course it is important to celebrate progress. Achieving equal power will not happen overnight, so the staging posts along the way do need to be marked and used as inspiration to reach the next milestone – but we should not lose sight of where we want to get to. A world where power is genuinely shared is possible, instead of one where a few women are allowed to play the boys' game as long as they don't rock the boat.

I remember a male colleague talking about how as a party the Lib Dems had a good record of getting women into local government, as then about a third of our councillors were women. While this was a little more than the other parties had managed, I challenged the suggestion that a third was good. Some of the practical challenges of being an MP don't apply to local government, and community groups and organisations are full of women getting stuck in in order to improve their local area. If we can't manage 50:50 representation at council level, we should at the very least be recognising the problem and actively trying to find solutions, not just patting ourselves on the back for being marginally less rubbish than the others.

Too often, the space women take up is exaggerated. Research has shown that the public's estimate of the proportion of women MPs is higher than the reality,[41] and I don't think that can entirely be explained by broadcasters attempting to balance their panels and therefore women being more prominent on our screens.

Even in Parliament itself, not everyone sees the true situation. I was stunned when in a debate in the House of Commons in 2015, Conservative MP Simon Burns disagreed that Parliament was overwhelmingly white and male, citing that there were more women and ethnic minority MPs than before.[42] I did the maths. At the time, fully two-thirds of MPs were white men, compared to 42 per cent of the population. How he didn't see that as overwhelmingly white and male was fascinating. But we all see the world through our own eyes - as a white woman living in the UK, I am less automatically aware of the racial diversity in a room than someone who has regularly experienced discrimination, prejudice and feeling different due to the colour of their skin. I have certainly been aware of my race when visiting countries in Africa - when you stand out as a minority, you feel it. Men often say the same thing when they suddenly find themselves in a room full of women.

We need at least to see the symptoms to have a chance of fixing the problems. Political power is not just in Parliament, so the visibility needs to extend beyond the traditional focus of measuring political participation by elected representatives alone.

You can do this yourself. Put your postcode into www.theywork foryou.com and count the men and women who represent you, on your council and in Parliament and any other positions. Are there equal numbers of men and women? Find the councillors page on your council's website and check out the different party groups. Where they don't have parity between men and women in their groups, contact them and ask what they are doing about it. At election time, you can do the same thing with the lists of candidates, and ask questions in public hustings meetings. When you read the coverage of politics online or in the newspaper, notice the journalists' names at the top. Are they mainly men? Ask the publication why. The answers you receive might seem less than enlightening, but just asking the question has power - it is so rarely asked by members of the public. There are committed political activists, councillors and MPs in all parties who put huge effort into tackling under-representation and improving diversity, but the lack of public pressure means far too many politicians spend hardly any time thinking about these issues and what they might do to address them.

If you're involved in a political party, you can apply the same questioning there. Who are the members of the local and national committees, who attends the conferences, who wields the power of running the campaigns, overseeing the budget and making the decisions? Are the roles segregated along gender lines – do they assume the men will step in to be the candidate and the women will make the tea and cakes for the social event? By noticing, you can start to challenge and change – suggesting women who might like to stand for election and encouraging them along the way, enlisting men to help clear up after the annual dinner, asking for data to be published on the gender split of conference speakers so the party has to take note. Gentle highlighting and dismantling of gender assumptions by individual members in local associations across the country can be a powerful reinforcement to proactive action that the party organisation takes centrally to promote diversity.

Towards Equal Political Power

Electing more women is a vital stepping stone to a society where we have equal power between men and women. The more we can all do to hasten that, whether as voters, activists or candidates, the better. And we all stand to gain from a more equal distribution: more different perspectives and less groupthink leads to better decision-making and policy solutions.

I've been on a journey about what we need to do to achieve this goal. There is a chicken-and-egg situation here. Many of the structural and cultural barriers that stand in the way of electing more women would begin to be broken down if you had more women in elected positions of power. But we can't wait until we get equal representation to deal with those barriers, so we need to be tackling them at the same time. That's one of the reasons why I was so opposed to all-women shortlists in the Lib Dems: I feared it would give the misleading impression that we had solved the problem, leading the party to be complacent, when in fact it would only be a cosmetic change to our group of MPs in the House of Commons, masking the enduring prejudices and problems throughout the party.

Labour have undoubtedly made huge progress in parliamentary representation with all-women shortlists, and they now have 119 women MPs, making up 45 per cent of their total. Yet it's telling that the underlying issues of gender have not gone away. In every election for the leadership of the Labour party, the women candidates have finished last. The Conservatives, with only 21 per cent women MPs, are on their second woman prime minister before Labour have elected a single woman as leader – despite there being a rich and much larger talent pool of Labour women MPs.

The Lib Dems went drastically backwards in 2015, with no women MPs at all. Sadly, my hope in 2001 that the huge gender inequality in the Lib Dem group of MPs would act as a catalyst for concerted, well-resourced action to promote gender equality across the whole party proved naively optimistic. Dozens of men and women gave up significant amounts of their time to talent-spot, train and support women to become candidates, and many thousands hit the streets and the phones to get those women elected as councillors and parliamentarians. But whether it was complacency, or distraction by the hurly-burly of the electoral cycle and dealing with what was urgent rather than important, subsequent leaders didn't really grasp the nettle, and so efforts were not on the necessary scale and didn't have impetus from the top.

Even well-meaning schemes like Ming Campbell's diversity fund to give additional campaign support to candidates from under-represented groups were essentially a PR exercise. After delving into the detail of the party's secretive processes for allocating campaign funds, I discovered that the diversity-fund cash was essentially just replacing funding that would have gone to those candidates from other sources, undermining its objective of channelling extra resources specifically to boost diversity. When I took the evidence that this was happening to Ming at his home in Edinburgh, nothing changed.

I gave Nick Clegg the benefit of the doubt on this time after time, too. Nick was a brilliant deputy prime minister, making the most of the Liberal Democrat opportunity to change the country for the better: helping poorer pupils with extra resources at school, supporting low-earners by cutting their income tax bill, and promoting equality through same-sex marriage. He is married to the inspiring and high-flying lawyer and feminist Miriam González Durántez. I wasn't really ready to believe, therefore, that when push came to shove, gender equality wouldn't make the cut for Nick.

But in reality there was a combination of just not seeing it, and it not being seen as important enough. I recall a fundraising event in 2012 where Nick made a speech name-checking several of our ministers – all men. He then listed past presidents of the party, and while reeling off mens' names he omitted to mention Baroness Ros Scott, who was sitting in the audience. The male bias was very obviously noticed by the women in the room, so as his parliamentary aide, I raised the issue with him afterwards. It just didn't compute. He clearly hadn't intended any slight, and was mortified at mistakenly missing out Ros, but I struggled to get him to understand why this kind of thing matters. Visibility is even more important when there is under-representation, and those people notice when their already minimal representation is airbrushed out of the picture.

Back in 2010 I had pointed out that Nick's appointments to the House of Lords weren't even managing to be 50 per cent women: given the existing Lords group was more than two-thirds men, there was a strong case for significantly more than half of each batch of new nominations to be women. Over the course of the Parliament, I consistently pushed this issue in private with Nick, including sending the names of brilliantly talented, liberal women who could be considered. By 2013 I was so frustrated that I was openly critical, and set out the problem at our parliamentary party away day, and Nick made the commitment that by the end of his time as leader, he'd ensure he had appointed at least 50 per cent women overall. The final tally of Nick's 40 appointments was just 43 per cent women, meaning our Lords group remains 65 per cent male. I used the opportunity of a call with Nick in early 2015 to highlight the importance of gender equality in the 'dissolution honours' - the nominations that happen after an election. Just 27 per cent of the non-peerage honours went to women.[43]

In the autumn of 2014, shortly after we had won the Scottish independence referendum, leaving a divided country that needed to heal, I leaned in. I made my case for promotion to Cabinet, and Nick listened politely. I made a further argument, that even if he chose not to promote me, he should not let our five years in government - possibly our only time in government for a generation - come to an end without a single Liberal Democrat woman serving in Cabinet, which would send out an appalling message for a party committed to equality and opportunity. It didn't have to be me - we had other talented and experienced women with plenty of ministerial experience, such as Lynne Featherstone, Sarah Teather and Susan Kramer. But it wasn't to be anyone. Nick said he didn't think it was all that important to have a woman in Cabinet. He was wrong.

I still believe that all-women shortlists will not deliver the cultural change that our political institutions and parties need, nor the mindset shift in how we identify and encourage activists and candidates. I still believe it is absolutely possible to make big improvements in women's political representation without all-women shortlists. But to make a step change in representation without quotas or hard targets takes strong leadership from the very top, with the leader making it a priority and driving different behaviour, day in, day out.

So in 2016 I found myself, 15 years on from leading the charge against all-women shortlists, proposing a motion at a Liberal Democrat conference alongside Scottish Lib Dem leader Willie Rennie which introduced all-women shortlists in Scotland. Willie is the first Lib Dem leader I've worked with who really, truly gets it: he's prepared to have the tough conversations, spend his own precious political capital, ruffle feathers in the old boys' club, make the controversial choice. Because that's what it takes – rewriting the rules of the game, appointing people who aren't the usual suspects – and it doesn't meet with unreserved admiration, especially from those who still don't recognise the need for change.

So what does this mean for you? Don't be put off when you agitate for change and it feels uncomfortable. That's a sign you're doing the right thing. The status quo is what many people feel comfortable with, but it's got to change. The heart of our democracy shouldn't feel like a step back in time, as it did to my grandmother at the State Opening of Parliament.

If you share my belief that a more equal politics would deliver better leadership for our country, here's an action plan for you, whether you're involved in the political system or not:

- **COUNT:** Notice the split of candidates and elected representatives, speakers at events, journalist bylines in newspapers – and challenge parties, organisers or media outlets when they are not representative.
- **GIVE SOMEONE A BOOST:** Look for opportunities to give others a confidence boost when they need it. A kind word of encouragement, or positive feedback, can make a difference.
- **SPEAK UP:** If you find it difficult to speak up, set yourself mini-targets to develop your own confidence in meetings and at events.
- **JOIN:** Join the political party that most closely represents your views – you can join online in just a few minutes.

- **GET INVOLVED:** Take that next step – volunteer to help in a campaign for a party or a single-issue group, attend a protest march or go to a conference or discussion event.
- **STAND:** Stand for election or, if that's not for you, volunteer to help others you support. Don't be afraid to ask those who have done it before for advice.
- **TALENT-SPOT OUR NEXT WOMEN POLITICIANS:** Be part of the #AskHerToStand campaign by encouraging women you know – friends, family and colleagues – to consider standing for election. Many women who would be excellent representatives have never even thought about it until someone else suggests it.
- **CONTACT YOUR MP:** Write to them or go to see them to ask what they are doing to make politics more representative, and urge them to use their role to implement the actions listed below.

Individuals have an important role to play, and so do political parties and institutions – they must work to:

- Get the big money out of politics with strict limits on spending and donating.
- Provide bursaries and financial support to improve access to political office.
- Link the state funding of political parties for policy work to their progress on diversity.
- Professionalise recruitment and promotion processes to assess skills and potential.
- Get over ageism in politics and value the broad spectrum of views from young to old.

- Run pilot schemes to work out how to make job-sharing successful for elected representatives.
- Implement the remaining recommendations from Professor Childs's review to improve the culture and accessibility of Parliament.
- Commence section 106 of the Equality Act, to force political parties to publish data about the diversity of their candidates.
- Policies and budgets should be analysed from a gender perspective to understand the impact on gender equality.
- Leaders should identify a diverse group of trusted advisers, to avoid the groupthink of homogenous cliques.

2

CHILDHOOD:
Learning the Ropes

From the very first moments of a child's life, their place in the world is viewed through the lens of gender. 'Is it a boy or a girl?' is one of the first questions on the lips of relatives, friends and anyone making polite conversation soon after a baby is born – and sometimes even before. It's the very beginning of a series of tiny and constant cues to parents and children alike about how that new little person should talk, dress, play, behave and generally relate to the world around them.

Equal Power is elusive because we are all complicit in preserving the status quo, even though we often do so unwittingly. From the very beginning, we embed sexism in the next generation. We repeatedly reinforce stereotypes and sexist messages through toys, books, clothes, television, our own behaviours and even the school curriculum. It becomes a subconscious part of how boys and girls – and in time men and women – navigate the world. It's not a case of men imposing sexist attitudes on women, it's all of us passing on what we have learned. Having been raised in this culture ourselves, we have all absorbed the assumptions of inequality, to the extent that we can even fail to recognise it. It is a difficult cycle of harm to break, but it can be done.

Colour-coding Conformity

Small children's capacity for seeing or hearing the same thing over and over again without getting bored is extraordinary, whether it's endless peek-a-boo, a favourite bedtime story or a TV programme. 'Again!' is one of the early commands a toddler will add to their vocabulary. As they explore the world, they quickly see and hear the same messages about boys and girls repeated on a loop – even colour-coded, to make it really simple.

History and science show us how society shapes the preferences of girls and boys in a gendered way. These days we associate pink with girls and blue with boys, yet a century ago these colour allocations were reversed. As the *Ladies' Home Journal* put it in 1918, 'the generally accepted rule is pink for the boy and blue for the girl. The reason is that pink being a more decided and stronger colour is more suitable for the boy, while blue, which is more delicate and dainty, is prettier for the girl.'[1]

The colours may have changed, but the societal expectations of boys to be bold and strong and girls to be meek and look pretty have persisted. We should not be surprised that children notice the myriad messages about gender and start to behave as they are expected to, just as they learn how to say 'please' and 'thank you', or wave goodbye, or put rubbish in the bin.

Researchers can even pinpoint when gendered preferences become apparent, and the magic age is between two and three years old. In an experiment where children from seven months to five years old were offered a choice of two different-coloured but otherwise identical everyday objects, no preference for pink was shown before the age of two, with the pink object chosen around half of the time, in line with random chance. By the age of three, girls showed a bias in favour of pink and boys were less likely to choose it. At age four, girls chose the pink item around 80 per cent of the time, while at five years old boys chose pink only 20 per cent of the time.[2]

When my niece was born I remember being absolutely delighted. As well as having a healthy and happy little addition to the family to love and nurture, suddenly I had an excuse to peruse the oh-so-cute children's clothes sections and buy the kind of things that you'd secretly love to wear as an adult. Kids can get away with anything – a bright-green dinosaur onesie, a big red strawberry-motif T-shirt, furry hats with bear ears, crazily patterned tights.

But I rapidly became dismayed by the pervasive panoply of pink. I like pink – indeed over the years I have enjoyed pink dresses, necklaces and shoes. Wearing pink is fine, but like many lovely things in life, it's about moderation and choice. The typical girls'-clothes aisle looks like a marshmallow has vomited up a florist's shop and then rolled around in some glitter at a tea party for unicorns. By contrast, as I found when my son was born, apparently little boys want to be permanently ready to camouflage themselves in a muddy forest on a dreich autumn day. Surely we can do better than wrap girls in bubblegum pink and cover boys in sludge-grey and khaki?

Then there's the literal labelling of children, with slogans on babygros and T-shirts that reinforce stereotypes and sexualise childhood. Bibs, tops and pyjamas for little girls often focus on appearance and being lovely: 'Beautiful like mummy', 'Pretty as a daisy', 'Little cutie', and even 'Sex kitten', 'Flirt' and 'So many boys . . . so little time'. For boys it is all about being rowdy and mischievous: 'Beware, mischief monster', 'Cheeky like my daddy' and even 'Hello ladies'. Trains and truck motifs for boys; flowers and fluffy animals for girls. In 2015, two much-loved institutions, Marks & Spencer and the Natural History Museum, teamed up to launch a dinosaur-themed clothing range – and marketed it exclusively for boys.[3]

Even sizing is different. There is practically no difference between the shape of boys' and girls' bodies, apart from the genitals, until they hit puberty.[4] But if you place a girl's T-shirt on top of a boy's one for the same age, you will find the girl's garment more fitted. Skinny jeans and leggings that show off the body are made for girls, and boys get roomy, comfy trousers that are practical for adventure. Boys' shoes have chunky soles with good grips and practical coverage of the whole foot, whereas girls are offered Mary-Janes that mean wet feet at the first contact with a puddle or high heels at a ridiculously young age.[5] Perhaps most worryingly from a health perspective, retailers offer significantly more sun-safe swimwear options (SPF material, covering the arms and legs) for boys than girls.[6]

And clothes are only the start. Nine in ten toys listed as being for girls are pink.[7]

When I was a girl, I spent hours playing with Lego, creating a whole town with houses, shops, parks, a hospital and airport, all connected by road plates in varying formations. Today's Lego has evolved, with many more colours and themes. It's great to have a wider range of brick colours, with not just pink, but also turquoise, purple and lime green. But these new colours seem to be marketed only to girls as part of the 'Friends' and 'Elves' sets, while the adverts and packaging for the majority of the other themes are very clearly aimed at boys.

It's a far cry from the approach Lego took in the 1970s, when they included a pamphlet in their boxes of bricks saying:

To parents
The urge to create is equally strong in all children. Boys and girls. It's imagination that counts. Not skill. You build whatever comes into your head, the way you want it. A bed or a truck. A dolls house or a spaceship.

A lot of boys like dolls houses. They're more human than spaceships. A lot of girls prefer spaceships. They're more exciting than dolls houses.

The most important thing is to put the right material in their hands and let them create whatever appeals to them.[8]

However, toy manufacturers have realised that if they create an expectation that toys are boy-specific and girl-specific, rather than just toys, they can sell more. Parents with both a daughter and a son can be encouraged to buy different scooters, or games, or puzzles, rather than using the ones they bought for their older child.

So we have separate 'Boys' and 'Girls' sections of toyshops and websites. The imagery on toy packaging and in adverts often defaults to lazy stereotypes. Boys playing with the science kits, construction sets and superhero toys. Girls are in the make-believe kitchens, playing with dolls and doing sparkly crafts. Women are in the domestic sphere, while men are doing exciting things outside the home.

Children love to play: it is one of the most important ways they learn about the world and develop aspirations for their adult life. Yet children's media, toys and books are channelling boys and girls into narrow roles from their earliest years.

Superhero v Princess

A professional woman I know took her four-year-old daughter to the doctor, only to be mortified when the little girl loudly exclaimed, 'She can't be a doctor, she's a woman!' Another friend on a hospital trip found their child was relaxed about the women doctors, but couldn't get over the nurse being a man. Others have had similar experiences, carefully raising their child free of gender assumptions, then being shocked when their son or daughter suddenly expresses a view steeped in stereotypes. Where do they get it from? Toyshops, in part.

In 2010, the Early Learning Centre changed the way they displayed their dressing-up clothes.[9] Instead of boys modelling doctor coats while girls wore nurse outfits, the new catalogue showed both boys and girls in a range of costumes. It was a victory for the letter and email campaign run by PinkStinks founders Emma and Abi Moore. Along with campaign groups such as Let Toys Be Toys, they have successfully put pressure on more and more retailers to remove gendered signage from their toy departments and websites, such as Boots,[10] Debenhams[11] and Toys 'R' Us.[12]

While there has been some progress, there is still a huge way to go. In 2014, the Early Learning Centre found themselves criticised again, for a dressing-up clothes promotion casting girls in helpless, passive roles while the boys as superheroes and a doctor saved the day.[13] Even where there have been wins, the assumptions are so ingrained that the campaigning needs to continue.

The different expectations for girls and boys are often still rigidly defined in play, as exemplified by Marvel superheroes and Disney princesses. These characters are everywhere: notebooks, toothpaste, lunchboxes, bedding, potties, breakfast cereals – you name it, it's branded.

The archetypal superhero is strong, active and exciting, casting the child in the role of saving the world but expressing no emotion or depth. The typical princess is beautiful, impossibly slim and patiently waiting for her prince, casting the child in the role of decoration without ambition or agency. Message received: girls should focus on looking good and boys should bottle up their feelings to project a strong, confident persona.

It presents children with a false choice between emotion and ambition, as if you can't have both. Thankfully there are some examples which buck the trend. Superheroes who are complex emotional characters, like Batman, are more compelling.

Princesses who deploy superpowers, like Elsa from *Frozen*, are much more interesting.

Zog, the princess story by former Children's Laureate Julia Donaldson, features a princess who decides to become a doctor. Recent Disney films *Moana* and *Zootropolis* have featured female lead characters, and refreshingly the plot is about their achievements rather than their love lives. Though Disney don't always get it right. Merida, the star of the film *Brave*, is a strong princess who rescues herself, yet the studio had planned to redesign her for the merchandise as slimmer, more sparkly and sexy – something they were forced to abandon when more than 250,000 people signed a petition to 'Keep Merida Brave'.[14]

Let's not forget the original combination of superhero and princess, the wonderful Princess Leia from *Star Wars*. But even Leia and her ilk are short-changed. Sci-fi geek and blogger Simon Ragoonanan noticed something strange happening with film franchises. The (female) characters of Princess Leia, Gamora (*Guardians of the Galaxy*) and Black Widow (*The Avengers*) seemed to be curiously absent from the merchandising on sale around the films' release dates. When *Star Wars: The Force Awakens* came out in 2015, he criticised the 'ridiculous' decision to exclude the main character, Rey, from many products, including a special-edition Monopoly set: 'It's like taking Skywalker out.'[15] Online outrage using the #WheresRey hashtag eventually shamed game-makers Hasbro into a U-turn, promising Rey would be included in a later edition,[16] but the fact that the lead character could be excluded in the first place – just for being a woman – speaks volumes about the assumptions in the industry.

Science is still widely presented as an interest for boys rather than girls – research in 2016 found that science toys were *three times* as likely to be listed as being for boys than girls.[17] It was only in 2013 that high-street retailer Boots announced they would remove gender signs for toys, after customer complaints that science toys were in the 'boys' section.[18] There are precious few women in science and engineering roles – areas where our economy has serious skills shortages. Just 9 per cent of engineers are women.[19] It's not such a surprising figure when you consider only one in five of those sitting A-level physics are girls – and this figure has barely moved for a generation.[20] The early message that science is not for girls is part of the problem. Research shows that the perceptions of science as for boys can put girls off, and significantly more boys than girls aspire to a career in science even at primary-school age.[21]

On the other hand, dolls are seen as exclusively for girls, mirroring the societal expectation that caring roles are done by women, not men. Yet our social-care sector is struggling to fill vacancies, and men are an obvious untapped pool of talent, as they currently make up just 18 per cent of care workers.[22] When I dared utter such sentiments in Parliament,[23] the media had a field day: 'GIVE LADS A BARBIE', screamed the *Sun*.[24] The backlash was fascinating, not just in the media but in wider public conversations and debate. Society seems fairly relaxed about girls playing with train sets, but rigidly resists boys playing with dolls. It's an interesting experiment to try: ask your friends or family how they feel about their son/nephew/grandson playing with a doll, and see what reaction you get. What is behind this discomfort?

Over the years there have been big changes in how femininity is perceived – today's girlhood embraces traits of adventure and achievement that would once have been labelled 'tomboyish'. We openly encourage girls to reach for the top, to be ambitious, and girls aspiring to traditionally male roles is largely seen as positive. But there has not been equivalent progress in the other direction: the notion of masculinity has remained much more fiercely defined. Girls can now join the Scouts.[25] There is no rush of people manning the barricades asking for boys to be allowed to join the Guides. From adults reinforcing 'boys don't cry', to the playground insults 'you're such a girl' or 'cissy', there is much less encouragement for boys to embrace traditionally feminine traits. This restricts boys' choices, as they can feel shame at pursuing activities like dance or even reading, because they are insufficiently 'masculine'. Career avenues such as teaching or social care may not be explored by them.

Somehow, a boy with a doll is seen as a threat to masculinity itself. Women and men alike should be alarmed at the brittle constraints on how to be a man today. Developing a modern vision of masculinity that is flexible and broadens the horizons for our sons is every bit as important as nurturing the ambitions of our daughters.

The Default Male

When he was two, my son was obsessed with butterflies. In any book, no matter how tiny or incidental a butterfly was to the illustration, he'd loudly proclaim 'Butterfly!' and point excitedly at it, rather than the main character. I think I know why. From a very early age he adored *The Very Hungry Caterpillar* by Eric Carle, just like millions of other children over the years. After reading it countless times, eventually I could recite it by heart – including getting the ten different foods that the caterpillar eats on Saturday in the right order. (I know – impressive, right?) This came in pretty handy for getting him back to sleep in the middle of the night without having to turn on the light. The final flourish of the book is, of course, the caterpillar becoming a butterfly, hence my son's firm attachment to these creatures.

Storytelling is at the heart of what it is to be human. We tell children stories from their earliest days. They don't understand the words at first, but the sound of parental voices and familiar words has a soothing effect. Later on they love the pictures, and demand repetition of their favourite books, often night after night.

Yet even the cosy world of children's literature perpetuates a male-centric view of the world.[26] In compiling a children's dictionary in 1972, Alma Graham and her team considered 700,000 printed slips from a computer that had analysed 1,000 children's books and magazines. These slips showed common words in three lines of context to help them pitch the definitions in a way that children could comprehend. Astonishingly, data from the slips showed that there were twice as many boys as girls written about in children's books, and seven times as many men as women.[27] Mothers, however, were more common than fathers, and wives were mentioned three times as often as husbands – demonstrating that men were cast in the main roles but women were still dominant when it came to caring.

A more recent study in 2011 which looked at 6,000 children's books published across the 20th century found that the characters were more than twice as likely to be male than female. By the 1990s this had improved to near parity for human characters, but male animal characters still outnumbered female animal characters two to one.[28]

Even though male characters are generally more numerous in books, there are exceptions. One day, while reading a nursery-rhyme picture book of 'Five Little Ducks', my son asked a simple but brilliant question: 'Where's Daddy Duck?' *Good point*, I thought. In the real world, Mummy Duck would soon be reported to social services for losing one of her children every day, but you've got to feel some sympathy for her, juggling five kids with seemingly no help from their father. Despite the overall male default, the traditional roles are still clear – parent characters are much more likely to be female, reinforcing views that caring is for girls, not boys.

We often use the male pronoun, even when gender is not known, and not just in books – it happens in everyday conversation. We talk about a squirrel scampering up a tree in the garden ('Look! There he goes!'), the tiger prowling at the zoo ('Isn't he big?') or the duck showing little interest in chunks of bread you've just thrown into the pond ('Maybe he isn't hungry today'). I catch myself doing it many times – making the default male – even though I'm writing this book and immersing myself in issues of equality. It's such a deeply ingrained, subconscious linguistic pattern that it is difficult to shake off.

Do these words matter? The truth is simply that when we hear the words 'he' and 'his', we are picturing men and boys, not women and girls. And by allocating pronouns so everyone is either he or she, we ignore people whose gender doesn't fit neatly into a male/female binary. Visualisation and visibility are important. Words do matter if we want all children to see themselves reflected in our culture, and to keep an open mind about what they might go on to achieve.

Analysis of gender pronouns in US books over the twentieth century shows that the ratio of male pronouns to female pronouns fell from 4.5:1 in the 1960s to around 2:1 by the early 2000s, reflecting – or perhaps encouraging – improvements in gender equality over that time.[29] It's a trend that needs to continue.

But the male default in language is so ingrained – just how do you go about changing the subconscious habit of a lifetime? I used to alternate the gender pronouns in songs. So 'Five little monkeys, jumping on the bed . . .' would be followed by 'one fell off and bumped *his* head' or '*her* head' depending on whether it was an odd- or even-numbered verse. We made sure our son's cuddly toys had a range of names, which made it easier to remember to refer to them not always as 'he' – so we have Amanda the Panda, Cilla the Gorilla and Gina the Lemur. When choosing books for children, remember the hero doesn't always need to be a little white boy. If you're reading to children and the characters are all blokes, you can even it out by changing some *he*s to *she*s or *they*s: it won't harm the story if Steve the monkey becomes Steph, or if you read Daddy Duck where the words Mummy Duck are printed.

When we use gendered qualifiers, we are also making a statement about what is the default. A female engineer, the FIFA Women's World Cup, a woman CEO – these all imply that the people in question are a deviation from the norm. It's hard to imagine the same phrases used with the gender swapped:

a male engineer, the FIFA Men's World Cup, a man CEO. On the flipside, we see the words 'male nurse' and 'male nanny' (or worse, 'manny'), but not 'female nurse', 'female nanny'.

Films show a real gender bias, too. Characters in family films are still more than two-thirds male.[30] I remember my friend James Millar telling me how he was going to see the film *Tinkerbell* at the weekend. When I expressed sympathy, he explained why he had to go. As a keen observer of gender inequality in childhood – he and his partner co-wrote *The Gender Police: A Diary* – his family has a rule that when they take their son and daughter to the cinema, they alternate films with a male lead and a female lead. The dearth of children's films with a female main character meant that *Tinkerbell* was a must-see (though he later reported the film was not as bad as he'd feared).

Computer games are even more skewed towards the male gender, which is a problem given that more than seven in ten children between the ages of six and fourteen play them, and it's worth noting that girls are as likely to play as boys.[31] Twelve-year-old Madeleine Messer noticed the apps her friends were playing on didn't always offer the option to play as a girl character, and she downloaded 50 top games to look at the scale of the problem.[32] The results were shocking – players had more than twice the chance of being able to play as a male character than as a female character, and they were *six times* more likely to have the choice of playing a male character for free than a female one. Put simply, if you wanted to play as a girl on screen in these games, you had to pay extra – on average $7.53, which was 29 times the average cost of the apps themselves. Many studies also document the frequent hyper-sexualisation of female characters in computer games,[33] and that their attributes often cast them as weak or frivolous,[34] with disadvantages for gameplay.

It's easy to imagine that manufacturers are simply responding to children's preferences. Like many men, Simon Ragoonanan had always assumed that pink and sparkly things were just what girls liked, and it didn't really matter anyway. Then he became a father, to a daughter who loves both superheroes and princesses. Now he sees the issue differently, and is worried about how implicit gender expectations in toys and culture constrain girls. He describes it as the 'cul-de-sac of girls' interests . . . like girls' interests are in a bubble, and everything else is for boys'.

That brilliantly captures the issue. The pervasive segregation of girls' toys with pink sparkly princess signposting creates the impression that everything that isn't pink and sparkly and princessy is for boys, reinforcing the fact that the default setting is male.

When the 13th Doctor Who was unveiled as a woman in 2017, the outcry from some quarters was essentially a backlash against any challenge to this male default.[35] After 12 white male Doctors in a row, the BBC's decision to cast a woman, Jodie Whittaker, to play the much-loved time-travelling humanoid alien was long overdue and, despite the negativity of some, was happily welcomed by most people. So there is certainly progress, but still so much more to do.

It's easy for people to dismiss as irrelevant the issues of what toys children play with, the books they read and the words we use when talking to them. Many people maintain that it is just up to the children themselves what they choose. Some of this *is* choice. But it's heart-breaking to understand the beliefs that underlie those decisions, formed at such an incredibly early age. Young primary-school children learn what is appropriate and expected for their gender, and self-select certain activities, narrowing their future options. Research has found that at the age of five, girls and boys were equally likely to associate their gender with being 'really, really smart'. By the age of six, there was a significant gender difference, with boys and girls more likely to associate brilliance with boys and niceness with girls. Crucially, this saw the girls opting out of activities and games they perceived to be for those who are 'really, really smart'.[36] These children are only six years old. After a decade of these choices, is it any wonder there is such a lack of girls taking A-level physics?

Brilliant v Nice. Superhero v Princess. Blue v Pink. We give children these messages over and over and over again, directly and subtly, in bedtime stories and real-life examples, through children's TV characters and Christmas presents, in every passing comment about brave boys and beautiful girls. We are naive if we think a half-day school careers workshop at the age of 14, and a few lightly funded programmes to encourage girls into science – and even-less-funded programmes to encourage boys into teaching – can ever compete with the powerful gendered indoctrination of early childhood.

Education, Education, Education

Even our school curriculum falls into the same trap. Seventeen-year-old student Jessy McCabe was doing her A-level music homework when she suddenly realised she had never studied a composer who was a woman. On looking in detail at the syllabus, she found 63 composers listed – every one of them a man. Confident this was an oversight and just needed pointing out to the Edexcel exam board, she emailed them to complain. She was shocked when they defended the omission, saying there weren't enough women composers to be included. Jessy started a petition on a Friday, put it on Twitter on the Saturday, and by the Monday, Channel 4 News had got in touch to run the story. The media attention was, Jessy admits, 'quite scary' – but it was also effective. The head of the exam board contacted her to ask for a meeting, where he backtracked and apologised, and agreed to start work to redraft the syllabus. Twelve women composers are now included across different musical genres.

What's interesting about Jessy's story is not only her success, but also that she assumed she would have been one of many people making the same complaint, and was shocked to be the first. She showed that one person with a worthy cause can make a difference. Her advice to others is to take action: 'It felt amazing . . . Go for it, don't stop yourself because it's a tiny bit scary.'[37]

Edexcel's old music syllabus is not some unusual bastion of maleness on an otherwise level playing field. Women's achievements have often been written out of history, or appropriated by men, and assumptions get made that there just aren't enough women who have done things of note to learn about. Dame Helen Fraser, who previously led the Girls' Day School Trust, has highlighted the lack of women across a range of subjects, from science to art to politics. In English literature, for example, the OCR exam board included just eight women on a list of 45 authors. She explains: 'Women are excluded, not deliberately, but thoughtlessly. The historic context is no excuse for leaving women out.'[38]

In an ironic twist, in 2015 the feminist movement itself seemed at risk of being written out of the education script in England, when a new A-level politics curriculum was proposed which omitted feminism from major political philosophies and included just one woman on its list of 14 key political thinkers. Again, it was a young woman who challenged the system, this time 17-year-old student and blogger June Eric-Udorie, who started a petition that attracted around 50,000 signatures. Ministers thought twice, and promised to include more women thinkers and ensure that feminism was included in the core syllabus.[39] Activism having firmly taken root, in 2017 June crowdfunded over £5,000 to organise a free cinema screening of *Hidden Figures* in east London for more than 400 black and minority ethnic schoolgirls from low-income families. The film tells the story of the black women mathematicians who helped secure NASA's success in the space race, and who were subsequently erased from the narrative.

I remember an interview I did with a journalist about gender equality in nursery education, shortly after I returned to work from maternity leave. The journalist had been exploring the Swedish system, where educational institutions, including preschools, have had a responsibility to promote equal opportunities between boys and girls since 1998.[40] The government there states 'gender equality should reach and guide all levels of the Swedish educational system'.[41] I was suddenly struck by a pang of horror that despite my best efforts, and songs with girl monkeys and boy monkeys jumping equally on the bed, for ten hours a day my son was in the hands of other people, and while I knew they were wonderfully caring, I had no idea whether or not gender stereotypes were being reinforced, and whether it was even on the radar.

Schools play a formative role in how we learn about the world, and should be about opening up the horizons of children, not funnelling them down specific gender pathways. And if they aren't consciously thinking about equality, then like the rest of society they will default to the pattern of male dominance and gendered assumptions. Whether it's a teacher announcing 'I need four strong boys to carry these chairs to the assembly hall' or telling children to 'remember to give the letter in your schoolbag to your mum tonight', the stereotypes are reinforced in myriad ways.

The prevalence of women in the teaching profession is no antidote, because all of us – women and men alike – have internalised society's assumptions and prescriptive gender roles. In fact, the skewed proportion of female staff in early-years settings just ends up reinforcing the assumption that 'women = carers' and does no favours for young boys, who miss out on having a wide range of role models. Just 15 per cent of primary teachers in England are men[42], and in Scotland it's even lower at 10 per cent.[43] Only one in five trainee teachers are men – and worse, this figure has actually fallen in recent years.[44] The situation is dire in nurseries, with men making up a meagre 2 per cent of staff.[45] As well as a better gender balance among staff, awareness of equality issues and how to promote equal opportunities in the classroom should be a key part of teacher training.

Conscious effort is needed to change the default settings. We should follow Sweden's example, and require schools to be proactive about embedding gender equality in the learning environment from the very beginning. Guidance should require nurseries and schools to ensure that the delivery of the curriculum does not default to an exclusively white male view of history, literature, music, science, philosophy and so on. Instead, a variety of men and women from a range of ethnic backgrounds should be included as examples, case studies and subjects of study. A gender-neutral school uniform policy means all children can choose more practical clothes (no more telling girls they can't turn cartwheels in their school dress), and it also makes life that little bit easier for children who are exploring their own gender identity. School inspections should assess specifically on gender equality as a stand-alone measure. Existing programmes to encourage men into the caring and teaching professions need a significant boost from government, not just in funding but in profile and priority.

Of course, in many countries girls still struggle to receive an education at all. Around the world, more than 60 million girls are missing out on school.[46] The barriers are varied, and include practical challenges as well as cultural assumptions. Poor sanitation may mean girls spend up to six hours a day collecting water, leaving little time for school. Many girls drop out of education when they start to menstruate if there is no safe place at school to keep clean during their period. (Shockingly, period poverty even means girls in England miss school or end up using socks or tissues as makeshift sanitary protection.)[47] Girls may be required to help with domestic duties or family care, and child labour can interrupt girls' education as young as five.[48]

Every day, 38,000 girls are married as children, which often brings education to an abrupt end, as can teenage pregnancies.[49] While child marriage is more prevalent in the developing world, it is not confined to those countries: 167,000 girls under 18 were married in the United States in the first decade of the 21st century, some of them as young as 12.[50]

In some places, girls risk their own safety when they go to school, such as the 276 schoolgirls kidnapped by Boko Haram in Nigeria,[51] or Malala Yousafzai, who was shot in the head by the Taliban in Pakistan at the age of 15 when she was travelling home on the school bus. She made an amazing recovery, became a global advocate for girls' education, won the Nobel Peace Prize in 2014 and continues to be a beacon of inspiration.

The astonishing thing is, educating girls is a no-brainer – it saves lives, strengthens communities and increases economic growth. As esteemed economist Professor Lawrence Summers said when he was Chief Economist of the World Bank, 'The education of girls may well be the highest-return investment available in the developing world.'[52] We shouldn't have to campaign for something so obviously good, yet we do. The Malala Fund website has lots of resources to encourage young people around the world to take action – by contacting elected representatives, writing blogs or articles for local newspapers about the importance of girls' education, fundraising for the charity, or inviting friends to read the book I Am Malala and hosting a discussion group about it.[53] You don't have to be as brave as Malala or be a Nobel prizewinner to make a difference.

The Good Girl Game

I went to my local state comprehensive school, Douglas Academy, but bog-standard it was not. The kind of school with a crest and a motto,[54] it had a strong ethos and high standards were expected. I became a bit of a swot, and it paid off with top grades. Each year there was a prize-giving ceremony, and in my fifth year I won the Senior Dux prize, for overall academic achievement. The prize included engraving my name on a trophy and a book of my choice to be presented to me at the ceremony. The book I chose was something of a revelation. Authored by Kate White, who later edited *Cosmopolitan*, it was called *Why Good Girls Don't Get Ahead . . . But Gutsy Girls Do: Nine Secrets Every Career Woman Should Know*. Black, white and bright pink with clashing fonts, the cover evokes the 1990s, when the slightly exotic – not entirely positive – concept of a 'career woman' was represented in the media by power suits, shoulder pads and briefcases.

As a 16-year-old, many of the office dilemmas described in the book felt far beyond my daily life, as my work experience had consisted of a week in the Glasgow *Herald* newspaper office, a paper round and a Saturday job at McDonald's. Kate White's lessons on delegation, breaking up big projects into small tasks and embracing feedback proved very useful later on in my career, but it is the core message of the book that was – and remains – so stunning in its truth and simplicity.

Through family relationships, celebrated role models, media representation and the education system, we encourage girls to play the 'Good Girl Game': work incredibly hard, follow the rules, keep your head down, be liked, and wait patiently to be recognised with a pay rise or a promotion. It is a recipe for staying in the slow lane at work, for being overtaken by others who are less talented or less hard-working, but play by different rules.

Top headhunter Sue O'Brien OBE has seen the impact of the Good Girl Game over many years recruiting for senior positions. Over a friendly cup of tea after I lost my seat in 2015, she asked me to think about the first time I fancied someone, and what advice my friends gave me. I recalled my first teenage crush. My best friend had taken a shine to the same boy, and together we would engineer scenarios where we might 'bump into' him. We hung out at a park near where he lived. I started taking the bus to school, as he also got the bus – all in pursuit of opportunities where he might notice me. We did this for *months*. Sue explained this was a typical female response, and that men will commonly answer that their friends suggested asking the person out, and if they said no, to move on and find another: 'Even at school, boys are conditioned to ask for what they want, while girls are not. So is it any surprise when it comes to asking for a promotion, or a pay rise, that women are less well practised?'

As a Member of Parliament, I regularly visit schools and talk to the pupils about my job, how democracy works and topical issues of the day. I always invite questions, yet with wearying regularity, around nine times out of ten, the first child to put up their hand to ask a question is one of the boys. How is this behaviour embedded at such a young age?

Sometimes the divide is so stark and the girls so quiet that

I specifically address the point to try to encourage questions. I explain how I'd experienced that little voice of doubt in my head when it came to speaking up: sitting through a discussion, thinking about what I might ask or the point I might make but then discarding or dismissing possible options, telling myself it would sound silly or obvious, or I'd somehow communicate it wrongly. And then typically, lo and behold, some bloke would ask what I'd been thinking of asking, but do so less eloquently than the words I'd formulated in my head, and he would be applauded for his insight. Then there's the problem that I often had, like when I was in the audience of BBC *Question Time* as a university student, that if you don't pluck up the courage to put up your hand until halfway through the time for questions, you're less likely to be noticed. So, after all that psyching yourself up, you end up saying nothing anyway.

There are myriad ways we socially condition boys and girls differently. From sloganising T-shirts and segregating books and toys, to contrasting sugar 'n' spice with slugs and snails – we make it very clear to little girls that they should be good, and 'ladylike'. This basically translates to quiet, prim and proper, reserved and certainly not even thinking about breaking the rules. The Girlguiding Attitudes Survey shows seven- to ten-year-old girls already have strong associations between character traits and gender: boys are strong, adventurous and brave whereas girls are caring, helpful and shy.[55]

At school, I had learned to play the Good Girl Game and excel at it. In the workplace, I had to unlearn many of my 'good girl' habits in order to get things done. I loved the 'gutsy girls' in the Kate White book: breaking the rules, taking risks, acting like a winner and asking for what they want. Doing these things often earns girls censure from teachers, parents and classmates, who can take a different attitude to the same behaviours from boys – 'boys will be boys', after all.

When women behave assertively, we are judged on a different basis to men. Like when I challenged a businessman whose company had presented an appalling piece of research about shared parental leave. His widely reported press release had wrongly suggested that only 1 per cent of new dads were using shared parental leave, but his data confused take-up rates for eligible fathers with the millions of men who hadn't taken the leave for the obvious reason that they hadn't just become a father. Demolishing his arguments with facts and logic, I'll never forget what he then said: 'I'd thought you were nice.' *Nice?* As if he thought I'd driven policy changes through government in the face of firm opposition just by smiling sweetly.

Then there was the memorable critique of Prime Minister Theresa May by Kenneth Clarke, caught on camera when he thought the microphone was off, calling her a 'bloody difficult woman'.[56] And President Donald Trump's dismissal of Hillary Clinton in the presidential debate as 'such a nasty woman'.[57] Women are even expected to prioritise niceness over achieving their objectives, and the very act of being successful means they are perceived as less likeable. As Sheryl Sandberg points out in her book *Lean In*, success and likeability are positively correlated for men, but negatively for women.[58] Girls see this and learn to behave accordingly.

Changing the Script

When as a minister I was devising policies to get more women into senior roles in the workplace, I hosted roundtable discussions with women who had made it to the top. I was often struck by how, even when exploring boardroom success, our discussions would keep coming back to childhood – role models, toys, school subject choices, and how gendered assumptions about what men and women do take root at such an early stage. One of the biggest barriers to a world where power is shared equally between men and women is that childhood currently functions as an apprenticeship in gender inequality. Again and again, children are bombarded with messages about girls being pretty, passive and pink – and boys being strong, active, in charge.

In *The Prime of Miss Jean Brodie*, the teacher famously says, 'Give me a girl at an impressionable age and she is mine for life.' She rightly recognised the power of influence during childhood. We absorb so many gender prejudices and stereotypes during our early years, and the fact that we've all grown up doing so is one of the reasons why change can be so difficult. It's also why challenging the sexist assumptions that permeate childhood is so important in the fight for Equal Power. We need to change this script, and give the next generation the benefit of an open mind about gender roles. Here's how you can help.

- **OPEN CHOICES:** Don't assume what a child will like because of their gender. Encourage them to experience the books, toys, clothes, after-school clubs and activities that are marketed at both boys and girls (but don't over-correct either – remember there's nothing wrong with boys enjoying football and girls playing with dolls).

- **THE POWER OF PRAISE:** Children notice what they are praised for, so take care to praise boys for being kind/caring/gentle/ thoughtful, and girls for being daring/strong/adventurous/ powerful – as much as the other way around.

- **FIND ROLE MODELS:** If you find one gender is over- represented – whether it's in an education syllabus, a film or a workplace that your child experiences – go online, seek out and celebrate alternative examples as role models, to prove that gender does not need to constrain their ambitions. If you're involved with a school, encourage them to invite role models who challenge the stereotypes to talk to pupils. Websites like inspiringthefuture.org and speakers4schools.org can help connect you with people to come and speak.

- **MIND YOUR LANGUAGE:** Words matter. Think about how you talk to children, whether as a parent, teacher, relative or friend. Resist reinforcing the 'brilliant v nice' division. Instead of the temptation just to comment on a girl's clothes or a boy's favourite sports team, ask questions: What is their favourite book? If they could have a superpower, what would they choose? Get them talking.

- **EXPAND HORIZONS:** Parents have a huge influence on career aspirations. Check out guides like 'Your Daughter's Future'[59] from the National Careers Service, or resources at the Prince's Trust,[60] and use them as a starting point for a chat with children or young people you know about what they might do with their lives.

- **MAKE EQUALITY THE DEFAULT:** Try to notice when you default to the male or make gendered assumptions when talking about a particular occupation. Make an effort not to fall into that trap – and correct yourself when you do.

- **CONTACT YOUR MP:** Ask them to support gender equality being embedded within education, through changes to school inspection criteria and curriculum guidance.
- **JOIN FORCES:** Link up with other parents to encourage your child's school or nursery to consider gender equality more comprehensively in what they do, in everything from school shows to the contents of the library.
- **SUPPORT EDUCATION FOR GIRLS GLOBALLY:** Visit the Malala Fund website[61] for ideas on how to take action to support education for girls around the world.
- **TACKLE PERIOD POVERTY:** Even in the UK, girls from poorer backgrounds can miss out on full participation in education due to a lack of funds for sanitary protection. Donate sanitary products to your local foodbank – it can be as simple as buying an extra pack at the supermarket and putting it in the foodbank donation trolley that most stores will have.
- **ASK WHY BEFORE YOU BUY:** Be thoughtful when shopping for clothes, toys and books for children. Avoid stereotypes, and buy products that are gender-neutral and positively feature a diverse range of characters.
- **JOIN THE CAMPAIGNERS:** Sign up for news from groups like Let Clothes Be Clothes and Let Toys Be Toys. They include links to gender-neutral products and retailers. You can use their template letters to complain, and add your voice to the regular challenges they make to retailers and manufacturers. Campaign for schools to adopt gender-neutral uniform policies.

- **LISTEN:** Hear what girls and boys say about their experiences, and ask them what they think. Discuss and explore ideas of gender and assumptions, so they have the language and confidence to challenge stereotypes themselves.
- **TALK:** Initiate a conversation with family or friends about issues like boys playing with dolls, as a springboard to chatting more widely about gender in childhood and challenging stereotyped assumptions. If you're a parent, let your children know about the action you are taking, and get them involved.
- **SHARE:** Use the power of your social media in your networks to spread the word. Celebrate products and projects getting it right, and put pressure on those getting it wrong. Whether it is Facebook, Instagram or Twitter, let companies know what you think.
- **REPRESENT:** If you're a girl, young woman or are genderfluid, stand for your school council or the Youth Parliament, or join a debating society. Find your voice. If you're a boy or young man, you can do these things, too – and use your voice to challenge gender inequality.
- **REMEMBER, ONE PERSON CAN CREATE CHANGE:** Draw inspiration from the campaigns of people like Jessy McCabe, who changed the A-level music syllabus, and June Eric-Udorie, who inspired hundreds of girls. Individuals can make a difference, so if you see an injustice, take action to challenge and change it.

3

BODIES:
Blood, Sweat
and Tears

In 1983, Sally Ride became the first American woman in space. When a team of (male) engineers were working out what needed to be in the flight kit for her one-week mission, they suggested 100 tampons. 'No. That would not be the right number,'[1] she gently replied.

The taboo around women's bodies and their natural functions fuels ignorance, suspicion and shame, from a girl's first period to the menopause and beyond. That some male readers may now be wondering whether 100 tampons for a one-week space flight is too many or too few is indicative of how even today we shy away from discussing the basic biology that affects the lives of half of the population on a regular basis. In some parts of the world, menstruating women are seen as unclean and are confined to live in spartan 'menstrual huts', often exposed to the elements.[2] Pre-menstrual tension is the butt of a thousand 'jokes'. President Donald Trump suggested reporter Megyn Kelly's tough questions were due to her being on her period, saying, 'You could see there was . . . blood coming out of her – wherever.'[3]

Supermarkets and chemists display tampons, sanitary towels and menstrual cups under the banner 'feminine care' or 'monthly hygiene', as if the words 'period' or 'menstruation' might offend. Indeed, even saying the word 'period' has been taboo – the actor Courtney Cox, best known for playing Monica Geller in *Friends*, was actually the first person to say the word 'period' in a sanitary protection commercial on US television,[4] in a Tampax advert in 1985.[5] In a House of Commons debate on abolishing the 'tampon tax' (sanitary protection products were classed as 'luxury' items and therefore had VAT charged on them), MP Stella Creasy was so frustrated by the linguistic dancing around the issue, she successfully challenged Conservative MP Bill Cash to say the word 'tampon'.[6]

Tampon and sanitary towel adverts themselves have been laughable.[7] Bizarre stereotypes of roller-skating women walking dogs, and those scientific tests about absorbency – always with that weird blue liquid. Guys – just so you know – period blood isn't actually blue.[8] In 2016, Bodyform broke new ground with their Red.Fit campaign, depicting active women and actual blood (from sporting injuries: a rugby player's nose, a rock climber's hands, a ballet dancer's feet).[9] While they still didn't represent the 'curled up on the sofa with a hot-water bottle' part of periods, it was nonetheless a refreshing change.

To the extent that it's acceptable to talk about it, it's the 'time of the month', 'having the painters in', 'Aunt Flo visiting', 'on the rag', 'surfing the crimson wave' or even 'shark week'. These euphemisms are common across languages – from 'strawberry week' in German, 'little sister has come' in Chinese, or the memorable 'there are communists in the funhouse' in Danish.[10] Amusing and creative though some of these are, the very number and scale of the ways to say it without saying it points to the taboo – why not just 'I'm on my period'? It's only blood, it's every month and it's happening to half the population, so why the social discomfort?

An international development charity, Plan UK, produced a brilliant video to promote their #JustATampon campaign, where blokes were presented with various sanitary products and asked what they knew about them.[11] 'Is this a Shewee, like they use at festivals?' one says, picking up a Mooncup. 'So the string is literally left dangling . . . ?' asks another in a tone of disbelief, holding a tampon after reading the instructions. 'Do you change it daily . . . or weekly?' (It's every four to six hours, actually.) Fair play to the guys who took part – probably not the easiest thing to volunteer for, and yet it was an important film, demonstrating the gap in knowledge. At school, first lessons about puberty tend to take place with boys and girls separated, which makes a lot of sense to reduce the snigger factor and enable children to feel comfortable asking questions. While many will have had some conversation about these changes at home, others will be taking in a huge amount of information – information that can be quite shocking – for the first time. But it is not right for boys to be left in the dark about what happens to girls, or vice versa.

Menstruation is not the only biological aspect of women's bodies that we recoil from in public discourse. Reproduction and fertility issues are endured silently, so that many women who experience problems conceiving, miscarriage or early menopause feel isolated in private grief.

Yet women's bodies are anything but private. They are talked about, touched without consent, judged and damned. The lens that sees breasts and vaginas as primarily sexual also sees breastfeeding and periods as things to be hushed up and hidden away. Our society frames so much of women's value in the physicality of their bodies, and maintains a narrow view of what those bodies should do: conform to a particular ideal of attractiveness, be just the perfect amount of sexually available, reproduce and then snap back to the standard beauty ideal as quickly as possible.

Combined with impossible beauty standards, girls and women are left feeling inadequate and pour huge amounts of energy into body maintenance - energy that could be otherwise directed.

Men and women alike reinforce these beauty requirements through their behaviours. The price of women not conforming to the beauty ideal is often so prohibitively high that they are really not in a position to choose to challenge it - but by conforming, they reinforce it for everyone else.

Reproduction Values

Exercising some control over fertility is empowering, enabling women to make choices about when to focus on their studies or career and when they would like to become pregnant, rather than leaving it to chance. The advent of the contraceptive pill in the 1960s,[12] and more recent alternatives such as hormone injections or implants, have been game-changers. As a young woman, I got my information on what was available from magazines like *Just Seventeen*.[13] There would be whole features on different methods of contraception, case studies and a handy list of contacts of where to go for more information. One article had a table setting out the advantages and disadvantages of different contraception methods, as well as their effectiveness rate. The intrauterine device (or 'coil' – a copper device inserted into the womb to prevent a fertilised egg implanting) seemed rather intrusive, the latex cap loaded with spermicide seemed fiddly and unspontaneous as you had to insert it before sex, and the 'sponge' had an effectiveness rate of about 80 per cent, which I remember thinking were not the kind of odds I was going to accept. Condoms and the pill were 99 per cent, and seemed the best bet for me. So I found out about sexual health clinics where you could be more anonymous than at your local GP practice, and when I decided I wanted to have sex for the first time, I went along to be prescribed the pill. My boyfriend and I were terrified of me getting pregnant, so we used condoms as well for good measure.

Over the years, I used the pill or contraceptive injections, happily with few of the side effects that I watched friends experience as they tried one type of pill after another to find the best option for them. I was unsettled, however, when it took almost a year for my periods to return when I stopped the contraceptive injections. So by the time I was in a relationship with the man I knew I wanted to spend the rest of my life with, the swift return of fertility once you stop taking the pill made it an obvious choice. I mused on how for all of my sexually active life I'd focused on absolutely not getting pregnant; suddenly it was strange to recognise that when I next stopped contraception, it would be because I actively wanted to conceive.

Most of the responsibility for thinking about contraception tends to land on women's shoulders. Men wear condoms, but even then women often end up buying them, or insisting on their use. Over the years, various pharmaceutical companies have invested in developing a male contraceptive,[14] which would not only empower men who want to have confidence about whether and when they will father a child, but also give couples more choice about what method of family planning would work best for them.

In 2016, a medical trial of a male contraceptive injection found a 96 per cent success rate in preventing pregnancy, but the trial was halted when 20 of the 320 men dropped out due to side effects ranging from depression and mood swings to muscle pain and acne.[15] Women using the contraceptive pill are familiar with side effects and risks. They face a higher risk of deep vein thrombosis and breast cancer, and the pill can also cause headaches, nausea, breast tenderness, irregular bleeding and mood swings.[16] Of course medical researchers should properly understand side effects and ensure the safety of drugs, but considering dozens of different pill brands are prescribed to women because no one type suits everyone, a trial result that finds 75 per cent of participants happy to continue with a contraceptive injection is a stunning result. We shouldn't expect that male contraception can only be successful if one drug can be found that works for all men without any side effects.

If contraception is seen as largely a woman's responsibility, then what happens after conception is even more so, and often in a very public way. In the media, high-profile women face acres of coverage and speculation around their pregnancies. When top human rights lawyer Amal Clooney addressed the United Nations about the need to investigate the rapes, kidnappings and genocide committed by ISIS in Iraq,[17] *Time* magazine tweeted: 'Amal Clooney shows off her baby bump at the United Nations'.[18] There is so much that's wrong there. Being pregnant and wearing clothes does not mean you are 'showing off' your baby bump, even if those clothes are not a sack and your baby bump is visible. I await the *Time* headline describing a male leader 'showing off' his beer belly, when he is in fact negotiating an important issue. Seeing the pregnant woman as just 'pregnant', and no longer a 'woman' with thoughts and ideas and talent, reduces her value to her pregnancy status alone, as if her brain has stopped working. One US lawmaker even described pregnant women as 'hosts' – an extreme example that sounds like it comes from dystopian fiction.[19]

In an everyday context, pregnant women find themselves fending off strangers reaching out and stroking their bump, and a steady stream of unsolicited judgement and 'advice'. This covers everything from the size and shape of her bump (*too big, too small?*), to the appropriateness of her attire given her 'condition', to being told what to do during pregnancy (*You must sit down and rest . . . You're eating for two now*) and when the baby is born (*sleep when baby sleeps, breast is best, set a routine* . . . the list is endless).

I can almost hear the shrill call of the 'political correctness gone mad' brigade complaining that now we aren't allowed to talk about pregnancy. On the contrary – it is amazing to grow a person, and as a society it is not only kind, but smart and in our own interest, to support the people who are doing it. And it's perfectly possible to be considerate to pregnant women without pawing or patronising them.

I found myself at the centre of a fairly ridiculous pregnancy story in 2013. Seven months pregnant, I had been spotted standing at the back of the House of Commons during Prime Minister's Questions. A journalist from the *Independent* rang me afterwards to ask me about it. I told him it wasn't a problem, I was happier standing, leaning against a wooden pillar. (In fact, one of the most uncomfortable experiences I had in the Commons while pregnant was sitting through a six-hour debate. Those green benches aren't so comfortable after a while, and I was experiencing back pain. I ended up nipping out to the ladies' loo in the voting lobby, getting on my hands and knees and doing back stretches before coming back into the debate.)

Anyway, this journalist decided that it didn't matter whether I actually wanted to sit down or not, and he wrote that I had been 'forced' to stand. Well, that's utter bollocks, I thought: *I chose to stand, and you know that because I told you so.* I was annoyed that he didn't accept my answer, and thought it was pretty sexist of him to assume he knew better than I did whether I wanted to stand or sit. Anyway, some Chinese whispers and a slow news day, and suddenly the story was out there that I thought it was sexist for people to offer seats to pregnant women. Cue a front-page splash in the *Daily Mail*,[20] a column entitled 'Does Jo Swinson hate women?'[21] and a *Spectator* blog from Rod Liddle calling me 'air-headed' and saying he'd give up his seat for any pregnant woman except me.[22] For the record, it's not sexist to offer your seat to a pregnant woman, it's lovely.

So, please do offer to give up your seat or help a pregnant woman with heavy bags – but accept her answer. Don't tell her she is wrong if she declines your offer. For women you know, ask how she's feeling today and if there's anything you can do to help, and listen to what she says. If you are offering advice to pregnant friends – and I confess I probably overdo this myself, tempted by various eureka moments of parenting that I wish I'd known about sooner – then at least frame it in the context of 'this is what worked for me/us', recognising that everyone's experiences are different.

For many people, fertility isn't that fairy tale of sperm meets egg, then happy ever after with a healthy, bouncing baby. One of my friends went through the menopause when she was in her early twenties, a condition called premature menopause that is very rare in women that young[23] but happens to about one in a hundred women before the age of 40. I've known countless couples who have struggled to conceive with round after round of IVF, rolling the dice in what feels like a cruel life lottery, a rollercoaster of hormones, procedures, false hopes and dashed dreams.

One in four pregnancies ends in a miscarriage, and it happens to 200,000 couples in the UK each year.[24] Sometimes it is at such an early stage it is mistaken for a late period; sometimes, as happened to my sister, it is tragically revealed at a scan appointment, staring at an ultrasound screen when no movement or heartbeat are found. Other times bleeding just starts and doesn't stop. One friend told me movingly of how heart-breaking it was, while the physical experience involved her sitting on the toilet as if she were weeing – but it was blood not urine, and it went on like that for more than an hour.

Miscarriage is still such a taboo subject, despite the fact it happens to so many people. Many go on to healthy full-term pregnancies after miscarriage; others experience the pain of miscarriage time after time. People's responses are different, but feelings of guilt, failure and grief are common, as is isolation. By not even talking about this issue – because it freaks us out, because we don't like to think of the details, because we're a bit uncomfortable, because we don't know what to say – we make experiencing it much harder for the women and men who are coming to terms with it. The charity Tommy's launched its #misCOURAGE campaign encouraging people to talk about miscarriage and how it has affected them, to help people understand what it is like and to help them better support friends, family or colleagues who experience miscarriage.

Scotland's First Minister Nicola Sturgeon has spoken out powerfully about her own experience of miscarriage, and the damaging assumptions people make about women's choices and lives.[25] Before she talked publicly about her miscarriage, the media's constant barbs and questions about the fact that she did not have children were in stark contrast to how they rarely if ever raised the issue with her predecessor, Alex Salmond, who also has no children.[26] Society's assumption that a woman is incomplete without a baby – in a way that a man is not – is underpinned by placing so much of the value of women's bodies on reproduction.

Many women do not have children, either by choice or circumstance. Women find their 'childless' status remarked upon and judged; if they are in the public eye it will be frequently mentioned in articles and interviews in a way that men in the same position largely escape. Actor Jennifer Aniston wrote brilliantly about the frenzied speculation and forensic body-scrutiny that accompanies her own life, in particular the constant assertion that she must be craving a child. Photos of her are pored over for any sign of pregnancy, to the extent that when she 'had a burger for lunch and was photographed from a weird angle' it would be seized upon as an early 'baby bump'.[27] The subtext is clear – she cannot possibly be happy without having a baby. Yet, as she says: 'We don't need to be married or mothers to be complete.'

For those who do give birth, along with natural joy in the arrival of a new baby and genuine well-wishing, there is body-shaming and criticism. The impossible standards expected were highlighted when the Duchess of Cambridge left hospital cradling the newborn Prince George, with post-pregnancy tummy rather than washboard abs. OK! magazine was forced to apologise for splashing a headline on the cover about 'KATE'S POST-BABY WEIGHT LOSS REGIME',[28] and various commentators sounded puzzled that a bump was still clearly visible.[29] No matter that she looked happy and delighted, radiant with immaculately blow-dried hair and make-up in a way that most women would thankfully not have to consider a necessity at that moment (can you imagine the reaction if she'd emerged, perfectly reasonably, in comfy maternity jeans and a nursing top with her hair in a ponytail?) – according to some, she had still not achieved the required perfection.

Pregnancy, birth and caring for a newborn take a huge toll on women physically and emotionally, and around one in ten women develop a mental illness during this time. Yet maternity mental health services are patchy, and often no local specialist teams are available to support women in these circumstances.[30]

Right to Choose

When women's value in society is seen through the lens of sex and bearing children, ending a pregnancy is viewed as a political act. Indeed, the issue of abortion is still one of the most emotive and hotly contested issues in politics even now, half a century after the 1967 Abortion Act moved the procedure from dangerous backstreet practices or DIY knitting needle attempts, to a safe, clinical and hygienic environment within the NHS. Before it was made legal, dozens of women in the UK died each year from abortion, and it was the leading cause of maternal mortality.[31]

Many people believe abortion is wrong in principle, and I've yet to meet anyone who thinks it is desirable, not least as it can be a physically and emotionally difficult experience. Clearly we should equip people with the information and confidence to make good decisions, through quality relationships and sex education, and ensure everyone has access to contraception to minimise unwanted pregnancies. We should provide excellent antenatal care and screening so that any problems are picked up early and can be treated – or, if that is not possible, that there is plenty of information available about all the options, and time to make decisions. We should continue to fund research and invest in neonatal care, so that babies can survive with conditions that would not have been possible in the past. We should ensure our adoption processes are sensitive and supportive for birth parents and adopters. All of these things increase choice.

Ultimately, however, a woman deciding whether to continue with her pregnancy is making a personal, not political, decision about her own body. She should be the one in control.

Rights to safe and legal abortion have been hard-won (just half a century ago) here in Great Britain, but remain denied to women in Northern Ireland, where women are still prosecuted for having abortions. In 2017, a small but important victory was won when Stella Creasy assembled a coalition of MPs from all parties, to force the government into a climbdown and stop charging Northern Irish women for NHS abortion care when they receive it in England. The fact remains, however, that women in a part of the UK face prosecution for choosing not to continue with a pregnancy.

The 'Change'

Consistent with women's value being inextricably linked to having babies, society dismisses and discards women as they age and experience menopause. Who talks about the menopause? I'm 37, so within the next 10 to 15 years I can expect to experience it, yet I realise when confronting this subject how little I know. Other than anticipating that my periods will become irregular and gradually cease, and the vague references to hot flushes, I don't have much of a clue. Come to think of it, what exactly is a hot flush like? How long does it last, how do you deal with it, how uncomfortable is it? I asked my mum, who said she didn't experience many symptoms, having been prescribed hormone replacement therapy. Her answer was helpful to an extent – I discovered that the menopause isn't a big deal for everyone – but questions about HRT now loom large in my mind: what are the risks, are there different types, is it a good idea? I'm sure there are excellent health websites with helpful information if I go looking for it, but where is the equivalent of the *Just Seventeen* magazine articles that informed me about my body when I was a teenager? Articles in mainstream magazines and newspapers discussing this issue that affects half the population are few and far between.

That I – and I expect probably many other thirty-something women – feel uninformed about menopause, despite knowing loads of women who have been through it, speaks volumes. We don't really talk about it as a society. In a world which tells women their power comes from appearance, fertility and youth, why would older women volunteer information that reminds people of the ending of their fertile years? Older women are so absent from the power structures we see, while corporate boardrooms, media empires and parliaments are teeming with older men, feted for their wisdom and experience. The parallel wisdom of their generation's women is left on the fringes of debate, ignored or even dismissed.

Body of Evidence

Even medical science has typically viewed women's bodies largely through the lens of sex and reproduction.

'People thought I was crazy in the 1990s,' the esteemed academic and clinician Dr Marianne Legato told me down the phone line from her New York base, in between seeing patients and heading off to teach a class. One of the world's authorities in the field of gender-specific medicine, her sense of mission was clear as she talked about forthcoming international conferences and the launch of her new scientific journal, *Gender and the Genome*. Her revolutionary idea that saw her 'accused of being a feminist' two decades ago was to study men and women's health separately.[32]

Previously, medical research on women was largely confined to the 'bikini zone' – areas of the body where female and male biology very obviously differed. This restriction was partly done as men's bodies were thought to be more stable, without periodic hormonal fluctuations, and partly done for protective reasons: the thalidomide scandal[33] was an example of how devastating the unknown consequences of new drugs can be, if taken by women who are pregnant.

In fact, excluding women from trials has been bad for women's health. Assuming that women are just like men apart from their lady bits led science into a 'most appalling intellectual error', Dr Legato told me. In researching coronary disease in women, she found significant differences compared to men in terms of the age of onset, the clinical manifestations and the way they responded to preventative and therapeutic measures. Researchers around the globe have now found that the human response to physiology and disease varies according to biological sex, and that at 'a molecular level, men and women are profoundly different'.

The Impossibility of Beauty

Throughout history, women's bodies have been altered to make them acceptable, or beautiful. In China, young girls had their feet bound so that their toes broke, to create the desirable pointed 'lotus feet'.[34] Girls in the Padaung tribe in Thailand have heavy brass coils wrapped around their necks from the age of five, pushing down their collarbone to create the illusion of an elongated neck. By the time they are a woman they may have up to 25 coils.[35]

One of the mothers of feminism, Mary Wollstonecraft, published her ground-breaking book *A Vindication of the Rights of Woman* in 1792. Reading it, I feel transported back in time, listening to one of the few women to have a political voice in the 18th century. Her insights are enlightening, but also depressing when you realise how so many things are familiar more than 225 years on. She railed against how societal norms meant that for middle-class women 'strength and usefulness are sacrificed to beauty',[36] and how 'to preserve personal beauty . . . the limbs and faculties are cramped with worse than Chinese bands', a reference to the restrictive corsetry fashionable for well-to-do ladies at the time. Corsets squeezed women's internal organs, and reduced their ability to breathe. Women often passed out as a result.[37]

Deathly pale faces were considered fashionable in Elizabethan times and for centuries after – ironically, the lead-based Venetian ceruse that many women and men applied to their skin hastened death itself. Lead poisoning led to muscle paralysis, hair loss, skin scarring and weakened immune systems. When the famous beauty Maria Gunning, Countess of Coventry, died at the age of 27 in 1760, it was dubbed 'death by vanity'.[38]

The standards of beauty have changed, but the pursuit of an unattainably perfect female form continues. Naomi Wolf wrote her bestseller *The Beauty Myth* in 1990, and suggested that the situation was getting even worse: 'The more legal and material hindrances women have broken through, the more strictly and heavily and cruelly images of female beauty have come to weigh upon us.'

The 'beauty ideal' is deliberately unachievable, to encourage us to keep spending our money. And this never-ending work to attain beauty demands time that women and girls might otherwise use productively on activities that enhance their power or improve their well-being. The pursuit of 'beauty' can lead to extreme outcomes.

A Westernised beauty ideal, elevated by global brands pushing the same type of model in adverts right across the world, has created a market for light skin, glossy hair and Caucasian features. Billions are spent each year on 'skin lightening' creams[39] – a euphemism for applying harsh bleach and sometimes toxic chemicals to the skin, resulting in skin damage and increased risk of skin cancer.[40] Skin lightening is widespread in many parts of Africa and Asia, with one study finding half of all Filipino women, six in ten Thai women, and three-quarters of Nigerian women using such products.[41] Ghana recently banned hydroquinone, the chemical used in many skin lightening products, and the Ivory Coast and South Africa also regulate the industry.

Bans on the most damaging ingredients are a first step, but are easily flouted – an investigative trip to beauty shops in south London by gal-dem magazine journalist Charlie Cuff found illegal products readily available.[42] And adverts for formulations that don't contain illegal ingredients still fuel the belief that white skin is superior – big-brand products in Asian markets such as L'Oréal's 'White Perfect',[43] Lancôme's 'Blanc Expert'[44] and Unilever's 'Fair and Lovely'[45] are, in essence, telling people of colour there is something wrong with their natural skin tone. In South Korea, one in five women have had cosmetic procedures, the most common being eyelid[46] and nose surgery to achieve a more Western look, with some people opting for extreme procedures that break and shave their jawbone to change the shape of their face.[47]

Many black women endure the burning pain of creams to 'relax' their afro curls, which over time can weaken and break the hair.[48] Endless hours and lots of money are invested in weaves, extensions and treatments to achieve the 'right' texture; despite making up less than 10 per cent of the population, black women account for more than 80 per cent of hair product sales in the UK.[49] But this is no vanity project. Powerful social norms create expectations.

I met the journalist and author Hannah Azieb Pool in the upstairs café at the Southbank Centre, where she curates cultural events. As part of the Women of the World Festival she has run discussion panels on the politics of afro hair. Over a juice looking out onto the Thames, she told me how the messages start young. Children have been sent home from school for wearing braids or their afro being too big. One school went to the High Court to try to defend its ban on children wearing their hair in the traditional cornrow style.[50] Black women are told their natural hair is 'not professional', and if they have an interview they are told to 'fix their hair'. And fix = straighten. The subtext is, she explained: *Can you be a bit less black?*

Caucasian women also struggle to live up to the beauty ideal, though their whiteness puts them in a privileged position compared to their black sisters. Hair on the head has to be glossy, but anywhere else it is forbidden, and must be removed. A furore erupted when Julia Roberts waved to the crowd at the premiere of her film *Notting Hill* in 1999 and, shock horror, showed an armpit with fuzz.[51] Ever wondered why there's a hair or beauty salon in almost every parade of shops? Across the country there are more than 30,000 – an industry worth £4 billion a year. Some 'treatments' are actually a treat – manicures can feel relaxing, and who wouldn't enjoy a massage? Hair removal is not a treat in any way – whether at home with a razor or foul-smelling dissolving cream, or at a salon with electric currents targeting individual hairs or hot wax being ripped off your skin. Waxing makes up between 30 and 40 per cent of beauty salon revenue.[52] What would you like waxed? Half leg/full leg/half arm/full arm/underarm/upper lip/chin/eyebrows/bikini line/landing strip/Brazilian/bum? If you fancy shelling out a bit more, why not try laser hair removal at up to £160 a time?[53] These treatments are a mainstay of beauty salons; repeat business, month in, month out, as customers maintain their personal grooming regime. One of the simple pleasures about winter is wearing thick black tights that makes my lower-leg wax feel optional.

Human beings have played with display and colour through the ages, we enjoy trying different looks – from children's face-painting to changing make-up trends. As a student, one of my favourite parts of a night out was getting ready with my girlfriends beforehand, a party atmosphere with music and chat, deciding what to wear and helping each other do our hair and make-up. The time with my bridesmaids doing the same before my wedding felt like a warm embrace of female bonding, a beautiful start to one of the most special days of my life.

Yet our ability to change our facial appearance through

cosmetics becomes oppressive when we feel compelled to do so. One day, a woman, Barbara,* came to my MP advice surgery deeply concerned about her teenage granddaughter who was living with her. Barbara found it hard to get her to attend school, as the girl didn't feel confident unless she had spent an hour applying make-up. While that story shocked me, in reality it is simply a more extreme version of how many women might feel about going to work without any make-up. In many workplaces, wearing make-up is seen as necessary for women to look professional. When that is the case, it ceases to be a choice, and is one more beauty chore eating our time.

Fat Is Still a Feminist Issue

Once, a voluptuous figure was a sign of plenty, wealth and status; now thinness rules supreme. The word 'fat' is an insult. Rib-squeezing corsets are back, renamed 'waist trainers' and promoted by selfie-posting celebrities including the Kardashians, Jessica Alba and Amber Rose.[54]

Despite – or perhaps because of – the fact that most women have thighs that meet at the top when they stand with their knees together, achieving a 'thigh gap' is a thing. Websites peddle dangerous imagery with tips on how girls can apparently starve or exercise themselves to this state, when for most it is impossible. Fat is indeed a feminist issue, as Susie Orbach wrote back in 1978. Thirty years later, her testimony convinced the Lib Dem policy group I was chairing to make it a political issue, too.

---

* Name has been changed.

Susie is a leading psychotherapist, and also a writer, campaigner and activist, keen to recast the frame through which we view our bodies. Over the past decade we have worked together on these issues – before, during and after my time in government. Susie is particularly concerned about new mums: at a physically and emotionally draining time, an obsession with 'fixing' their body can have an impact on their relationship with their new baby, and body anxieties can be learned by children from their parents. Shockingly, she says she has seen 'new mums having a tummy tuck at the same time as a C-section', such are the pressures.

While beauty has been prized since time began, it was deemed important for women in a particular social class, for a 'very short period of their lives . . . no one had to look like a movie star from the age of six until eighty'. What started with a commercial focus on women's bodily imperfections has spread to men, too. Encouraged by industry and cultural norms, Susie says, 'now men are supposed to be buff'.

The documentary The Illusionists by Elena Rossini[55] explores body image in countries all over the world. It also concludes that the pressure on women is extreme, and it is increasing for men, too. The film uses the example of GI Joe, a kind of US Action Man toy. Comparing the toys over the years is fascinating. In the 1960s, he was a normal-looking guy; by the 1970s his waist had narrowed, and he had acquired built-up pecs and a six-pack; and by the 1990s, he had a beefcake-on-steroids look.[56]

So why the unrealistic body shapes and sizes? The fashion industry is certainly part of the problem. Sketches of clothes follow a set ratio between the head and body of 1:11, when the human form is typically more like 1:7.[57] This means even on paper the look is unrealistic, so tall, skinny models are required, and naturally slim people are recruited, then directed to lose weight. Fashion designers send magazines 'sample sizes' of their clothes months in advance, so the fashion shoots can be done and editorials published at the same time the new season's collection is launched. These sample clothes are typically a UK size 4–6,[58] in contrast to the average size of UK women, which is 16.[59] So the glamorous fashion images we all see are routinely featuring the exact same size of model. Designers, magazine editors and model agencies pass the buck of responsibility in an elaborate display of sloping shoulders that seems always on trend. The agencies say they hire only slim models because that's who magazines book. The magazines say they need to have people who will fit into the sample garments. The designers say they have to send sizes that fit the models. And so a healthy, slimmer-than-average size 12 is considered 'plus-size', with fewer than 1 in 75 models in advertising campaigns being size 12 or larger.[60]

The organisers of exclusive catwalk shows at fashion weeks in London, Paris and New York say that it is more expensive to showcase different sizes on the runway. When models are a range of different sizes, the clothes have to be matched in advance to a particular model, rather than using an interchangeable army of mostly underpaid, very slender young women available to act as human coat hangers displaying the art of the garments to best advantage.

Teenage models are at the frontline of this battleground for thin. Former *Vogue Australia* editor Kirstie Clements spoke out about coming across models with scabbed knees from regular fainting, the normalisation of extreme dieting, eating tissues to keep hunger at bay (the tissues apparently swell up and fill the stomach), breast reduction surgery, and even hospitalisation.[61] But that is just the start of the human toll of the thin obsession, which then seeps out into every aspect of society, causing misery for girls and women stuck in the constancy of feeling fat.

Even dolls are complicit – the proportions of Barbie are famously impossible: if she were real she would not be able to stand up and would not menstruate.[62] Barbie's manufacturers, Mattel, have finally responded to pressure from parents who voted with their purses and stopped buying the doll for their daughters – 'we realised we had a problem with moms,' said Evelyn Mazzocco, Barbie's global brand general manager.[63] In 2016, a more diverse range of Barbie dolls was launched with 7 skin colours, 3 eye colours, 30 hair colours, 24 hairstyles and textures, and 3 different doll sizes, including one which vaguely resembles an actual woman's proportions. While 'Curvy Barbie' is in fact very slim – a UK size 8 – this is still an important move, and it shows the power that consumers have in demanding change from major brands.[64]

I am mystified by the pretension of some top fashion designers and their disdain for women's bodies, when they talk of how designs just hang better on thin models, because natural curves ruin the lines. If so, maybe that's the fault of the designer? Perhaps they could channel their creativity and skill into making stunning clothes for different body shapes? It's as if their work is designed to be viewed in a glass case rather than to dress living, breathing human beings.

In 2009, fashion commentator Caryn Franklin, fashion PR director Debra Bourne and top model Erin O'Connor founded a campaign, All Walks Beyond the Catwalk, to shake up the world of fashion. Through high-profile campaigns, they captured the attention of the fashion industry and succeeded in getting plus-size models walking the runway in Mark Fast's show at London Fashion Week.[65] Working with fashion colleges, they are equipping the designers of tomorrow to practise their craft with emotional intelligence and an appreciation of the diversity of the human form. Through course modules and competitions, students learn to design and cut clothes for different body shapes and sizes, and all of this is supported by a new Diversity Network across fashion colleges.[66] All of this is done on a shoestring, channelling the amazing energy and creativity of the founders and like-minded supporters.

In 2010 I co-founded the Campaign for Body Confidence with my Lib Dem MP colleague Lynne Featherstone, and set up the All-Party Parliamentary Group on Body Image, a cross-party group of MPs dedicated to highlighting the problems of body image pressure, and campaigning for change. We worked with All Walks, and also with groups like Girlguiding, the eating disorders charity Beat, Susie Orbach's campaign group AnyBody,[67] the YMCA and Mumsnet. We raised the issue up the political agenda by hosting film screenings in Parliament, conducting an inquiry in Parliament and producing the report 'Reflections on Body Image',[68] as well as organising the first UK Body Confidence Awards ceremony[69] and regularly generating media debate to drive change. Against the odds, my colleague Lynne and I ended up in government after the coalition was formed. Lynne was a Home Office minister and also Minister for Women, and she drove body image onto the government agenda, which I continued when I took over the portfolio two years later.

Of course, governments can make laws, but I found the power of generating public debate and the gentle pressure of government on an issue often more effective in driving change quickly. The advertising industry started to respond. Their think tank, Credos, began researching attitudes to the imagery of bodies displayed in adverts – first how teenage girls were impacted by excessive retouching to make models look thinner,[70] then around the minimal and often stereotypical portrayal of minority ethnic groups,[71] and more recently about how boys are affected by body ideals presented in ads.[72] Some retailers changed their tack – Debenhams banned body retouching in lingerie and swimwear adverts, and introduced size 16 mannequins into some of their stores.[73]

The ubiquity of the Internet and camera phones – and the way confidence is measured by 'likes' online – has ramped up the pressure even further, and different generations develop different norms in their use of social media apps. I spoke to Isabelle, the 21-year-old daughter of a friend, about the stress of creating and living up to social media images. 'Behind the scenes it's the most miserable thing . . . it's just fake,' she said. People waiting until they are somewhere special, or spending ages taking the best selfie but looking nonchalant, as the current trend is for 'candid'; applying filters and then taking down the photo if it doesn't get enough likes within ten minutes – 11 likes was a key minimum figure. 'One per cent was about the photo, the rest was about the analytics.' She was even part of a WhatsApp group of friends who had a pact to 'like' each other's Instagram posts. The group chat was only used to notify others about Instagram posts: *Gram*, one person would type, and all the other members were expected to go and like the new post. If people didn't respond quickly enough, they would be checked up on and challenged. Isabelle told me that the other 14 members of the group were all guys; she had been added on a night out once. I don't know why this surprised me, but it did.

It feels sad for social acceptance and status for young people to be so dependent on a crude metric of likes. As it happens, Isabelle had deleted Instagram a couple of weeks before we spoke. She described the extra free time she now enjoyed, and said simply, 'I feel lighter.'[74]

The beauty ideal is so unattainable that we go to extreme ends to approximate it, from restrictive diets to intensive exercise regimes, and altering how we look digitally, or even physically through cosmetic procedures. Women whose livelihoods depend on their looks invest huge amounts of time and money maintaining the standard, yet give off an air of effortless ease, as is demanded by the myth that this idealised notion of beautiful is normal.

Too often when we see famous women working out, it is a sanitised, unreal picture of exercise, where make-up is perfect and hair is gently bouncing, not the dishevelled sweaty state that actually accompanies hard physical effort. The imagery of normal women out of breath, red-faced, sweating and jiggling in Sport England's This Girl Can campaign is so powerful and refreshing for this very reason.

Through the ages, beauty has been a currency, particularly for young women. Without property rights or the chance to be taken seriously in a career, a woman's success depended significantly on making a good marriage. Jane Austen's novels give us a glimpse of how high society rated girls on beauty. In Tudor times, we know Henry VIII used portraits of potential brides to help choose a future wife.

Despite progress in legal rights and opportunities for women to engage in our economy ostensibly on similar terms to men, meeting rigid beauty standards is still part of the requirement for women to succeed in many roles – most obviously in high-profile positions in the public eye that include appearing on television and in news media. This filters down to a general expectation in all sorts of jobs – from receptionists in office buildings being instructed what height of shoe heel and shade of eyeshadow *must* be worn,[75] to workers deemed attractive tending to earn more.[76] Some of this applies to men, too, and the bias in favour of tall men in leadership positions is both stark and ridiculous.[77] I would argue that instead of the trend to hold men to increasingly higher standards of 'beauty', equality would be better served by giving everyone a break and judging individuals on their actual contribution to an organisation, not how they look while they are doing it.

While beauty has always been prized in adolescence, as Susie Orbach points out, what is new is the enduring expectation that we should be aiming for perfection throughout our lives – from young children judging themselves on fatness, to striving for unattainable beauty standards as we age.

When beauty is a currency, and the ideal is so impossible, we end up investing a huge amount of time and money trying to live up to the standards. The make-up and cosmetics market is

£9.3 million[78] a year in the UK and growing, and men's grooming is now the fastest-growing part. Dieting is big business, too, even though it doesn't actually work. Different fad programmes to lose weight fast come in and out of fashion – denying carbs, the Atkins diet, eating only raw food, fasting, juicing. There's even one plan that consists of only drinking a mixture of maple syrup, lemon juice, water and cayenne pepper. Most people can't stick to these kind of restrictive regimes, so they lose a few pounds initially then end up putting more weight back on. Dieting in itself isn't the root cause of eating disorders, which are complex and have many risk factors, but as one academic put it to me, 'most eating disorders begin with a diet'. Certainly, banning entire food groups is a sign of disordered eating.

When changing our bodies through strict control over calories and exercise doesn't achieve the required results, some turn to permanent alteration through surgery. Cutting through skin and fat and removing flesh is one way in which people try to achieve an 'ideal' figure. Others insert foreign objects into the body to plump up areas such as buttocks and breasts, with sometimes calamitous health impacts, as the leaking breast implants scandal showed us in 2013.[79] People pay to have poison injected into their face in an attempt to hide wrinkles, and this also renders their face unable to communicate with the usual range of human expressions. Even the areas not on display are deemed to need 'fixing' – labiaplasty has increased fivefold in recent years.[80] Typically, this is women undergoing unnecessary surgery on their perfectly healthy genitalia, to achieve a supposed 'ideal' look. We rightly rail against female genital mutilation (FGM) being carried out on girls, but why is a Harley Street doctor charging thousands of pounds to cut into the labia of healthy women not similarly denounced? The normalisation of cosmetic surgery is evident in all sorts of ways – the gaming apps aimed at children that enable players to choose which surgeries to perform,[81] the concept of surgery as a birthday or even wedding gift, and personal loan products tailored to finance cosmetic surgery procedures.

Sexuality as Power

With the senior levels of business, politics, sport and the media dominated by men, most of the women who punch through into our consciousness as powerful and influential are celebrities, rather than political or business leaders. It is images of women from Hollywood, our television screens and the music industry that girls see the most. For these women, beauty is part of the job description, and increasingly their sexuality is, too.

When I was growing up in the 1980s and '90s it was Kylie, Madonna and the Spice Girls. Think of the most memorable images of these women at the height of their success and you'll recall Madonna in her conical bra, Kylie gyrating in gold hot pants or dancing braless in a revealing white jumpsuit, and Ginger Spice's knicker-revealing Union Jack dress at the Brit Awards. These events were controversial at the time, but look tame compared with what's on display nowadays.

Women in the music industry who resist revealing photoshoots report it is much harder to secure airplay and promotion for their work. Charlotte Church delivered a powerful BBC lecture in 2013, describing her own experiences. 'When I was 19 or 20, I found myself in this position, being pressured into wearing more and more revealing outfits. And the lines I had spun at me again and again, generally by middle-aged men, were "You look great"; "You have a great body, why not show it off?" or "Don't worry, it'll look classy. It'll look artistic."'[82] You could debate for hours whether women who do the shoots are exploited and encouraged to display more skin that they would like – or whether they are the ones in control, creating risqué imagery through personal choice. Either way, the message is clear – sexual portrayal secures attention, space and relevance.

Girls look up to these icons and learn that their sexuality is a key source of power, and often the only source of power.

I want girls to love – and feel the power of – their bodies. Bodies are amazing: running, breathing, dancing, changing, swimming, embracing, relaxing, growing, kissing, healing, loving, thinking. The physical exterior is such a minor part, yet takes up so much attention. Sexuality is wonderful, yet too often girls are encouraged into actions they hope will make them feel powerful, and they are instead not in control.

The pressure teenagers are under to send naked and sexual images by text or social media is intense, with most teenagers saying they have been asked to send such pictures.[83] Yet often, private intimacy is not respected and girls are publicly shamed by these images instead. Women (and also some men) of all ages have been victims of 'revenge porn' – where intimate photos taken in private are later shared widely in a deliberate and malicious act of revenge after the relationship's breakdown. This became illegal in England and Wales in 2014[84] and in Scotland in 2017.[85] The UK government also introduced a helpline for those affected by this crime, which can be reached on 0845 6000 459.[86]

The Goldilocks Paradox

Women owning the power of their sexuality face the Goldilocks paradox: there is no right amount of sexuality; somehow there is always either too much or too little on display.

Four armed men clad in black, towering menacingly over a frightened woman on a beach as they force her to remove her clothes, and her daughter cries: the photograph went viral and underlined this paradox. France had banned the 'burkini' – a swimming costume which covers the whole body, essentially a wetsuit – from its beaches, and here was a police officer enforcing the policy. In this case, a former air hostess sitting with her family on the beach wearing leggings, a top and a headscarf was issued with a fine for not wearing 'an outfit respecting good morals and secularism'.[87] It's ridiculous that law enforcement officers in a supposedly liberal country could require women to remove clothes in a public place. This was literal policing of what women wear, a concept women are familiar with even if it doesn't always involve actual police officers.

And at the other end of the scale are debates about topless sunbathing – whether and where it should be allowed. But there is never any suggestion that surfer dudes can't wear full-body wetsuits, or that topless guys are a problem on the beach.

Sometimes, even a hint of cleavage is judged too much for women in the public eye, as if the men will need smelling salts to recover from a glimpse of décolletage. 'She knew exactly the effect her outfit would have' . . . 'Who do these breasts belong to?'. . . 'She hogged the limelight in a plunging top'.[88] Then, at other times, women are criticised for looking frumpy or mumsy, with no sense of style, as if it is that, rather than their actual job, which matters.

Women are derided as 'frigid' if they show too little sexuality, and 'slags' if they admit to enjoying their sex life. We have a situation where more than a third of people say that if a woman is sexually assaulted while wearing a short skirt, she is totally or partly to blame.[89]

Women must be allowed to own, enjoy and celebrate their sexuality, but in doing so they are often pilloried or slut-shamed for stepping outside the conventional norms. Madonna knows this better than most. Throughout her life she has broken the rules, challenged taboos and embraced her sexual power. I love Madonna: her music, her passion, her fearlessness. She is an inspiration to so many. In a 2016 speech, she showed a rare vulnerable side when she opened up about her experiences as a woman in the public eye: 'There are no rules if you're a boy . . . but if you're a girl, you have to play the game. You are allowed to be pretty and cute and sexy, but don't act too smart. Don't have an opinion . . . You are allowed to be objectified by men and dress like a slut, but don't own your sluttiness and do not – do not, I repeat – share your own sexual fantasies with the world . . . Finally, do not age, because to age is a sin.'[90]

It's as if the female body is so dangerous that it has to be closely controlled. That's certainly the subtext behind the requirement for women to cover up to varying degrees across different cultures. Blaming a rape victim for wearing revealing clothes has the same roots as forcing women to wear a headscarf or a veil. In both cases, the woman has to take responsibility for the actions of men. Far better to require men to keep their hands, lewd comments and penis to themselves unless explicitly invited.

Muslim women find themselves at a fiery intersection of misogyny and Islamophobia, and bear the brunt of spikes in hate crimes.[91] Debates about 'banning the burkha' have become totemic - despite the burkha being incredibly rare in the UK. I can count on my hands the number of times I've seen someone in a burkha (which is a full head and body covering with just a gauze to see through). The niqab, which is a veil with an opening for the eyes, is less rare. The hijab, which is just a headscarf, is fairly common - and let's face it, not all that different to the practical 'scarf tied under the chin' that has been popular with Western grandmothers for decades. Yet for some parts of society, there is something about women choosing to cover up that seems threatening or hard to accept. Consequently, abuse becomes a depressing part of daily life for women wearing the hijab. Nadiya Hussain, who shot to fame when she won *The Great British Bake Off*, described how it feels: 'I expect to be shoved or pushed or verbally abused, because it happens, it's happened for years.'[92]

I've often found people who spew hate towards Islam suddenly proclaim their deep concern for women's rights and the injustice of women being forced to cover up, using this issue as a stick to beat an entire religion with. Their fiery demands for women to be treated with respect are undermined by their ridiculous assertion that every woman wearing a headscarf is doing so under duress, robbing women who choose to wear the hijab of their agency. These people are blind to their own double standards - many of the same anti-headscarf brigade blame victims of sexual assault for not covering up. Women can't win.

Toxic Girlhood

All of these pressures add up to a toxic girlhood, as young women learn they will be judged on how they look but also that their bodies are wrong because they do not meet the impossible beauty ideal, so they must constantly monitor and 'maintain' their bodies to be deemed acceptable. Counting calories, competing to eat less, styling hair, applying a mask of make-up, regular hair removal, exercise driven by the desire to weigh less rather than to feel fit, and choosing clothes, language and attitudes that achieve the right balance of sexually attractive yet not 'asking for it': the time and energy that teenage girls pour into these activities is time and energy they aren't pouring into other aspects of their lives.

And stop blaming the girls. When I speak about these issues in the media, the responses are predictably patronising: 'surely there are more important things to worry about', 'they shouldn't care what others think', 'women should just stop buying those magazines', 'but we do have an obesity problem', 'so we're not supposed to try to look good now?'

Of course there's nothing wrong with caring about your appearance; people have played with their looks and celebrated beauty through the ages. The problem is how out of proportion appearance has become – and with understandable reason, when girls rightly see how the world judges women constantly, comprehensively and critically on how they look. We should be encouraging people to adopt healthy lifestyles, but there is not a shred of evidence that fat-shaming is a successful strategy to tackle the problem of obesity, and plenty of research shows these attitudes actually prevent obese people from taking exercise that will improve their health.

There are no easy answers, and we all bear part of the responsibility. The fact that women as well as men have internalised and then perpetuate the impossible beauty myth does not mean we shouldn't challenge it. Wondering why girls don't just ignore the pressures to look a certain way while being bombarded with images of 'perfection' is like asking why most people don't eat their ten portions of fruit and veg a day when they are surrounded by adverts and offers for tempting foods laden with sugar, salt and fat.

Low body confidence feeds low self-esteem and insecurity: these girls are more likely to behave in ways that risk and damage their health and well-being: unprotected sex, abuse of drugs and alcohol, self-harm, disordered eating. Girls also say that low body confidence stops them putting their hand up in class,[93] wearing the clothes they would like to, exercising, socialising, having fun with their friends, and even, in some cases, attending school.[94]

And it's not just girls. The problem is affecting increasing numbers of men. More young men are taking their own lives, while more young women suffer from anxiety and depressive incidents. Boys suffer more mental health problems than girls around the age of 10, but by 14 this pattern has reversed.[95] Trans children experience higher rates of anxiety and depression, though when they are supported in their identity this increased risk disappears.[96] All children, whatever their gender, need to be supported in order to nurture good mental health, and this includes reducing the pressure to conform to unrealistic body ideals.

Poet and author Sabrina Mahfouz created an art project where she asked more than 1,000 young women about their lives, hopes and fears. In one exercise they had to choose their most essential items from a list of everyday objects. Some of the most frequent choices are no surprise: bras, smartphones, lipgloss, jeans, laptop. The top item shocked me, however. It was headphones. What a symbol of a hostile environment, of a need to retreat into your own world and block what is happening outside. Wearing headphones says don't talk to me, and don't worry, I'm not speaking out either; I can blend in, be part of the wallpaper, not participate; I can pretend I don't hear men's catcalling and lewd comments; I can create my own soundtrack for the world.

It's the world that needs to change its tune. We need to compose a new score.

So choose your instrument of change . . .

- **LOVE YOUR OWN BODY:** If your children see you look in the mirror, sigh and self-criticise, they learn and copy. Being positive about your own body is one of the best ways to cultivate body confidence in your children.
- **CURB COSMETIC SURGERY:** Write to your MP to push for stricter regulation and to ensure such surgery is properly subject to VAT. And support the campaigns (such as #SurgeryIsNotAGame) to make tech companies stop advertising inappropriate cosmetic surgery 'games'.

- **INSTILL RESILIENCE AT SCHOOL:** Ask your child's school how they cover body confidence in personal, social and health education.

- **BREAKING THE TABOO:** All children should have access at school to quality education about sex and relationships – covering consent, fertility, contraception and the full lifecycle of reproductive health, including the menopause. Ask your child's school how they do this, or contact your MP to raise the issue.

- **LOG OFF:** Step away from social media. You could delete one or more of your apps, like Isabelle did, or even just put the phone down a day a week, or have a digital detox while you're on holiday. You may find you feel better without it.

- **PUT YOUR MONEY WHERE YOUR VALUES ARE:** Be aware of how commercial organisations are advertising to you, and what messages they are sending with their imagery. Support brands that promote body confidence.

- **BEAT EATING DISORDERS:** The charity Beat does amazing work. You can support them with a donation,[97] by volunteering or by joining their campaigns.

- **LISTEN TO PREGNANT WOMEN:** Offer help, support and a kind word, and don't assume you know what they need.

- **INFORM YOURSELF:** One in four pregnancies end in miscarriage, so it is likely someone you know and love will go through this experience. Find out about the issue from the Miscarriage Association[98] and support Tommy's #misCOURAGE campaign[99] to raise awareness, so that when someone close needs you, you are there to support them.

- **ORGANISE A SCREENING OF *THE ILLUSIONISTS*:** Find a room, grab some popcorn, and bring people together in your school, college or organisation to watch the documentary and discuss the issues.[100]

- **'DON'T TELL YOUR DAUGHTER SHE'S BEAUTIFUL':** The *Telegraph* ran this misleading headline about an interview I gave on body image. Of course I didn't suggest never praising a girl's looks, but my point was this: if a large chunk of the praise a child hears relates to their appearance, don't be surprised when they get the message that looking good is what matters. We are much more likely to talk to little girls about their pretty dress or shoes or hair than we are to little boys, so consciously think about what you say. Give praise for being kind, brave, patient, curious, helpful, creative, loving, trying hard . . . the list is endless.

- **DITCH THE FAT-TALK:** Agree with your friends to stop the shaming chat – 'I'm sooo fat', 'I put on four pounds', even the supposedly complimentary 'you look great, have you lost weight?' – which just reinforces the thin ideal. How we interact with our friends can have a huge impact on our self-esteem – it's not easy to change the habits of a lifetime, but among friends we can notice when we fall into old critiques, and try to move to more positive conversations. In some US universities, there is an annual Fat Talk Free Week to encourage people to break the negative habit.[101]

- **TRY MAKE-UP FREE:** Make-up can be fun, but when it becomes essential for just walking out of the door, we have lost some freedom. If you always wear make-up, challenge yourself to go without for a day, or to dial back your routine, and see how it feels. Relish those extra minutes in bed.

- **USE YOUR VOICE:** Contact your favourite magazines and retailers asking them to include a diverse range of models in their photoshoots and adverts: including a variety of body shapes, sizes, skin colours and ages, plus people with disabilities, is much more inclusive and promotes body confidence.

4

PARENTING:
It Takes Two to Tango

I had a good pregnancy, back in 2013. I had no morning sickness, apart from some slight nausea for a few days, which annoyingly coincided with a weekend away at a cottage in Norfolk to celebrate our second wedding anniversary. I was able to keep working right up until the end. As I demanded more gas and air in the small hours of that Sunday morning, in the dark, clinical, windowless birthing room at St Thomas' Hospital where time seemed to stand still, just 72 hours earlier I'd been up with the larks to do the rounds of ITV, BBC and Sky breakfast TV interviews. Even my labour was relatively quick and straightforward (though it didn't feel like it for those ten hours).[1]

Yet I still had weeks in the first trimester where I was overwhelmed by fatigue. I'd get home from work and plonk onto the sofa, and need twenty minutes just to summon up the energy to make a cup of – urgh, decaf – tea. I had the almost-constant weeing as your bladder is squashed to make room for everything else; during long debates in Parliament, where the rule is that ministers are supposed to be present on the green benches throughout, I'd give a heads-up in advance to my opposite number on the Labour side that I wasn't being rude by nipping out every so often for a couple of minutes. And as the pregnancy progressed, I started to feel like a whale, lumbering, clumsy and out of breath climbing a few stairs. I needed more sleep, so hefty ministerial boxes of paperwork that would take till 1 a.m. to work through were not possible – we got ruthless with the diary and axed non-essential daytime meetings, so that more decisions could be taken during the day to reduce the overnight box (which incidentally was an excellent exercise in prioritisation). Non-pregnant, even wearing heels I could easily jog from my departmental office to the House of Commons voting lobby in the eight minutes between the bell ringing and the doors being ceremonially locked – but the eight-months-pregnant me had no chance, so we moved meetings from the Department building to rooms in Parliament in case of votes. I even got over my usual aversion to ministerial cars, recognising that being ferried efficiently from A to B actually enabled me to do my job well in those final few weeks.

I was lucky that it was absolutely possible for me to carry on with a few adjustments throughout my pregnancy, and that I had a job where those around me were determined to do what they could to help. Not everyone has it so easy. Many employers take a much less positive attitude, and many pregnancies are much less medically straightforward. The list of common pregnancy problems includes backache, constipation, deep vein thrombosis, cramp, high blood pressure, faintness, bleeding, piles and sleeplessness. One of the mums-to-be in my antenatal group arrived at the first session, 34 weeks pregnant and on crutches, suffering intense pain even to walk. Many women do a lot of throwing up in the first 14 weeks, and for some the morning (or all-day-long) sickness can be extreme, with vomiting up to 50 times a day and lasting throughout the pregnancy.[2]

In short, it's a pretty big deal physically to grow another person inside you. And emotionally – well, let's just say I shed a *lot* of tears at the John Lewis Christmas advert that year, the one about the Bear and (*sob!*) the Hare.

Then you have birth itself. Intense, traumatic, a whole new experience of pain, heightened senses (the innocent crinkling noise of a cereal bar packet being opened mid-contraction evoked fury in me), joy, dismay, desperation, search for relief. Every birth is unique – the method, length, pain relief and challenges. Yet there's also a quiet bond between women who have experienced it, often manifested in a desire to pass on knowledge, advice or practical help to others soon to give birth. We remember. And simultaneously forget, so that we do it all again, in a brilliant twist by Mother Nature.

That's where the story often stops. TV programmes like *One Born Every Minute* and *Call the Midwife* have a successful formula and an emotional arc that ends with welcoming a newborn into the world. It's a special and amazing moment to be sure, and a compelling narrative.

But just as love stories that end with a wedding and 'happily ever after' conveniently miss out the hard work, daily learning and compromise that create a successful marriage, looking at parenting through the lens of pregnancy and birth misses the vast majority of actual parenting. And while pregnancy, birth and breastfeeding are physically a woman's domain, the rest of parenting is not intrinsically female, contrary to prevailing attitudes.

Historical perspective is useful here. Pregnancy, birth and nursing a newborn are intense experiences that require the devotion of significant energy. When there were high levels of infant mortality and women had little control over their fertility, it was common for women to experience many pregnancies: on average, women from the 1500s right through to the 1890s gave birth to between four and six children.[3] One child would start toddling and another would be on the way very soon. During women's reproductive years, they would spend a significant chunk of time pregnant or breastfeeding – often almost continuously. Given the physical impact, that was a pretty effective method of controlling women and preventing them from participating in power structures and decision-making in society outside of the domestic sphere, whether that was the intention or not.

These days, in the developed world and increasingly elsewhere, women spend much less of their life pregnant. The UK has a fertility rate – the number of babies born to women on average – of about 1.9,[4] and four out of five countries have a rate of less than three. Out of a working life of more than 45 years, that means women now spend on average two to three years pregnant and nursing, and if they are in good health with low-risk pregnancies, then most of that time will be spent in work, too. That is a radically different situation. It's nothing short of a game-changer for how we organise society.

Infant mortality plummeted in the first half of the twentieth century in the UK. At the end of Queen Victoria's reign, one in six babies died before their first birthday, and by the 1950s this was down to one in forty.[5] The advent of the contraceptive pill in the 1960s and the sexual revolution was half a century ago. Yet around the world, women do between two and ten times the caregiving and domestic work that men do.[6] Even in the most equal societies, women still do double what men do. Why are women the ones metaphorically and literally holding the baby when it comes to raising children?

The Myth of Choice

Daniele Fiandaca runs a diversity initiative in the advertising industry, Token Man. He told me that one day he was talking to his co-founder Emma about the choice women make to go on maternity leave. She told him, 'That's interesting, that you think it's a choice.'[7] Her simple statement prompted Daniele to reconsider his assumptions.

To look at the current division of responsibilities and assert that it is purely down to women's choices fails to recognise the social conditioning, legal framework and economic realities driving these decisions.

The social conditioning is particularly strong. From the earliest months of a child's life we begin the process of telling little girls that caring for children is what they should do, and telling little boys not to bother – by encouraging girls to play with dolls and ridiculing boys who want to do so. The law has reinforced this, too: legal rights to two weeks of paid paternity leave didn't exist until 2003,[8] and it wasn't until 2011 that men could take more time.[9] Parental leave after the arrival of a new baby didn't become fully flexible between both parents until I changed the law to introduce shared parental leave in 2015.[10] It sent a clear message: mothers were the main parent, with fathers playing a secondary role. Women's role as mothers is prominent in the media, in storytelling, on screen, and even where it is frankly irrelevant to the narrative. By contrast, men's role as fathers is ignored. I recall making a speech on these issues as a minister, arguing that men are too often written out of the family script. The *Daily Mail* wrote up the speech and clearly wanted to illustrate it with a photo of me and my son.[11] Only one photo was in the public domain, which we gave to the local newspapers in our constituencies when we announced Andrew's birth, depicting me and Duncan cradling him in a big white snowsuit, just a few days old. The *Mail* literally cut Duncan out of the picture they printed to accompany the article about me criticising the media for the way they treat fathers. You couldn't make it up.

The gender pay gap means that, on average, women earn 19 per cent less than men,[12] so when considering constrained family finances after the birth of a child, it's understandable that many couples will opt for the mum to take the lion's share of the leave to protect family income. These combined 'choices' end up reinforcing the gender pay gap, however, as time out of the labour market is one of the key contributing factors. It's not a lack of ambition, as the ground-breaking Project 28-40 survey found. Women are confident and ambitious in their working lives, but they feel nervous about the impact having children will have on their career.[13] In debates about equal parenting, some people cling to the argument that it is natural for women to stay at home with the baby while men go out to work to bring home the bacon, because he earns more. This argument is rarely taken to its logical conclusion – that in the increasing number of mixed-sex couples where the woman earns more, the man should be staying at home looking after the baby.[14] While current financial realities do drive rational choices, we shouldn't be accepting the gender pay gap as an immutable given, to be used as a convenient excuse for outdated attitudes about men's role as fathers.

The Myth of Mother's Intuition

I've lost count of the number of times I've heard people tell me, truly believing it, that women are just better with babies, that they instinctively know what to do, so it makes sense for dads to get more involved when children are a bit older. This is nonsense, and it's dangerous nonsense.

Rewind to the many times as a twenty-something woman that a friend or relative would ask if I wanted to hold their new baby and I'd freeze, knowing that the polite thing to do was say yes, but simultaneously full of trepidation as the tiny fragile bundle was passed across. Terrified of dropping or breaking the child, I'd hold on for dear life in a rigid, nervous cradling pose, until the inevitable wail would come and then there would be the whole stressful how-do-you-hand-them-back gymnastics, seemingly impossible to do while supporting the baby's head so it doesn't fall off and your hands are in the way and it's all a bit awkward and thank heavens at least it's over now. The first time I got comfortable with a baby was when my sister's daughter, Charlotte, was born. It helped that she had chronic colic and cried constantly for the first four months, so there was no sense of judgement or doing something wrong when she kept crying as I held her. Rather, seeing how frazzled my sister was by the endless torture of her baby's distress, I knew I could be genuinely helpful by taking my tearful niece into another room for a while and holding her safely, softly singing and trying to give her comfort. With the space to practise, and the confidence to ask the really simple questions of my sister and brother-in-law, I learned that it is possible to move a baby from a cradle hold to resting on your shoulder when your arm gets tired or they fancy a change of scenery, and their head doesn't actually fall off.

Despite having had some exposure to babies, I remember arriving home from the hospital with our little boy in his car seat and sitting him down in the middle of the living room, looking at my husband and just thinking: *So, what now?* We didn't have a clue. By trial and error – and googling on the iPad at 4 a.m. – we muddled through. Things that seem obvious now were mysterious and otherworldly in our sleep-deprived, new-parent haze, when you're taking shifts for a 90-minute sleep and screaming in frustration at the endless advice about breastfeeding that just keeps repeating how great it is rather than telling you how to actually make it work when it isn't happening.

Fast-forward a few months and I was taking part in a constituency campaign meeting via Skype. As Andrew was awake, I'd put him in the Ergo baby carrier and was bouncing him up and down to keep him entertained while I chatted with my team about canvass figures and leaflet-distribution plans for the forthcoming Scottish independence referendum. After an hour or so of the meeting, Andrew was bored, restless and fussing, so I got him out of the baby carrier and held him up with his tummy on my head in a flying pose, at which point the wails ended, he laughed and was in his element. It must have looked a bit odd to those watching via the video call, and my campaign organiser Sam was struck by how he'd suddenly stopped crying: 'How on earth did you know he'd like *that*?'

'You try *everything*,' was my response.

That's my top tip for parenting. Lots of experimenting. And practise, practise, practise. It may not make perfect – there is no such thing as perfect in the world of parenting – but it just about gets you through the day. There's a theory that practising something for 10,000 hours makes you an expert. That's about 18 months, at 18 hours a day (and in the early weeks you'll be lucky to get six hours' sleep a day).

So, yes, it seems amazing to the uninitiated that a baby will stop crying when passed back to its mother (oh, the power of the smell of milk), and that she seems to know exactly how to entertain or soothe the infant. It's easy to assume this is some instinctive gift that mothers have. The reality is far more prosaic: she has spent hours trying everything. How the baby likes to be held, stroked, fed, have their nappy changed, bathed, cuddled, what songs, stories, toys and games they like best, and what sends them to sleep – she will have spent many hours practising that especially. And here's the thing: breastfeeding aside, men can do every bit of this as well as women, if they put the hours in.

The idea that men's and women's brains are somehow hardwired differently from the start and don't change or adapt to circumstances is outdated.[15] While pregnancy, birth and breastfeeding lead to hormone production and changes in women's brains that support nurturing behaviour, research has shown that the act of caring for babies leads to similar changes in men's brains, too, with the extent of the change directly related to the amount of time spent caring for the infant.[16] In short, mothers are not inherently better at caring for children. People who spend a lot of time caring for children are better at caring for children.

Sharing parenting doesn't just mean splitting the hours spent caring for your child. It also means sharing the joys. After all, no one else will ever be quite as obsessively enthusiastic about your little one's every gurgle and smile as your fellow parent (though grandparents come a pretty close second). I've found that some men underestimate these early joys – certainly my husband Duncan did.

I love our son; what dad doesn't? Perhaps a little more surprising is how much I have loved the experiences that our son has already given me, as a dad. After all, we dads are not that good at passing this news on to prospective fathers. Sure, there are the heartfelt congratulations, but even chat about how great it is will be invariably accompanied by banter about lost sleep or being glad to get back to the sanity of the office, while the strongest enthusiasm is reserved for activities like sports days and football training that are still a very distant prospect.

The reality can be much better than that, and certainly needn't wait until your child is capable of conversing with you about sport or current affairs. Uncontrolled joy, playfulness, hero worship and, at the heart of it, unconditional love – these screaming, whining, weeing, sickly poo-monsters have so much more to offer their dads than a regular supply of filled nappies and sleepless nights. The key thing I've learned is that babies reward practice: the sooner you are involved, and the more practice you get at looking after your baby, the more confident you become, and somehow they realise and begin to co-operate. So I've resolved to talk to the new and prospective dads I know about the joys and practicalities of looking after baby, and challenge the casual 'big talk' about what they'll be leaving for the mother 'to take care of' which sadly I still come across as well. There really is no need for the joys of looking after children to be a secret we can't talk about with other men – most of them will be dads themselves at some point or already.

As a couple, you can accelerate the learning process by sharing your breakthroughs – 'I've noticed he really likes being held while bouncing gently on the fitness ball next to the fairy lights on the Christmas tree' or 'last night, singing "Five Little Monkeys" really helped him sleep'. Parenting a newborn really made me appreciate how amazing single parents are. For so many reasons, lots of people parent on their own, and do it brilliantly, but my goodness it must be hard, given how difficult it is when there's two of you. Hats off to them. Plus anyone who has twins. Just. Not. Enough. Hands. And you're outnumbered on a regular basis. At least for most people, by the time they have two small children in their care on some outing on their own, they've had plenty of time to get expert at it by practising with just one.

Each stage of parenting brings its own challenges. As mum to a four-year-old, making it work in the early years is most vivid for me. Looking at friends and relatives who have older children,

I can see what is coming down the track: the mental checklists and organisation for school uniform, gym kits, packed lunches, parents' evenings, dentist appointments, play dates, swimming lessons, sleepovers, birthday parties, friendship advice, school transition, after-school clubs, developing independence, exam stress, puberty, teenage crushes, social anxiety ... the list goes on. Parenting is a lifelong endeavour – and just when you're getting the hang of part of it, it changes.

Hapless Dad and Can't-Win Mum

Popular stereotypes about mothers and fathers help neither parent. The assumption that 'mother knows best' disempowers men in their parenting role, and piles the pressure on women.

We've thankfully moved on from a view of fathers as distant from children. In the 1950s, it was rare for men to be present at the birth of their child, and their main task afterwards would be to 'wet the baby's head' in the pub with their mates, rather than getting familiar with nappy-changing at home.[17] The father was often a figure to be feared for his role in enforcing discipline, especially at a time when corporal punishment was seen as acceptable. Nowadays, 86 per cent of men are present at the birth of their child;[18] however we've replaced the stern and unemotional caricature with Hapless Dad – a bumbling but well-meaning chap who never quite gets it right because, you know, men are slightly rubbish as parents. Think Homer Simpson, or the 1980s comedy film *Three Men and a Baby*.

It's hugely patronising, and so ingrained in our psyche that people on public transport or in the street find it acceptable to approach men out and about with a baby or small child and impart unsolicited advice, ask if they're 'babysitting' today, or even – no doubt trying to be lovely – tell them that what they're doing is amazing. As Simon Ragoonanan puts it, 'What woman has ever been told they're a great mother because they're feeding their baby a bottle of formula in a supermarket café?'[19]

The Hapless Dad stereotype sets our expectations of fathers so low that covering the absolute basics of clothing, feeding or comforting a child is seen as overachievement. Dare I say it, this suits some people. Men who have figured out that it's bloody hard work looking after a child may find conceding their inferior talents is a passport to an easier life. Women who feel frustrated with male dominance in practically every other sphere of society may want there to be one area where they are the unchallenged experts. Unravelling the false assumption that men are crap parents means men taking responsibility for childcare, and women letting go of their monopoly on caregiving expertise.

The flipside of Hapless Dad is Can't-Win Mum. It doesn't matter what the decision is, there is no escape from the maze of parenting paradoxes for women, with guilt and shame lurking behind every choice.

The first issue is whether to have children at all: either way, as a woman this will be used to define you. 'Childless' is used as an accusatory or pitying adjective for women, as if to pour shame on them for not doing their womanly duty and popping out a sprog. Lots of people choose not to have children; lots of people want to have children but can't. We don't tend to question the men about it, but a woman's lack of children is often seen as suspicious and leads to intrusive questioning[20] or an irrelevant 'justification' for their suitability for a role. My friend Sarah Teather was an excellent Minister for Children and Families, but that didn't stop Conservative MP Tim Loughton criticising her with the catty jibe that she did not 'produce' a family of her own.[21] Equally, a woman's status as a mother will often be referenced when it has no relation to the issue at hand – when Rona Fairhead was appointed to chair the BBC Trust, for example, the *Sunday Telegraph* headline read 'MOTHER OF THREE POISED TO LEAD THE BBC',[22] with her maternal status seemingly more important than her name or business acumen.

If you do become a mother, welcome to the guilt-laden world of Can't-Win Mum. Depending on your age, you may be a feckless teenage mother, a slut with an unwanted pregnancy, or perhaps you got up the duff deliberately so you could get a council flat and have a cushy life, struggling to make ends meet on benefits. 'Have you left it too late?' magazines scream at women, with much less fanfare devoted to how men's fertility also drops with age. Are your ovaries shrivelling as we speak, is your biological clock loudly accelerating towards the day when you will be barren? Will you drain NHS resources by selfishly undergoing IVF to bring a new life into the world?

If you are disabled, how dare you consider that you could also be a mum! When Paralympian athlete Tanni, Baroness Grey-Thompson told a medical professional she was pregnant, one of the first things they did was to offer her an abortion.[23] Shocking – but, according to Tanni, not an uncommon experience for disabled women.

When you get pregnant – or as common parlance often puts it, 'fall pregnant', just to emphasise the original sin that we women commit by virtue of being 'unvirtuous' – then your body belongs to the rest of society.

Complete strangers will feel empowered to remark and pass judgement about the size and shape of your bump,[24] and in some cases reach across and have a good feel. Women in the public eye who are pregnant are micro-analysed and body-shamed, normalising this kind of scrutiny of pregnant women generally.[25] And your behaviour as a whole is now seen as fair game for comment – your choice of footwear, your physical activity, what you're eating.

When baby arrives, there's still more judgement. Women who give birth by C-section are derided as 'too posh to push'. Women who opt for a home birth are seen as irresponsibly bohemian. Women who have pain relief are made to feel as if they somehow 'failed' by not enduring the full onslaught of labour pains in blissful serenity singing 'Kumbaya'.

Breast or bottle? Society will make you feel wrong whichever you choose, or if you use both. The benefits of breastfeeding are well documented, but it doesn't work for everyone. Our current approach of demonising mothers who don't breastfeed, yet providing very poor breastfeeding support, is unsurprisingly ineffective at boosting breastfeeding rates while being devastatingly effective at making new mums feel like they're failing from the word go. And if you do breastfeed, make sure you are not doing so 'ostentatiously',[26] or you'll be told to cover up[27] or run the risk of social media vilification, like the woman who was the subject of these tweets from a BMW employee: 'Had a new one today – sat down with a customer and without saying anything, this woman just gets her tit out and starts breastfeeding . . . I had absolutely no idea where to look or what to do.'[28] Despite a legal right to breastfeed in public places, women breastfeeding their babies have been asked to leave all sorts of venues: cafés[29] and restaurants,[30] the Jobcentre,[31] a primary school,[32] a Sports Direct,[33] the local swimming pool,[34] a town hall[35] and even a branch of Kiddicare, a shop which sells baby products.[36]

If you dedicate yourself to your new baby as a stay-at-home parent, you're written off as a lazy yummy-mummy, leaving your employer in the lurch. If you go back to work, you're branded a career-obsessive who doesn't care about her children. If you take less than a year of maternity leave, then the official government line now is that you're going back to work 'early',[37] as if there's a single, 'correct' amount of time to take.

Look at the reaction to Yahoo CEO Marissa Mayer in 2015 when she announced she'd be taking two weeks of maternity leave after the birth of her twins before returning to work. A deluge of criticism followed in the media and from the public, with Mayer accused of setting a 'bad example',[38] and of being responsible for shrinking maternity leave in the US.[39] In fact, Mayer had increased paid parental leave at Yahoo and it was well used, suggesting she had fostered a positive culture about taking leave.[40]

Yet a double standard was clearly on display: at around the same time, Facebook CEO Mark Zuckerberg was lauded for his decision to take two months of paternity leave – *Time* branded it a 'win for women'[41] and a photo he posted of him changing his daughter's nappy attracted more than two million likes.[42] A salient question was posed: could a powerful woman ever post a baby picture like that?[43] The reality is she wouldn't: it would only reinforce the stereotype that harms women's careers, and she would be showered with misogynistic comments rather than praise.

How often do we even know when a male CEO becomes a father? How often is he asked? I'm delighted that Mark Zuckerberg took parental leave, and that he shared photos and was open about it. That is exactly what we need powerful men to do, to reset the expectations. But it is sad that we still have such a problem with women making their own choices, and the reaction to Marissa Mayer really does epitomise Can't-Win Mum.

Motherhood Penalty/Fatherhood Bonus

Women who have children face a motherhood penalty at work – they earn less, are less likely to be promoted, and are more likely to have careers stall and be placed on the 'mummy track', where bosses assume they have no interest in new challenges. Yet men who are fathers earn 21 per cent more than their male colleagues who don't have children, in a daddy dividend.[44]

The scale of pregnancy discrimination in the UK is shocking: 54,000 women each year are forced out of their jobs as a result. In an antenatal class of nine women, one of them will be sacked, or treated so badly she is forced to leave her job as a result of her pregnancy. It's a shameful situation for 21st-century Britain, and it's getting worse. A decade ago, the figure was 30,000.

Employers complain that to deal with maternity leave or support pregnant women in the workplace is a hassle and costly. Of course it takes some time and attention to get it right. I know this myself, having once had three members of staff in my small office on maternity leave in the same year. But just as you plan for other unexpected events or risks in an organisation, it's entirely possible to manage the process of a member of staff being away for a few months – and with generally fairly predictable timing and a decent amount of notice.

Business and society benefit from the next generation. Apart from the obvious 'continuation of the species' imperative, without children there would be no customers and workers of the future, and no one paying taxes to fund services and pensions when the current generation retires. This is increasingly recognised as a real problem. In most rich countries, the number of children being born is below the replacement rate of 2.1 for each woman. In some, like Japan, it is as low as 1.4,[45] and these countries are frantically trying policies to encourage procreation, from payments when babies are born, to subsidised childcare, to bizarre campaigns to encourage people to have more sex like 'National Night' in Singapore, 'Do it for Denmark' and Russia's National Day of Conception, where lucky couples who conceive can win a car.[46]

So while parents of course contribute by far the lion's share of the investment of time, money, love and energy into raising children, it's perfectly fair for society and business to be expected to do their bit to support this, even if there are better ways than cringeworthy YouTube videos. The state provides education for children and some financial support for parents. And business has to accommodate its employees going on leave when a new child arrives. Complying with the law is a basic essential for any organisation. Good employers also recognise that human beings are the ultimate engine of corporate value, but that they are also people - mothers, fathers, daughters, sons and friends, with relationships and responsibilities outside of work. By enabling staff to integrate work into the rest of their life, businesses can reap the benefit of enhanced loyalty, better staff retention and productivity gains.[47]

I've often heard women talking about the calculation they have to make about going back to work after having a baby, based on how much more (or how little more) they would earn than the cost of childcare. It's almost as if caring for children is seen as 'woman's work', so childcare costs are hypothecated to a woman's salary. But a different way of thinking about it is deducting half the cost of the childcare from each parent's salary. It doesn't change the household sums of a financially difficult time, but it does change the perception of responsibility. Childcare - whether provided free of charge by a parent or other relative, or in a paid setting - is essential for all working parents, not just mothers.

We do need to change the sums too, though. The lack of availability of affordable, quality childcare is a major structural problem that perpetuates gender inequality in the workplace and at home. Some families are spending up to 45 per cent of their disposable income on childcare. In many areas, there are simply not enough nursery, childminder and after-school-club places. And it is even harder to find childcare for the increasing number of people who work different shift patterns and irregular hours, or for those who have a disabled child.[48] The government must do more to help.

A New Division of Labour

We need to ditch the constant guilt and micro-judgements over every parenting decision, and jettison the outdated notions of who does what. Men and women are equally capable as parents, and each couple needs to find the way of sharing the responsibilities that works best for them.

The sexual revolution of the 1960s and '70s is unfinished business. We only changed one side of the equation, so it's no wonder things have ended up out of kilter, strained and not quite working. Women were accepted into the workplace, more or less. Paid less, promoted less, respected less, for sure. But they were there. At the same time, men did not gravitate back towards the home. Working women were also working at home, doing the double shift. Some 'new men' would 'help out' with the kids, or cook Sunday lunch, and revel in how enlightened they were. But the prime responsibility for running the household, caring for the children and organising their lives stayed with the women. On top of the day job.

When mothers experience workplace discrimination, and burnout from trying to do it all, it's not encouraging for men who are keen to be hands-on dads. They have understandable – and rational – concerns about the impact on their job. Yet sharing domestic responsibilities more equally is the key to a better, happier workplace, and a win-win for both men and women. The younger generation is already prompting employers to change ways of working, embracing flexibility and shunning presenteeism in favour of judging on outcomes. This more modern approach to working is better for parents, and also benefits a much wider group of people who, you know, want to have a life outside of work, too.

In the autumn of 2012, when Deputy Prime Minister Nick Clegg summoned me to his grand Whitehall office overlooking Horse Guards Parade and asked me to become a minister in the Department for Business, Innovation and Skills, the first thing I said was, 'Do I get to do shared parental leave?' The answer was yes, and I was over the moon. Shared parental leave was a long-standing Lib Dem commitment, which I had promoted through a policy working group I chaired back in 2008. We had got it into the Lib Dem 2010 manifesto, and then the coalition agreement with the Conservatives – the document that was the foundation stone of the government's plans for its five-year term.

In theory, everything in that document should have been certain to happen. In practice, it is a challenge to drive any major change through the maze of vested interests, bureaucracy, legal opinions, spending constraints and inertia that is government, and even more so when it is a coalition and the bigger party is sceptical about the policy. Turning shared parental leave from a commitment to a reality was a significant challenge, and my dream job.

The system we inherited was that women could take up to twelve months' maternity leave, and men could take two weeks' paternity leave. In 2011 we had implemented some flexibility, but with heavy restrictions. Additional Paternity Leave enabled couples to transfer leave en bloc from the mother to the father. But this didn't kick in until the baby was six months old, there was no option for them to take leave at the same time, and once the transfer was made there was no room for further flexibility.

Shared parental leave, by contrast, would give parents the ability to split the year of leave however they liked, other than a basic requirement for each parent to take at least two weeks. So the father could take a year of leave, or the mother could do so, or they could split it equally, or anything in between. They would have the opportunity to take leave at the same time, for example to have more than two weeks together as a family at the beginning, or to have a 'handover' period when leave switched from one parent to the other. They could even take separate blocks of leave, for example if a parent wanted to return to work for a specific project, event or busy time of year, and then go back on leave. The new flexibility would apply to heterosexual couples, same-sex couples, and those becoming parents through adoption or surrogacy.

A positive, modern change – what's not to like, you'd think. But scratch the surface and parts of society remain stubbornly traditional about gender roles at work. As my Liberal Democrat colleague Ed Davey described the policy to a group of employers, he explained that dads would now be able to take significant chunks of parental leave. One dinosaur businessman remarked in horror, 'You mean I won't be able to employ men now too?'

Various Conservative ministers – Grant Shapps in particular – fought to weaken and block shared parental leave at every turn as it progressed through the phases of consultation, drafting of legislation, and decisions about practical implementation. We won many of the battles, helped by the strong support of the Deputy Prime Minister Nick Clegg, who was personally very committed to the policy. I brought implementation forward to April 2015, so it couldn't be stymied by a change of government in 2015. We ensured the Civil Service set an example to other employers by enhancing pay for those taking shared parental leave, in line with maternity policy. Yet some elements were impossible to secure, like extra weeks of leave given to dads, on a use-it-or-lose-it basis, which we knew from international experience was important for driving take-up. Post-2008 austerity meant increasing basic maternity and shared parental pay were out of the question for now.

The business response was intriguing. Most business groups welcomed the changes. Some grumbled about the additional burden, which given we hadn't in the end been able to increase the overall amount of leave parents could take, I thought was an illuminating argument. While I accept that any new law means employers have to familiarise themselves with the changes, the subtext was clear: some bosses felt that men taking leave was more of an inconvenience than women doing so. They basically thought the men were more indispensable, more important.

Then there was the slightly depressing research about how men felt about taking shared parental leave.[49] Lots of enthusiasm for the policy, but many men commenting that they were worried about the impact on their career. Discussing views on taking shared parental leave with men was like watching the penny drop, as if the workplace consequence of parenting had never before been appreciated – welcome to the world of the working mother, guys! As Gideon Burrows powerfully expresses in his book *Men Can Do It!: The real reason men don't do childcare*,[50] there is also a selfishness deeply rooted in this. Couples will make their own choices, and there's no one-size-fits-all, 'correct' approach. But where a man in a relationship decides not to take parental leave due to the impact on his career, he needs to recognise that he's implicitly deciding that he's fine with the impact falling on his partner's career - and that's the person he presumably loves so much that they've started a family together.

The prize is to create a workplace where there aren't huge career penalties for parents and carers. I believe we'll get there much faster if both men and women are engaged in that challenge, one of the reasons I was so determined to make shared parental leave happen.

In April 2015, in the midst of the general election campaign, I was knocking on doors and speaking to voters in my constituency. It was a beautiful, sunny spring evening, but I was exhausted from the toll of campaigning over many weeks, coupled with broken sleep (what a time for Andrew to be teething!). As I told myself I would do five more doors before heading home for something to eat, a pregnant woman answered the next door, and we had a brief chat about expecting a baby; she was at eight months, so awaiting her new arrival with excitement and a little trepidation. When she told me that she and her husband were going to be using the new shared parental leave, suddenly my tiredness vanished, my mood matched the crisp evening sunlight and I practically skipped home. Since then, I've cherished that feeling whenever people have told me they've used shared parental leave: from Twitter exchanges to family gatherings to drinks with colleagues. It's a heady combination of feeling that you've helped someone as an individual while simultaneously changing the world a little. I caught up with former colleagues from the Deputy Prime Minister's office a year after we left government, and one of the civil servants, Ross, told me how excited he was to be taking shared parental leave – or his 'Swinson leave', as he called it.

In changing the law, my refrain was simple: shared parental leave is good for children, good for families and good for equality in the workplace. There is compelling research that both parents being involved in the early weeks and months of a child's life is good for the child's development.[51] Close contact between parent and baby in the initial phase is important for bonding and attachment. Enabling fathers to spend this time with their newborn is an investment in that child's future.

Adapting to the arrival of a new baby is a wonderful, though hugely stressful, experience. Sleep deprivation and constant demands from a newborn mean a difficult time with a huge, steep learning curve. The state shouldn't be making it harder by dictating how parents split the responsibilities, so giving families choice is a no-brainer. Perhaps the biggest impact shared parental leave can have, though, is outside of the family unit: improving gender equality.

Contrary to the popular narrative, a key reason that women's careers are so heavily impacted by having children is not due to the biology – it's the unequal distribution of childcare and domestic responsibilities after the newborn phase that is so instrumental.

When mum has spent six, nine or twelve months intensively looking after baby, and dad has done so for two weeks, mum is the clear expert. She's better and more efficient at feeding, nappy-changing, dressing, soothing and sleep-inducing. So, even when she returns to work, a cycle is reinforced where she is the primary caregiver, and dad plays a supporting role, helping out when she is exhausted, taking direction on how it should be done, but not taking overall responsibility. Playdates, packed lunches, birthday parties, gym kit, homework, doctors, dentists, new clothes, school trips, swimming lessons – so much of this rigmarole of parenting ends up falling on the mum's shoulders. Often this is compounded by other domestic tasks: doing laundry, making meals, grocery shopping, cleaning the house and so on. Interestingly, research has found that where domestic chores are shared evenly between parents, girls grow up with broader career aspirations.[52] The father's approach to household tasks was the strongest predictor of young women's professional ambitions. So, men, if you want your daughter to aspire to a stellar career, make sure you're pulling your weight at home.

Shared parental leave has the potential to nip in the bud this pattern of chore inequality. When each parent spends time in sole charge of an infant, both become experts, and sharing the tasks and overall responsibility is more intuitive and practically easier. There can still be division of labour, but based on individual preferences and aptitudes.

A review of shared parental leave is due to happen this year, looking back over the first three years and recommending any necessary changes. We should, I hope, get some official figures on take-up rates. Survey data and shared parental pay figures from HMRC that exist so far suggests that take-up is in line with our published expectations for the early stages, of between 2 and 8 per cent of eligible couples. What fascinates me, however, is the regular stream of media stories proclaiming the policy a failure, using bogus data to claim that hardly any dads are taking leave, when the numbers are just what we predicted.[53] Publicity-seeking firms have cottoned on to the fact that if they do a bit of research and slam a shocking but false statistic on the top (such as saying only 1 per cent of men take the leave, but including men who aren't even dads in the 99 per cent who don't), they get acres of free coverage. This lazy media narrative that men don't really want to take leave, or that they can't, because unlike women they are indispensable in their work roles, needs to be challenged. It is actively harmful, because it labels men who do want to take leave as extremely unusual, reinforcing existing cultural barriers. Shared parental leave should change and evolve; it was always a crucial first step towards more equal parenting. Employers need to be encouraged to enhance the pay, as they do for maternity leave, and fathers should get a bigger chunk of leave allocated just for them on a use-it-or-lose-it basis. Couples who currently miss out, for example, due to the father being self-employed, or the mother not working, need to be included. And statutory maternity, paternity and shared parental pay should also increase.

In the first six months of our son's life, my husband and I had a rough rule that I did inputs, he did outputs. Of course, sometimes I changed nappies and Duncan gave Andrew bottles of milk, but I spent a huge amount of time breastfeeding and Duncan certainly perfected a much slicker nappy-changing technique than me. When I went back to work, however, Duncan took responsibility for the pureeing stage: cooking, blending and freezing cubes of various fruit and veg for the weaning process. When Andrew was ill and couldn't be at nursery, we'd compare diaries and work out the least disruptive solution, often sharing the care during the day – I'd look after Andrew while Duncan did a media interview in the morning, and we'd swap so I could take part in a parliamentary debate in the afternoon. It wasn't always easy. I remember running across Westminster Bridge one evening with Andrew strapped to me in the baby carrier, dashing to the doctor's before they closed, then picking up the antibiotics prescription, only to realise that this meant Andrew couldn't go to nursery for 48 hours. Duncan was in his constituency in Wiltshire, yet the next day I had a long-planned ministerial visit to the Trading Standards team who were seizing dangerous imports at Southampton docks. Duncan ended up doing a 220-mile round trip while I rejigged my diary for later on, and we both managed to do most of what we'd planned. Looking back at our combination of ministerial responsibilities, representing two constituencies at opposite ends of the country, both of us campaigning hard to hold on to marginal seats and becoming parents to Andrew, I wonder how we did it. But at the time, we just did. Parents across the country just do, in all sorts of circumstances even more challenging than ours.

Does one parent always have to be the one taking the primary responsibility? Certainly one way many women combine being at the top of their profession with motherhood has been to flip the gender roles, with mum as breadwinner-in-chief and dad staying at home or working in a supporting role. Anne-Marie Slaughter, the writer and former Hillary Clinton aide who penned *Unfinished Business*, suggests that one parent taking on the primary caregiver role is inevitable, even when couples try to split the responsibility. And while it may be true in some of the biggest, most intense jobs – US Secretary of State, or CEO of a huge corporation – even then there may be opportunities to pass the baton, with different parents taking primary charge of the children at different points. Some couples try this 'turnabout' parenting by swapping responsibility from week to week, or fitting in with shifting work commitments. I think there are also alternative models that pioneering couples are exploring and creating, like archaeologists meticulously dusting away on a dig, with different people in the team uncovering varied elements as the whole find takes form. Instead of uncovering the secrets of the past, they are unlocking the potential of the future.

A parallel and related journey is that of same-sex couples who are parents. Over pizza in a bustling Italian restaurant in 2016, Tara Kaufmann told me that she always knew she wanted children, but when she came out as a 19-year-old in the early 1980s she just thought it would never be possible. There were some gay parents then, but the role models were few and far between. As Tara put it, 'I didn't want to be one of those pioneering lesbian mothers . . . basically raising their kids in communes.' She described the open and outright hostility towards gay people, where even those who 'tolerated' homosexuality took for granted that it wouldn't be 'right' or 'fair' for gay people to have roles as teachers or parents. But attitude shifts and legal changes over the years meant that Tara and her partner Andrea were able to become parents 11 years ago, and now have two daughters, Ava and Georgie. They divvy up the school-run responsibilities according to their work – Tara doing it on the two days she works from home and Andrea, a writer, covering the other days. Andrea has caring responsibilities for her own parents at the weekend, when Tara spends more time with the kids. It's a good model that other couples could emulate, making it 'much more about practicalities', rather than every decision being 'overlaid with gender expectations'.[54]

Fitting a new parenting model into our lives requires a reshaping of the workforce, not just with more flexible, agile working patterns and a focus on results, but with a wider appreciation of employees as individuals who are more productive, loyal and motivated if they are enabled to thrive personally as well as professionally. There are many organisations that require workers to have a stay-at-home spouse if they want to have a family and do a given job – but those business models are broken. As attitudes change, in the future there just won't be sufficient talented people for them to employ if they continue to restrict themselves to fish in the recruitment pool of people whose partners do not work. Whether it's the military, the diplomatic service, investment banking or management consultancy firms, they need to change to adapt to the needs of the modern workforce. It also means a resetting of assumptions in society.

How Do We Get There?

So what can we all do to create a world where parenting responsibilities are shared more equally between men and women? In short, we need simply to start doing it more equally, and making it easier for others to do it more equally.

As parents, we can all take an honest look at ourselves and see what assumptions and excuses we make for how it 'just has to be the way it is'. Time and time and time again I've seen couples at similar levels in their career pre-children, who swiftly fall into the parenting stereotypes against their stated wishes. The dad will lament how it's such a shame that he doesn't have the kind of job that enables him to commit to picking up his child on time. Often the mum doesn't have a very different kind of job, but as someone has to make sure they're there when school or nursery ends, she has made it a non-negotiable condition that she will leave at a specific time. In the other direction, I've often heard mums talk about how they 'have' to arrange the playdates, choose the child's clothes and be there for bedtime, as if their other half is incapable of human conversation, basic motor skills or comforting their own child.

The change starts with us, and here are some ways you can make it happen.

- **STOP ASSUMING:** Let's stop assuming things about parents, and indeed whether people are parents or even want to be parents. There must be a more interesting question you can ask people than 'are you planning to have children?' and a pregnant woman doesn't need to hear 'oh, you'll feel differently and take the whole year' when she tells you she's returning to work when her baby is five months old. People have individual circumstances and make their own decisions about whether and how to have and raise their children, so let's banish the guilt trips.
- **START TALKING ABOUT DADS:** One of the most powerful ways to change outdated perceptions is to talk about the new normal. Dads being open and frank about their role as fathers, the time they devote to it and what they love about it all helps other men to see it as part of the deal of being a man, rather than the domain of women. This can be online, at work or with family

and friends. There are loads of great dad bloggers out there, charting their experiences and providing inspiration for others. Try:

- http://manvspink.com/
- http://dadbloguk.com/
- http://www.citydaduk.com/
- https://candledave.wordpress.com/

Or why not start your own? Meanwhile, in the workplace, men being open about their parenting responsibilities is also important. If the boss is leaving early to watch his child in the school play, rather than pretending he's off to a key client meeting, it's better people know the actual reason – then it's easier for others in the organisation to ask for the flexibility they need at work, too. And within family and friendship groups, being open about sharing parenting more equally helps to shift attitudes.

- **GIVE EQUAL ADVICE:** Children do affect your life, so if you want to have children it does make sense to think about when you might do so and how you might combine it with your work – but this should be considered equally by men and women, and indeed girls and boys considering their career choices far into the future. If you're in a position to advise people, whether as a parent, youth leader, teacher or friend, don't assume men and women need different advice about combining family and career. Help people test their assumptions rather than just reinforcing them.
- **ENHANCE SHARED PARENTAL LEAVE:** The government and employers need to build on shared parental leave. There needs to be more dedicated leave for dads, enhanced pay,

and promotion of the concept by government and business leaders. Employers can ensure they have policies for paid shared parental leave to encourage take-up, and ultimately the government needs to find ways to increase pay for maternity, paternity and parental leave. Far too many new parents have no real choice – finances dictate the parenting split, and indeed the overall length of leave. One interim step might be to increase flexibility, so that more pay per week could be taken – for example by giving couples the choice to concentrate the existing pay for 41 weeks into fewer weeks at a higher rate.

- **MAKE PARENTING CULTURE INCLUSIVE:** Just as the male-dominated workplace presents cultural challenges for women, the female-dominated realm of parenting can be culturally difficult for men. Imagery and language on everything from posters in doctors' surgeries to the names of groups for young children ('Mother & Baby Rhyme Time') can scream to men that they are not welcome, but these are also easily fixed with a little thought. Parenting magazines and media stories often focus on women to the exclusion of men, and advertising imagery all too easily falls into the stereotypes of who does what – so those in the media can do their bit to present a more balanced view of parenting. Those not in the media can turn their yelling at the telly or tutting at sexist articles into feedback or complaints to media outlets and brands applying lazy stereotypes that assume 'parent = mum'. And on an individual level, if you're a woman somewhere where there's nine mums and one dad, remember how it feels when the tables are turned, and make an effort to include him in the conversation and activities.

- **PARENT-FRIENDLY PUBLIC SERVICES:** Too often, a father is shut out in the earliest hours of his child's life, as many hospitals make no provision for dads to stay when mum and baby are kept in overnight after the birth. This is destructive to families at a time that is both exciting and vulnerable – and leads both men and women to feel frustrated that they can't support each other in their early experiences of parenting together. The NHS must find ways to allow families to be together – bonding as a unit – immediately after birth, and some hospitals are already showing how it can be done.[55] I lost count of the number of forms we filled in after Andrew was born that asked us to give details of the 'primary' parent. Not only does that jar when you're sharing the care, it actually promotes the idea that there ought to be a primary parent. Simple changes to official forms across children's centres, nurseries and health services would make space for the view that parenting is a shared endeavour. Schools and nurseries often assume that mum is in charge, despite what parents tell them. After I talked about these issues at an event, a woman called Shelley came up to me to say she was driven round the bend that her child's nursery rang her every time her child was ill – even though they'd clearly stated on the forms that her husband was to be the first point of call, due to the different situations in their jobs. She told me she had resolved to challenge them on it rather than seethe in silence, as that's the only way they would ever change their assumptions. Shelley is right – we need to point it out to public service providers when they make sexist parenting assumptions.
- **QUALITY, AFFORDABLE CHILDCARE:** Contact your MP and ask what they are doing to increase the availability of good

childcare, and the financial support offered to help parents struggling with the cost.

- **GENERATIONAL CHANGE:** When grandchildren arrive, the passing down of advice through the generations can be a source of tension. Couples wanting to share parenting differently today aren't saying their parents got it wrong. Advice on putting baby to sleep on their back/front has changed with time, and in so many other ways the experience of parenting today will differ from decades ago. Parents' choices should be respected, however, rather than expecting them to conform to how it used to be. With increased longevity and good health as we age, grandparents are often very active in their grandchildren's lives – and in many cases for grandfathers today, more hands-on than they were able to be when their own children were small. This is an opportunity to embrace changing parenting roles and rethink old attitudes.

- **JUST DO IT:** Dads need to step up and take responsibility, and mums need to relinquish the role as sole omniscient gatekeeper to the world of parenting. It's not easy, especially when the world sends out messages that a man doing 25 per cent of the childcare is a phenomenal dad, and a woman doing 75 per cent is being a rather selfish and neglectful mum. But the benefits are significant: involved fatherhood helps children to thrive, makes men happier and healthier, and helps women and girls achieve their potential. One dad of two gave me a list of ideas for new dads unsure of where to start: 'Sign up for a class with your child, and take them regularly. Make a whole batch of food and freeze it, and do it regularly. Buy baby clothes online, a size ahead. Be in charge of shoes (it's fun).' It's not about achieving a precise 50/50 split every day. What's more important is genuinely sharing the responsibility rather than one person being in charge and directing the other, and being able to share frustrations when this isn't quite working out, rather than letting them fester.

5

WORK:
The Unlevel
Playing Field

'I think it's changing,' he said to me over a posh cup of tea in a swish private members' club, one of those places where the teapots look like antiques and you have to remember to use the silver tea strainer and place it delicately back on its dinky little saucer. I was chatting with Antony Jenkins, the former CEO of Barclays. We'd first met a couple of years earlier in the House of Commons, when we were both invited to speak at a breakfast event on how to get more women into senior positions in the workplace. I remember being impressed – I had literally never before met a male banker who 'got' the diversity issue in anything like the same way. It was so refreshing.

As we sipped our tea, he told me how the testosterone-driven leadership styles of the past were no longer working, and companies were having to change their hierarchies and culture in order to survive the new world of fast-paced technological innovation and disruption. He's absolutely right that getting to 50:50 in organisations is crucial for success. But I don't share his optimism, certainly not on the speed of change. It's true we are seeing some business leaders recognise how vital diversity is to their organisation, and the scale of the action they need to take. However, much more common is for companies to find a relatively tiny amount of money for a few initiatives and events, but leave the core power structures intact.

We spend a huge chunk of our waking lives at work. Our experience of work not only affects our income, but also our health and self-esteem. Bad management practices cause huge stress, and there are far too many workplaces where people are treated appallingly – men and women alike. On the flipside, when people are valued, trusted and well supported, work can be a big boost to their quality of life.

The dynamic between employer and worker is already one where there is a power imbalance. In large organisations power can become very concentrated, resulting in faceless bureaucracy. On top of all of this is a toxic gender power differential, leading to huge inequalities that harm our whole economy.

Some people argue that this will correct itself in time. Women, after all, make up more than half of all graduates. Girls are outperforming boys at school and are now a third more likely than boys to go to university.[1] But girls made up more than half of university students twenty years ago when I started my degree, yet positions of power in the workplace for those in their late thirties and early forties are not even close to equally divided between men and women. In the field of medicine, women have outnumbered men at university since the early 1990s,[2] yet cohort studies[3] consistently show that men are more likely to become consultants[4] and to do so more quickly. Even when you control for factors like time out for maternity leave or part-time working, there is still a gender pay gap for doctors of around 5 per cent.[5] Women now make up almost two-thirds of law students,[6] and since 1993 more than half of those entering the profession have been women, yet less than a quarter of partners at law firms are women.[7] Since 2000, equal numbers of men and women have been 'called to the Bar',[8] which means they have completed their training and are eligible to advocate in court. Barristers with 15 years' experience can apply to become a Queen's Counsel, but in 2016 less than a quarter of the new QCs appointed were women.[9]

It doesn't matter what line of work you look at, the story is the same. Achieving a 50:50 intake is just the start. Any assumption that girls doing better at school will translate automatically into an equal workplace is misguided. There is nothing inevitable about achieving gender equality at work.

There are a range of reasons for this, as we will explore, but the link between school performance and workplace power is an important one to highlight. It is the ultimate extension of the Good Girl Game. While girls at school worry about getting it perfectly right – preparing, planning, revising, waiting their turn to speak – they are practising behaviours that are not widely rewarded at work. Keeping your head down, quietly doing a good job and hoping someone will give you an A* is not the best advice for the workplace – though managers should certainly be reassessing why their supposedly meritocratic hiring and promotion practices are not rewarding employees who follow this approach.

Playing the Good Girl Game works at school in terms of securing academic grades, though the constant desire to conform, to meet others' expectations, and to be a Good Girl is sadly effective at keeping young women's spirit and character in check, with seven in ten of them feeling they are not good enough.[10] In the workplace, though, it's checkmate. Women seek permission, take fewer risks, self-select out of opportunities and wait until they're certain before they act. And they watch men, who never had it drummed into them that they had to be a Good Girl, get the big promotions, pay rises and positions of power.

Jobs for the Boys

It was a beautiful spring afternoon, and the sunshine was glinting off the ripples on the River Thames. I was sitting on the terrace outside the House of Lords with Baroness Greengross, discussing changes in the world of business during her lifetime. In her eighty-plus years she has worked in various sectors, been a chief executive herself, and now advises Fujitsu on corporate responsibility when she's not scrutinising the law in Parliament. She matter-of-factly told me that when she started out working for an electronics firm in the 1960s, she would sign letters with 'Lee Hunt' instead of 'Sally Greengross'. That way, she said, 'the letter would get read'.

It's easy to marvel at such an anecdote and consign it to history, relieved that we no longer have to resort to such tactics. But maybe the outcomes would be fairer if we did use pseudonyms:

these gender biases remain right across the workplace. Even in a supposedly evidence-driven field like science, there is a huge gender gap. While almost four in ten of those working in science are women, if you exclude the health sector this drops to one in four.[11] Across the scientific disciplines in academia, the proportion of women reduces throughout the career stages (as it does for black, Asian and minority ethnic people and disabled people), with a sharp drop between senior lecturer and professor.[12]

It's not just that fewer girls study science subjects at school. An experiment which submitted job applications for a lab manager position from identical candidates with either male or female names found that the male applicant was rated as more competent and was more likely to be hired.[13] The senior academics rating the candidates also offered a starting salary to the men that was on average 14 per cent higher than to the women.[14] Notably, both male and female assessors displayed this bias. As in the rest of society, the world of science defaults to a deeply ingrained view that men are inherently more capable than women, even when looking at identical credentials. The challenge is that this bias is not applied knowingly. That is, after all, why they call it unconscious bias.

Like when you look at an optical illusion of two lines that are the same length but appear different, our brain takes two identical CVs and applies our own in-built bias onto them. It tricks us, effectively. So to attract and retain the best talent, the scientific community needs to be alert to these biases and be proactive about correcting them: citing and sharing work by women academics, reaching out to the next generation and encouraging young women into science and to progress their careers.

Space scientist Maggie Aderin-Pocock has done exactly that. Over the past few years she has spoken to more than a quarter of a million children to encourage their interest in science. We met in a functional train station coffee shop, and despite recovering from the flu, Maggie spoke quickly and was positively fizzing with enthusiasm. It was easy to see why she's a hit with kids, whether in person or on TV presenting *The Sky at Night*. 'Science has been seen as very unemotional,' she explained. In pursuit of the scientific method, people have become so detached that 'we miss the wonder'.

The coffee machine steamed noisily into life behind us as Maggie told me how in her first job, at the Ministry of Defence, her boss's boss had 'girly pics on the wall'. Or the time when as a PhD student she arrived at a contractor's site, in a suit and carrying a briefcase, and was told 'here's the keys, love' and ushered towards the cleaner's cupboard. Meeting a combination of sexist and racist assumptions, she told me that at least the prejudice is easier to tackle when it is out in the open, instead of what someone is thinking quietly to themselves.

Engineering is another bastion of man-dom. Ninety per cent of the engineering workforce are men, and with 87 per cent of applicants to study engineering at university also being men, it doesn't look like this will change anytime soon. Worse than that, the small number of women engineering graduates are significantly less likely than their male counterparts to go on to work in the industry.[15]

Roma Agrawal, engineer and author of *Built*, has worked on a wide range of projects, including as part of the design team for the iconic building known as The Shard in London.

We met in an art deco diner, and she told me how she became used to being the only woman in the room, and determined it would not hold her back. Some of the challenges she has faced are practical: having to bring her own personal protective equipment (PPE) so it would actually fit, or being on construction sites with one (locked) female loo and having to chase around the site to find the person with the key. Then there are the familiar sexist attitudes: people questioning her presence, or assuming she'll make the tea. She too recalled seeing pictures of naked women in construction site offices in the early part of her career. Roma told me how puzzled she is by this 'weird notion that science is for boys and arts for girls' that is so prevalent in the UK and US. Having grown up in India, where girls are encouraged into science, she had a very different experience. India's engineering courses have more than 30 per cent female students[16] (though there are still barriers in employability). Closer to home, within Europe, countries like Latvia, Bulgaria, Croatia and Lithuania manage to achieve rates of over 25 per cent women in the engineering workforce.[17] This significant geographic variance should silence those who argue that gender innately determines interest in science or engineering.

Meritocracy?

In the midst of researching this chapter and the process of trawling through a lot of corporate-speak on diversity, one phrase hit me between the eyes. I was on the Clifford Chance website, one of the elite 'magic circle' law firms, and the sentence read:

'As a meritocracy, Clifford Chance is committed to setting out clear, transparent pathways to help people achieve their personal and professional goals.'[18] Intrigued, I had a quick check of their global executive team[19] – two women, eleven men. Their London office? Sixty-two per cent of graduate recruits were women but 80 per cent of partners were men.[20] Maybe it's just a matter of time? Nope – of the 33 new partners in the last five years, 23 were men[21] – that's 70 per cent.

So we have a firm that proclaims its meritocratic credentials, a majority of women recruits (and given what we know about law graduate numbers, we can safely assume that has been the case for some years) – and still men are dominating the promotion track to partner. I don't specifically single out Clifford Chance as an especially poor example, as other firms are similarly dominated by men at partner level: Slaughter and May 75 per cent,[22] Linklaters 77 per cent,[23] Allen & Overy 82 per cent,[24] Freshfields Bruckhaus Deringer 82 per cent.[25]

In fact, this pattern is wearyingly familiar, in all sorts of different workplaces and industries. Imagine a pyramid, with lots of men and women recruits at the bottom, working their way up. At each level, the overall numbers reduce, but the women reduce disproportionately. At junior levels it might only be a few percentage points of difference between men and women; you might not even notice. But steadily the gendered attrition continues, until you get to the top and, guess what, it's a sea of blokes, blokes, blokes.

Either the women are just choosing to do something else, or there's a problem. In fact, even if the women are just choosing to do something else, there's a problem. Our economy needs the talents of both men and women to thrive, and diverse companies make more money.[26] So let's debunk the 'choice' myth that underpins the 'meritocracy' nonsense.

Research shows that women are just as ambitious as men,[27] and women are the biggest underused asset for our labour market. Women want to work more,[28] whether that's getting back into the workplace after a period of caring, or increasing their hours because they are working part-time. And women are often in roles for which they are overqualified, not least because there is still a misplaced, arrogant snobbery about the possibility of working part-time at a senior level. More than one in five professional women downgrade to find the hours of flexibility they want, half of them moving to low-skill jobs, with women from managerial positions particularly badly affected.[29] There will no doubt be individual examples of women and men choosing not to work, but at the macro level the evidence is clear – women's unequal participation in the workplace is not some whim of choice that we needn't worry about.

The Structurally Sexist Workplace

So what's the problem? Simply, that the workplace is structurally sexist. Without conscious intervention therefore, a laissez-faire 'meritocratic' approach delivers the same male-dominated results time after time.

The way we work isn't governed by some law of nature. In fact, when our society was much more attuned to the natural world, we worked very differently. The hours of light and darkness governed how much could be done, and when. Work changed, peaked and troughed with the seasons – indeed, to this day in Scotland the schools have a week of holiday in October, which traditionally was because all hands were needed for the 'tattie howking'[30] and children swapped school for the fields, pulling up the potatoes to earn some extra cash.[31]

No, our 'modern' way of working was designed. Designed by men, and for men. Not out of some sexist master plan, but just responding to the challenges of the time. Henry Ford was an early adopter of the 8-hour workday more than a century ago, which is still the basis of the common 9 to 5, Monday to Friday pattern. Ford wanted to end the exploitative hours and conditions of many factories; on making the changes, he found that productivity increased.[32] When you need a big team of people working in unison to assemble a car, it makes sense for them to arrive and leave at the same agreed time.[33] Does it still make sense in our economy for everyone to keep the same office hours? Not at all. While some overlap between people's workdays is helpful for teams working on projects, or doing business with other companies, in a globalised economy with multiple time zones it actually makes more sense to stagger the workday. With congested roads and massive investment in public transport systems, it is also a no-brainer to spread the load over a longer period of time, rather than concentrate it into a rush hour. While for some jobs the location is determined by the role – providing personal care for an elderly person, putting out a fire, stacking supermarket shelves, operating on a patient, and many others – there are also many roles where it doesn't matter where you are. This is of course much more the case as technology has advanced, as we can easily and fairly inexpensively be connected to workmates through phones, tablets, laptops and other devices, and access most of the functionality that would traditionally have been provided by an office.

Yet we cling to the dated 1950s mindset of what 'work' looks like, long after it has ceased to be useful to us. In many workplaces, someone arriving at 10 a.m. is greeted with a 'good afternoon!' from colleagues. Or leaving the office at 4.30 p.m. attracts raised eyebrows and mutters of 'part-timer' – that such a phrase is even used as an insult tells its own story. Power between the sexes aside, this is a crazy way to behave in the 21st century. Organisations that can't adapt to new ways of working will lose the talent war, especially as they try to attract a generation of millennials who are far more likely to embrace flexibility in their working styles – and the connectivity and collaboration that brings – than conform to archaic corporate straitjackets.

The culture of presenteeism chokes organisations of innovation and creative thinking. If management send the message that it's all about being *at* work, then people will respond accordingly. They won't necessarily *do* more work, though – the possible distractions of our Internet age are legion, and much more varied than the age-old alternatives of daydreaming or discreetly doing the crossword. When people are judged on what they deliver and achieve, then suddenly the rules of the game change. Often you do still need to be present; for all that video-conferencing and collaborative software are helpful and cut travel costs, there is no real substitute for face-to-face interaction, relationship-building and generating ideas. But when outcomes are what matter, people can more freely design work that works around their lives.

Life-Work Balance

Everyone has a life outside of work. Whether it's family, friends, hobbies, religion, sport or involvement with their community, there are things we care about that are not work. Most, though by no means all, people will make a home with a partner and have children. And in most of those cases, both partners will work.[34]

There are many workplaces and occupations that are not designed for this reality. Their working practices, norms and culture were created in a different time, when the workplace was mainly the preserve of men and unmarried women, and mothers would stay at home and take care of the children and the domestic work. It was therefore possible for diplomats to be posted around the world with the assumption that their wife and any children would follow – and indeed that the wife would be available to play the dutiful, beautiful hostess for foreign ambassadors. It was possible for salesmen or consultants to spend weeks on the road, living out of a suitcase, returning home for occasional weekends. It was possible for clients to have their favourite lawyer, advertising exec or banker on call 24/7, working around the clock as some kind of badge of pride; as the old testosterone-filled ad agency mantra ran, 'If you don't come in on Saturday, don't bother coming in on Sunday.'[35]

There was never any suggestion that choosing to work in these fields meant you would not become a father. The contradiction didn't seem to arise, and that's because there was no assumption that in being a father you would have new responsibilities that impacted on your availability for work. As one professor responded to a research question about whether it was difficult to combine having children with being a scientist, 'No, absolutely not. That's why you have a wife.'[36] The underlying assumption is that you will have a stay-at-home spouse.

This business model is inherently sexist – and the caring responsibilities in society are unevenly divided between men and women. Yes, there are examples of high-profile, successful women who have made it and have a stay-at-home spouse, like top investment banker Helena Morrissey or former Education Secretary Nicky Morgan. But the proportion of stay-at-home dads is still tiny.[37] Even as a few more men adopt this role, trends also suggest that the number of stay-at-home mums will continue to decrease,[38] and therefore any business model that rests on the premise that people will have a partner who looks after all the home stuff is a broken anachronism and doomed to fail.

Nowhere is the deep-rooted shibboleth about the importance of an individual's constant availability for work more obvious than in society's attitudes to pregnancy and employment. Many women are anxious about telling their employer they're pregnant. They don't know what the reaction will be, but they fear, often rightly, that they will be seen as somehow letting the side down, imposing a burden on colleagues and demonstrating a lack of commitment.

I remember being worried about telling my ministerial colleagues – I felt I ought to tell them personally before it became public knowledge. Vince Cable had guessed already. A few days beforehand I'd missed the monthly question session in the House of Commons with just an hour's notice, as I'd rushed to the hospital with bleeding that I feared was a miscarriage (thankfully a scan showed all was fine with the baby). Vince had covered my questions, but he knew I would not have missed the session lightly, and a pregnancy-related issue was an obvious possible explanation. He was delightfully supportive. I didn't expect such a warm response from my old-school Conservative colleague Michael Fallon (I have unconscious bias, too), but I tracked him down in the voting lobby and asked to have a quick word for a minute. We sat on the green bench at the side, away from the hubbub of the MPs pouring through to vote. With trepidation I told him, and I was so relieved when he just squeezed my hand, smiled and warmly told me it was going to be the most wonderful experience.

I was incredibly lucky to be in a position of power while pregnant. Most pregnant women are not, and the combination of being powerless and feeling vulnerable is toxic for their health and well-being at work. One in twenty-five pregnant women end up leaving their jobs because their employer does not resolve health and safety risks, and this rises to one in ten for young women.[39] Pregnant women on agency or zero-hours contracts are much more likely to be discriminated against and treated badly.[40]

Despite legislation in place for decades to protect women in the workplace throughout and beyond pregnancy, bad practice and discrimination are scarily common. Partly we need better enforcement of the laws. I fought a long-running battle in government against the punitive fees for bringing a case to an employment tribunal, but I was sadly unsuccessful in making any headway against the Conservative part of the government. I was personally delighted that these fees were eventually deemed illegal by the courts in 2017. But even without that financial barrier, and even if we extend the time available for women to bring a claim, it's not sufficient. Understandably, new parenthood is one of the times in your life when you have the least energy and resilience available to challenge your employer at a tribunal, so many atrocious cases will never be pursued in court. We need a much stronger collective condemnation of bad treatment of pregnant workers, so that cultural and reputational pressure drives good practice. Currently, we effectively give tacit acceptance of employers behaving badly. When I was chair of Maternity Action, a charity which advocates for policy improvements and provides advice services to pregnant women and new parents, I regularly did media interviews on these issues. I was struck by just how often the interviewer said something like, 'But of course some employers can't really afford to deal with maternity leave.' At a 2016 panel discussion I participated in, a businessman in the audience actually said to me that while regrettable, pregnancy discrimination was in fact 'rational' for employers looking to minimise costs. And I was saying nothing more controversial than 'pregnancy discrimination is illegal and unacceptable' when the Conservative Woman blog accused me of getting on my 'feminist horse'.

At another event I attended about the importance of getting more women into senior positions in the workplace, the panellists were asked to share an anecdote about when they had supported a woman in their organisation. One of them described a talented woman who had applied for a senior role. He said he had decided to give her the job, but in the meeting when he was going to let her know she had secured the position, she told him she was pregnant. He said that as the position was already vacant, obviously he couldn't appoint her to that role because of her pregnancy, but he found another job for her when she came back from maternity leave and supported her later career moves. My jaw hit the floor. Here was a leader in a major UK consumer business, brazenly admitting to pregnancy discrimination to a room of 150 people, and thinking it was a good example of helping women at work. Whether a woman is pregnant (or not) cannot legally be a factor in whether to give her a job. Yet many women are still asked about marriage and family aspirations in job interviews. This happens to 1 in 30 white women and as many as 1 in 8 Pakistani women,[41] again underlining the multiple layers of discrimination that women of colour face. In the business world, there is a common view – often unspoken but definitely there – that sees maternity leave as a burden and one that, naturally, they will try to avoid and hope they don't get caught doing so. So whether it is not giving the job to the 30-year-old woman, suddenly judging the pregnant employee's work not up to scratch, or restructuring the company and not finding a role for the woman on maternity leave, there are myriad ways that women lose out unfairly – and illegally.

Just for a second imagine we're not talking about pregnancy discrimination laws. Imagine it's the minimum wage. Now, there's still some ridiculous flouting of minimum wage laws – and as a minister I increased the financial penalties and introduced routine naming and shaming of those who break the law, in order to help tackle that problem. But there isn't the same tacit acceptance in the business community of paying workers less than the minimum wage. Small business groups don't argue for an exemption from having to pay the minimum wage; people don't suggest that it would be 'rational' for employers to pay people less than the minimum wage as long as they can get away with it. The perception of pregnancy in the workplace speaks volumes about how women are valued at work.

Toxic Environment

The structural sexism in the workplace is not limited to issues around having children, however – that's just one of the most visible and obvious parts. The culture, the norms, the experience of work is different for men and women, and it's important to shine a light on all of this, too, because often people point to the challenges of combining work and family responsibilities and see that as a convenient explanation for the power imbalance between men and women.

Many firms casually attribute the lack of women in senior roles to women leaving after having a family, but this is rarely the full story.[42] Women may leave the organisation, but as they typically do not leave the labour market, this attrition should be recognised as an indicator of dissatisfaction with a toxic work environment, rather than something inevitable.

I met Therese Procter for a coffee shortly before she celebrated her 30-year milestone with Tesco: not many people these days can mark such a length of service with one employer. Other than a short spell at the Bank of England as her first job after leaving school, Therese had spent her entire career at the supermarket giant, steadily working her way up through the ranks from an entry-level position to become Chief People Officer at Tesco Bank. She spoke with passion and authority on the importance of creating a genuinely inclusive working culture and the productivity gains that result, and the challenges of building shared values across staff when setting up a new institution with more than 4,000 employees from scratch.

I could immediately see how the warm, engaging and clearly determined Therese had succeeded in leading others. Her mantra 'be kind, be brave, be you' seemed a pretty good piece of career advice. Yet I was stunned when she spoke about the career advice she had been given on her way to the top. She had been told to get elocution lessons, to make her hair 'less big', to change her wardrobe. Until she mentioned it, I hadn't even clocked that she was from the east end of London – why should anyone care what accent you make your point in? She summed it up: 'The advice I've been given to get on is to change who I am.'

Groupthink stifles innovation, while diversity of voices sows the seeds for better decision-making. When people spend valuable energy suppressing who they are and projecting a different persona – whether it is adopting a different accent, carefully choosing pronouns when discussing their same-sex partner, or fighting with their hair to make it 'acceptable' – they are less able to thrive. Workplaces need to let people be individuals.

On their own, the tiny slights that happen in the workplace seem almost not worthy of mention. But piled on top of one another, the compound effect is powerful. Clients talking to your more junior male colleague instead of you. The sexist 'joke' and banter in the office. Being talked over in meetings, the point you made ignored until a man says the same thing a few minutes later and is lauded for it. President Obama's women staffers banded together to challenge this, adopting a tactic they called 'amplification'. When one woman made a good point, other women would reference the same point, giving credit to the woman who first said it, so it was noticed rather than ignored and so that - importantly - the person who made the point would receive the recognition.[43]

Everything is set up with men at the centre, from the corporate hospitality default of men's sporting events, to the choice of speakers for company awards evenings. In 2015, the ill-judged 'entertainment' at the Construction Computing Awards led to attendees walking out and a social media backlash.[44] The comedian they booked made sexist jokes about the few women in the room, then launched into a tirade of Irish jokes when challenged by a male audience member who happened to be Irish - exactly the opposite of the kind of culture construction needs to create if they are to plug the skills gap. Men and women alike expressed their disappointment; the organisers apologised and gave assurances that they would work hard to prevent such problems in future.[45] But it's worth noting how the action of the attendees affected the outcome in this situation. By challenging the sexism directly, voicing concerns online, and in some cases voting with their feet, men and women in this industry sent a powerful message.[46]

Many organisations will blithely proclaim that they don't see gender at all, but what they actually don't see is that the default is male, not gender-neutral. A senior partner at a global professional services firm told me about their Thailand office, which had 70 per cent female partners. There was a nail bar in the building and they ran drop-in sessions at lunchtime for staff to get their bra fitting checked. It's not surprising that firms here in the UK with 70 per cent male partners end up seeming similarly organised around the needs of one gender, but the least they could do is recognise that's the case. When there is such a skew in the power of an organisation, it takes a conscious effort to change it.

Role models matter, not just to inspire individuals to achieve success, but also to change others' perceptions about what they can do. In most organisations it is easy to imagine a young white guy moving upwards and onwards to a leadership role, following a well-trodden path of so many before – and this enables people to look at his potential. The underlying assumption is that he will be competent and up to the task. A young woman or a young black man in the same organisation is instinctively viewed as more 'risky', and needs to prove their worth, demonstrating their skills and abilities before they are seen as credible candidates for promotion.

This 'prove it again' trap is well documented[47] – and you don't need to speak to many women about their workplace experiences to find countless examples. I suspect it applies in the other direction, too, for roles which have been historically done by women. How many male primary school teachers, I wonder, find that parents are wary at the start of the school year, then 'pleasantly surprised' that he turns out to be good at his job after all? But given the historic imbalances between men and women in positions of power, this presents a greater hurdle for women's career advancement overall.

Even when women do make it to the top, they still face the assumption that they're not up to scratch. Women CEOs are significantly more likely to face shareholder activism than men

CEOs,[48] and company share prices fall when a woman CEO is announced – despite evidence that women at the top deliver greater returns to shareholders.[49] In fact there's a phenomenon dubbed the 'glass cliff',[50] which details how when women are chosen to lead an organisation, it is often because it is failing. In good times, they'll appoint a bloke, but if nothing else has worked then what is there to lose by trying something as wackily different and risky as having a woman at the top?

Then there's the assumption that alpha male behaviour is the default, and a blindness to how others might feel. I remember taking part in a panel debate at an event hosted in Parliament, with an audience of businesspeople. The chair of the event started proceedings by telling people that they would have the opportunity to pose questions later on, but as we were in the House of Commons they should make sure that anything they said was worthy of our grand surroundings. Knowing how difficult it often is to get women to put their hands up to contribute at all, I sighed inwardly – this was the exact opposite of the message he needed to send to ensure we could have a lively discussion where everyone felt comfortable speaking up. Predictably, we were well into the debate before any women from the audience raised their hands. When convening or chairing work meetings or conferences, it is important to encourage contributions from a diverse range of people in the room, and recognise that those less used to speaking up, or those who are in a minority in the room, will often feel less confident.

When new projects or responsibilities are being considered, the default choice is often to ask men first. This is important when it comes to promotion to senior grades. Kirsty Bashforth told me about her time as a senior executive at BP, grappling with the issues of getting more women into leadership roles in the organisation. Analysis she carried out identified that the people who made it to the top had all had at least one international posting, all had run some kind of operation, and all had done a chief-of-staff type role for one of the company's top executives. Yet she told me that very often a certain discussion would be had about who to send to a particular project – say an operational site in a volatile country. Bob and Jane would be considered, and while it was well-meaning, the sense of 'let's not put Jane at that level of risk' meant she may never even know she was in the running, and she would never be asked. Kirsty's advice? 'Bosses should not assume what risks women are willing to take, or what assignments they would be willing to do – ask them.'

And in asking or encouraging women to go for a promotion or a step up, we should not be blind to socialised gendered differences. The classic example of response to the job description applies here. Women will look at it and only apply if they feel they meet all of the essential criteria. Men will look at the list and if they tick about half the boxes they'll stick in an application, assuming the rest is negotiable or they can just 'wing it'.[51] Even the way job descriptions are worded can make a difference. Research shows that the use of masculine or feminine words to describe the same job responsibilities can encourage or deter applicants.[52] So if you're trying to attract more women to your engineering firm, or more men to your care home staff, think carefully about the words you use.

Recruiters and managers can take this into account. If you want women to apply for a role, don't create a lofty job description full of 'essential requirements' that you don't expect applicants to meet and will be flexible on anyway: you'll reduce your pool of talented applicants. If you suggest to a woman she should go for promotion and she says she's not sure she's ready, then don't automatically interpret that the same way you would if a strident man said it. It's much more likely to be the default response from a woman, who maybe needs time to think about the idea and encouragement that she has the requisite skills and could be supported to do it. This isn't 'special treatment' for women, it's just stopping treating everyone like a stereotypical man. And while it can be frustrating when talented women hold themselves back, it's just as suboptimal to have pushy blokes bullshit their way into roles they aren't qualified for. I stress that these are generalisations of behaviour – not every man and woman acts as the stereotype – but being aware that the systems are often biased towards one type of behaviour is a good starting point in trying to deal with people as individuals.

Why don't more women speak up, then? Well, one explanation might be that when they do, they don't get the same positive response that men do.[53] Research on pay negotiations in Australia is fascinating, as the government collects data not just on pay, but also whether people have asked for (and whether they have received) a pay rise. It shows that women are actually just as likely as men to ask for a pay rise, but men are 25 per cent more likely to be given the extra cash.[54] Other research suggests women are indeed less likely to negotiate than men[55] – perhaps because they don't think something is even negotiable, or they worry how they will be perceived if they do ask.[56]

Women speaking up are often seen as pushy and aggressive, and it can result in real penalties in the workplace – from both men and other women. Hillary Clinton's approval ratings are an interesting case study here. When she was getting on with her job trying to improve the country as a New York senator, or tackling international issues as Secretary of State, she enjoyed high approval ratings. Yet when she was running for office – seeking power herself – then the ratings plummeted.[57] One writer brilliantly described it as the 'catch-22 of female ambition: To succeed, she needs to be liked, but to be liked, she needs to temper her success.'[58] The 2016 election campaign went further than not liking Hillary Clinton; it developed into a full-blown hate campaign, with slogans like 'Trump that Bitch'[59] and rallies of thousands chanting 'lock her up'. Little girls watching received a powerful message about what happens when women put themselves forward for the top job.

We need to drop this double standard. Easier said than done, of course, but awareness is the first step.

Just Banter?

A final way sexism endures as a structural problem within the workplace is sexual harassment. The figures are sobering. While it affects both men and women, women are three times as likely as men to experience it, and the vast majority of perpetrators are men.[60] Project 28-40 found that one in eight women had experienced sexual harassment at work,[61] and joint research by the Trades Union Congress and the Everyday Sexism project found this was as high as one in two, if women were instead asked about the individual behaviours that are defined as sexual harassment –

hearing sexual comments about themselves or other women, unwelcome sexual jokes, unwanted touching and unwanted sexual advances – yet four out of five women never report it.[62]

Sarah, a beauty salon owner, told me how common it was for older men to try it on with young therapists booked to give them a massage. Even in high-end, reputable health clubs, the sense of entitlement by some customers to some kind of 'extra' shocked me.

I remember when I was 16 years old, working my part-time job at McDonald's on Saturdays and Monday evenings after school. One night a guy came up to the till, and after placing his order, leered at me and asked, 'Would you do this job topless?' I felt mortified and had no idea how to deal with the situation, so just pretended to ignore it and silently prepared the order, burning inside with shame and embarrassment. I never thought about telling my manager – what would he have done? Yet my older self wishes I'd known that such behaviour was entirely unacceptable and I didn't have to put up with it just because I was being paid to serve customers. No, the customer is not always right, so if that's their attitude they can fuck off and eat elsewhere. If challenged, no doubt the man who said it would have used the excuse that it was 'just banter'.

As a 19-year-old medical student, my sister worked in a top Glasgow hotel, waitressing in the restaurant and taking up room service. On one occasion she was met at the door of a hotel bedroom by a middle-aged celebrity wearing just a towel, and he propositioned her. She made a hasty exit. These are not exceptional experiences, and much as I'd love to think things had changed in the intervening two decades, I don't think they have.

The research suggests young staff are just as likely to experience these kinds of situation nowadays, from customers – but also from colleagues and bosses.

Given the power dynamics, it's not surprising that young women experience more sexual harassment, as do women working in male-dominated industries like construction, the uniformed services and armed forces.[63] And while President Donald Trump's comments that came to light in the 2016 campaign invoked global revulsion, they betrayed a wider truth. He said: 'Just kiss. I don't even wait. And when you're a star, they let you do it. You can do anything . . . Grab 'em by the pussy. You can do anything.'[64]

Men often do get away it, in particular men in positions of power. And Donald Trump found that, ultimately, such comments were no barrier to him becoming the most powerful man in the world. Despite the outrage from tens of millions of decent people, tens of millions of others didn't think such behaviour made him unfit to lead his country.

As Inga Beale, CEO of Lloyd's of London, has said, 'There is an "automatic protectionism" amongst senior men . . . guys protecting each other, it's a club . . . they don't want to rock the boat.'[65]

I'm not saying that getting ahead at work is always a bed of roses for men. Men work hard and experience setbacks and disappointments in their careers, too. They feel no inevitability that they will rise to the top, or if they do, they understandably don't want to think their gender has anything to do with it, when they have worked hard to get where they are. I recognise that it's often difficult for men to see these challenges facing women, apart from occasional glimpses. It's like when I am suddenly reminded of my white privilege when I hear a racist comment. I usually don't see the myriad tiny cultural, visual and verbal cues promoting white people in positions of power. I might notice that a panel is all-white and think it's odd, but I probably haven't automatically clocked quite how unrepresentative industry conference halls, boardrooms and corporate brochures are, day in day out – and the impact that has on people of colour working their way up in an organisation. There's an oft-cited analogy of two young fish swimming along, and they meet an older fish going the other way. The older fish says to them, 'How's the water today, lads?' and the young fish look at each other and say, 'What's water?' That's an apt descriptor of how men proceed through the workplace, and indeed society. The water of inequality, sexism and misogyny is obvious to women or other under-represented groups trying to fight their way through it. For the young fish – or the men, or white women – it just invisibly helps them as they swim along.

Power and the Money, Money and the Power

'Power and the money. Money and the power. If you give us money, we'll send them a flower,' we rapped over the soundtrack of Coolio's 'Gangsta's Paradise' in a chilly auditorium back in 1997. My classmates and I were in the Dunbartonshire Young Enterprise regional final, pitching how successful our business had been against teams from other schools in the area. Our company – Young Enterprise Trading Initiative – had a mascot: our company secretary Richard dressed up in a black furry costume, supposedly resembling a yeti. Thinking back, I'm not sure black fur was the best choice for a creature fabled to reside in the snowscape of the Himalayas, but it did the trick in breaking the ice with potential customers on stalls at trade fairs. We won the regional final, and while our musical interlude no doubt provided some slightly cringeworthy light relief, our victory was more about our sales and profit numbers.

Money is not the only source of power, but it is a significant one, particularly because of the self-reinforcing capitalist loop between money and power. People with power generally find it easier to acquire money, and people with money generally find it easier to acquire power.

At the extreme end of the scale, this manifests itself in outright bribery and corruption, whether it's the decisions of politicians, sporting officials, law enforcement agencies or companies being influenced by the illicit exchange of money. But it's not just illegal activity where the power-money loop plays out.

Powerful brands and companies spend huge sums on media advertising campaigns to reinforce their dominant position, which delivers more profit and makes it even harder for firms with smaller budgets to compete – even if they have a better product.

Political parties that are in power – rather than opposition – raise funds much more easily, as companies and individuals want to pay to attend their conferences and events, which finances their campaign to continue in power. And of course these donors writing big cheques tend to encourage politicians to use their power to protect those capable of writing big cheques from increased taxation.

Wealthy tycoons and big businesses can make credible threats of expensive legal action to silence critics, changing the risk calculation for journalists and others about whether particular stories should be published.

And at the individual level, rich people can effectively buy confidence, connections and a career boost for their children, making it more likely that they will go on to hold powerful positions. Top private schools have the funds to invest in state-of-the-art facilities, but what many parents are buying is the assurance and confidence that such an education delivers, not least through the normalisation of privilege and power that comes from interacting almost exclusively with others in a privileged position.

There is a significant correlation between high family income and children going on to become successful entrepreneurs.[66] That is not to belittle the achievements of those entrepreneurs who have still had to innovate and persevere to succeed. But it is worth noting that those who can be supported by their parents or an inheritance are more likely to have the time to dedicate to making their ventures a success, and are more easily able to access seed funding from family, compared with those who are working in a bar to pay the rent and nurturing their start-up on the side. In many industries, unpaid internships are seen as a rite of passage – though, thankfully, far fewer now see this exploitative practice as acceptable – and again, those with money can buy their children a head start in an industry by financing them through periods of unpaid work, and often by introducing them to the connections that secure the placement in the first place.

So, money matters. We've come a long way from when wives were seen as 'chattels', possessions of their husbands along with other worldly goods, livestock and cash. It's almost 150 years since married women were first allowed to own property and wield financial power in their own right.[67] Yet financial power is still heavily concentrated in the hands of men. Not only does the power-money loop perpetuate this inequality, but men's monetary power reinforces their power in other spheres.

It starts early. Boys receive more pocket money from their parents than girls. I was staggered when I heard that. *Really? How can parents be doing that? Surely not.* But the research has been conducted for years by Halifax, and while the size of the gender pocket-money gap fluctuates (and, positively, last year was the lowest to date), the piggy bank is consistently weighted in boys' favour, every single year.

	Boys	Girls	Gender pocket money gap
2017	£6.35	£6.32	0.5%
2016	£6.93	£6.16	13%
2015	£6.25	£6.14	2%
2014	£6.50	£6.19	5%
2013	£6.67	£6.32	6%
2012	£6.16	£5.79	6%
2011	£6.41	£6.09	5%
2010	£6.08	£5.70	7%
2009	£6.88	£5.58	23%

So from the very beginning, we're sending a message to girls and boys about their relative value, mirroring the wider world which consistently pays women less, invests in women less and values women less than men.

The gender pay gap is stubbornly persistent. Measured as the difference in average hourly pay for men and women, the gap in the UK is currently 18.1 per cent overall, or 9.4 per cent if you only compare full-time workers.[68] This doesn't mean men and women doing the exact same job are being paid different rates – that has been illegal since the Equal Pay Act came into force in 1975.[69] While there are certainly still cases of that kind of direct pay discrimination, the gender pay gap is mostly driven by men and women working in differently paid sectors and jobs, caring responsibilities being shouldered largely by women, and men being disproportionately represented in high-paid leadership roles.

One of my most frustrating experiences in government was trying to get companies to seriously tackle the gender pay gap. While they were generally very happy to run leadership events for their women employees, and celebrate the tiny number of women they had in senior roles, the level of complacency on the pay gap problem was astonishing. Most didn't conduct any kind of gender pay audit to understand whether they had a problem, and only a handful – Friends Life, Genesis Housing, Tesco and AstraZeneca – were brave enough to actually publish their gender pay gap.[70] I became more convinced that making companies look at and explain their own gender pay data to customers, investors, shareholders and employees would prompt action. One senior executive from a progressive company said that they had carried out an equal pay audit purely to show leadership, not because they expected to find any issues: they were, however, appalled by the results.

Of course, gender pay gap reporting requirements would be new regulation, which my Conservative coalition partners viewed like some toxic chemical to be avoided at all costs, no matter how sensible or necessary the change. After years of stalemate on the issue, I spotted my opportunity in the dying days of the Parliament in February 2015. I rang the deputy prime minister, Nick Clegg: 'Are you up for another fight with the Tories on the gender pay gap? This time I think we can win.'

Nick immediately agreed. The Tories' vulnerability was their fear of failing to enact the Small Business Bill before Parliament finished up for the general election. We very much wanted the bill to become law, too, but I judged they would blink first. The ticking clock made delay risky to the bill's chances, and the proximity of the election raised the political cost of a public spat where their position would be unpopular with women voters. Amendments tabled by Labour in the House of Lords, where the government didn't have a majority, gave us the perfect opportunity to force the government as a whole to back the long-standing Lib Dem policy, and bring forward plans for organisations employing more than 250 people to publish their gender pay gap. When I heard that we'd secured government agreement, I literally jumped up and down for joy in my office.

Gender pay gap reporting is just the beginning, but the transparency should help companies pay rather more attention to the problem and how to solve it. In an age where consumers care more and more about the ethics of the companies they give their money to, this transparency will prompt many shoppers to ask searching questions before they buy. Nothing focuses the minds of CEOs and shareholders more than a tangible impact on the bottom line. But let's be clear, employers should not expect plaudits for paying men and women the same for the same job, when that has been the law for nearly half a century. It is not okay to see a quarter of leadership positions filled by women and pat yourself on the back for 'doing quite well'. By all means celebrate milestones on the way to equality, but the path and plan to close the pay gap should be clearly set out and reported on.

And while the pay gap is important, it's worth noting how in some ways it underestimates the power imbalance in society. The gender pay gap is measured on the basis of hourly wages, but the actual income gap between the sexes is much greater than the 18 per cent figure suggests. The total income for men in the UK is £516 billion, and for women it is £271 billion, which means men earn *twice as much* as women overall.[71] This difference is driven by greater numbers of men in paid employment, and the fact that men typically spend more hours doing paid work. Given the close link between money and power, this is deeply concerning. While there are many loving couples with very unequal individual incomes who pool their money with no problem, financial independence is important. It gives individuals the ability to make choices, including whether or not to stay in a relationship. Controlling and bullying behaviour around money – from restricting bank account access to unilaterally making important financial decisions – is now recognised as a form of domestic abuse.[72]

The concentration of money in men's hands has many knock-on effects. Take funding for start-up companies as an example. The world of investment can seem something of a mystery. When you imagine an 'angel investor', the picture is often of a very wealthy, white-haired businessman finishing his career by passing on his knowledge and some initial funding to exciting start-ups. That wasn't the picture in the glass-walled meeting room where I found myself one chilly October afternoon.

Twelve women and four men were sat around a big table, ranging in age from thirty-something to late fifties, and bringing together a medley of experience and money from the worlds of marketing, banking, health and television. We're here for an investor workshop – an afternoon introduction to how high-earners can use their wealth to support new businesses, while also growing their assets. By investing as part of a syndicate, you pool expertise and risk. Contrary to the image of *Dragons' Den*-type sums being put in by individuals, sometimes the sum will be as little as £5,000, an amount that senior professionals or executives without huge personal wealth might be able to invest.

Sara, a retired physiotherapist, explains apologetically that she has 'no business experience' despite the fact that she ran a successful physiotherapy practice for 20 years, which she then sold. The money she made is now largely gathering dust and little return in a series of safe investments, so she's keen to use some of it to 'take a punt'. She rates her risk appetite at five, on a scale of one to five.

In a case study of a fictional but typical investor, someone mentions buy-to-let investments, adding as a throwaway line, 'Who in London doesn't have one of those?' I look around and wonder if it's just me. I'm not here with a pot of money to invest, nor do I have a portfolio of buy-to-let properties in London or anywhere else, but I am fascinated by the concept of this initiative. Angel Academe was set up by Sarah Turner in 2013. She had a bit of money to invest, and when she went along to some angel investor groups in London she was 'horrified' at how few women there were.

The facts are stark. Just 8 per cent of venture capital firm partners are women,[73] and just 10 per cent of venture capital funding is invested in women founders[74] – and there's precious little ethnic diversity.[75] This matters, because not only do women entrepreneurs secure more funding when there are more women investing, but they have more chance of the business succeeding, too.[76] Yet while men do own more wealth than women, they are still disproportionately deciding who gets the dosh when it comes to start-ups seeking funds.

You might think that investors are objectively weighing up the best bets to deliver a return on the money they put in – after all, that would be the rational approach, wouldn't it? It is probably what they think they are doing. Yet a controlled experiment on video pitches by researchers at MIT found that when the exact same venture is pitched, with the exact same words, the male entrepreneur was chosen over the female entrepreneur 68 per cent of the time. This backed up their findings from looking at three years of recording from actual angel investor pitch competitions, where men were 60 per cent more likely to succeed in securing funding. Interestingly, they also found a link to attractiveness, with good-looking men outperforming their plainer counterparts.[77]

Demystifying the concept of investing in new companies not only opens up another channel for women to manage their assets, but it introduces start-ups to a more diverse pool of potential investors, who will see the value in business ideas that a homogenous group might miss.

The world of finance can seem like an impenetrable maze, but we can have influence even if we don't have a pot of cash to invest. Steve Waygood is an environmental campaigner who pivoted his career into fund management at insurance giant Aviva, and he is a passionate advocate for using the power of finance to drive better corporate behaviour. His message is simple: money talks, so you should find out what your money is saying. For most people, the biggest investment they have is their pension, but how many of us know which companies our pension contributions are funding?

When investors ask questions of corporate leaders, they listen. Investment expert Abigail Herron told me about meetings she had back in 2007 with leading companies, where she deliberately took a male colleague along to ask the questions about their progress on gender. She felt there was a 'stigma' around women asking these questions. The answers they got were pretty rubbish, with the top executives acting like 'rabbits caught in headlights, looking around the room for help' when the subject of gender came up. Now, business leaders expect these questions and are prepared for them. Organisations like the 30% Club Investor Group have driven this change – a group of investors all asking the same questions on gender, and using the power of their vote at the company's annual general meeting to say: *if you don't show progress, we won't vote to re-elect the chair of the nominations committee.* This creates a powerful motivation for that guy (and it usually is a guy) to make sure gender diversity is high on the agenda.

But what can you do as an individual? For most of us, our pension is our main link to corporate finance. There are key questions that your pension trustees should be asking of their fund managers, and that in turn those fund managers should be asking of major companies. Do they support the 30% Club Statement of Intent?[78] Have they signed up to the Treasury's Women in Finance Charter? You don't need to be a finance expert to do this: there's a standard letter you can download and send to your pension trustees – and if you have a financial adviser, send it to them, too.

One Small Step or a Giant Leap? Getting from 25 per cent to 50 per cent

Progress towards workplace equality isn't linear. The initial battles fought by previous generations were for the very concept of women being accepted in the workplace as equals. Pioneers across different industries broke glass ceilings by being the 'first woman' to be employed by a particular company, in a particular role, or to serve on a particular board. Some of these glass ceilings have been broken recently – it was only in 2014 that the last all-male board in the FTSE 100 appointed a woman.[79] Other glass ceilings stubbornly await a new generation of women to be the 'first' – most FTSE companies and many major institutions have not yet been led by a woman as CEO or chairman.

But the basic principle of women in the workplace has been normalised, to the extent that we often notice if there are no women at all in a large leadership group in an organisation. However, once there are one or two women, a new problem can arise. Organisations adjust to what they think is a new normal, with a smattering of women 'brightening up' the sea of dark-suited men on company websites. People look around the table, see there is a woman or two, check their mental diversity box, and promptly stop worrying about gender equality. Their benchmark is that there used to be no women, so it looks like progress to reach 15 or 25 per cent, and people heartily congratulate themselves.

If you look from a lens of equality, where 51 per cent of the population are women,[80] 25 per cent looks rather less impressive. A good staging post perhaps, worth a motivational celebration for sure, but the focus should be on how far we still need to go, on rolling up our sleeves and getting on with the next piece of heavy lifting.

Getting from 25 per cent to 50 per cent is hard. First, this step lacks the powerful binary comparator and catalyst of going from none to some. It appears more of an injustice for a group not to be represented at all than for it not to be proportionately represented. Take the group of Lib Dem MPs. In 2010 there were 7 women out of 57 MPs, and in 2015, no women out of 8 MPs. Let's explore the statistics here. If you were tossing a coin, it would be a much less likely outcome to get only 7 heads out of 57 tosses, than no heads out of 8 tosses. Neither is very likely, but 7/57 is by far the greater outlier. This suggests that alarm bells should have rung louder in 2010 than 2015. Yet there is no doubt that having no Lib Dem women MPs at all felt worse (and not just to me, with a personal interest in the matter – it is also portrayed as a more damning indictment by critics). Happily, the 2017 election delivered a brighter picture, with 4 women MPs out of 12, putting us at 33 per cent, our best ever proportion by far. Yet now there is a real risk that some people will think 'job done' when there is still a huge amount to do.

People also often overestimate how many of a minority group are actually there. In the wake of the progress in getting more women on boards, I encountered a (female) headhunter who said that since now so much focus was on women, hardly any men could get board director positions anymore. The reality was that about a third of new board positions were going to women, leaving 'just' two-thirds for men. Only the previous, higher benchmark point of men getting upwards of 80 per cent of directorships could make two-thirds feel like 'hardly any'.

Second, 25 per cent to 50 per cent represents a fundamental shift in power. People do not like to give up power. Men don't have to give up significant power to change group composition from 100 per cent men/0 per cent women to 75 per cent men/25 per cent women. While of course the men will not always agree with each other or coordinate their actions, they all benefit from the default setting, the norms and the culture of the group continuing to be male. The 25 per cent women have to adapt their behaviours in order to succeed, and all sorts of leadership programmes, training and support networks are deemed necessary. When the group changes to 50 per cent men and 50 per cent women, the men's inbuilt advantage is lost. The balance of power changes fundamentally. Even aiming for 50 per cent is hard – think of all the initiatives that have chosen a less threatening target: the 30% Club for women on boards, the Davies Review target of 25 per cent women on boards, raised to 33 per cent by the subsequent Hampton-Alexander Review, David Cameron's promise to make a third of his Cabinet women.

Getting to 25 per cent means women joining the men's 'club', and largely being expected to play by the existing rules. Getting to 50 per cent means rewriting the rules. And rewriting the rules is how we'll both reach Equal Power in the workplace and get the maximum benefit out of it.

Here are some ways you can rewrite the rules.

- **DESIGN OBJECTIVE PROCESSES:** Harvard academic Iris Bohnet has written an excellent book (*What Works: Gender Equality by Design*) about how to achieve gender equality by design – if you are involved in leading an organisation, get the book and implement its ideas. For example, in recruitment she found equality is helped by using structured interviews where all candidates face the same questions, and judging candidates on work-sample tests where they mimic parts of the job.
- **TIME TO CHANGE THE TIME?** Are key meetings held at times so people with caring commitments or those working flexibly can attend? If not, move them, and/or enable people to contribute remotely.
- **MIND YOUR LANGUAGE:** Thinking about the wording of job adverts can help to attract a diverse pool of candidates in the first place. You can quickly run your job advert through a free app to test how gendered it is: http://gender-decoder. katmatfield.com/
- **WHAT GETS MEASURED GETS DONE:** Creating a workplace with Equal Power is not simply a numbers game, but shifting the numbers does need to happen. Start counting: from promotions to bonuses, recruitment to retention rates, monitor and analyse for gender and other characteristics. Set targets and include people's work on improving diversity in their performance reviews.

- **VALUE OUTCOMES NOT INPUTS:** A culture of presenteeism is bad for everyone, but judging people on their willingness to work long hours particularly disadvantages women while domestic and caring responsibilities are not equally shared. Reward getting the job done, instead of incentivising inefficiency by those who have the luxury to stay late in the office checking Facebook.

- **PROMOTE ON POTENTIAL:** The great thing is, organisations know how to do this already; it's how they've been promoting men for years while subjecting women to an endless cycle of 'prove it again'. Structures for objective assessment of potential can help level the playing field, as can creating opportunities for sponsorship – not just mentoring – from leaders within organisations who can help seek out the next promotions for women executives.[81]

- **PUBLISH THE DATA:** Moves for greater transparency like gender pay gap reporting help to increase social accountability for gender inequality. Encourage your organisation to collect and publish data on gender representation at different levels. Use reported data to ask questions – as an employee, shareholder or customer – about what companies and organisations are doing to close gender gaps.

- **SIT AT THE TABLE:** If you are a woman, literally do it. If you're chairing a meeting, invite women to do it. And whatever your gender, encourage women to do it, and indeed anyone else who naturally shies away, such as introverts.

- **OBAMPLIFICATION:** Remember the Obama staffers who reinforced each other's points? Great strategy, and dead simple. It doesn't matter whether you are a man or a woman, when you see a woman make a point you agree with, make sure it doesn't get lost. Repeat it and give credit to her as you do so.

- **VISIBILITY:** You can't be what you can't see. Change the pictures on display in corporate HQs, company brochures and websites, and at panels at industry events and conferences to include more women, people of colour, people with disabilities, and those of different ages, so everyone can look at the imagery and feel included.

- **ASK THE QUESTION:** Ask about gender: how many women are speaking at that conference/event you have been invited to; what is the gender mix on the team pitching to a client or representing the company at that networking event? If it isn't balanced, ask why not and suggest names to rectify it.

- **UNUSUAL SUSPECTS:** One token woman on the panel is not enough – aim for equality. This may mean asking a *lot* more people – one TV show found that to get equal numbers of male and female guests on air, they had to start with lists that were 80 to 90 per cent female, and prioritise women for all the non-headline slots.[82] And don't just keep asking the same women or minority leaders to front up your initiatives. Go beyond the people that easily spring to mind, ask a diverse range of people to make suggestions and you'll end up with much more interesting events.

- **BE A LEADER:** Changing the culture of organisations to become inclusive demands leadership at the very top *and* throughout the organisation. In your team, speak up if you see something you think should change (like an all-male panel), look for ways you can celebrate difference, and in meetings notice who is talking and encourage unheard voices.

- **WE WERE ALL BABIES ONCE:** We need to challenge the tacit acceptance of pregnancy and parental discrimination. The law is there for a good reason: as a society it is in everyone's interests for babies to be born healthy, bond with their parents and have a good start in life. It is also in everyone's interests for parents to be able to contribute to our economy – we all prosper as a result. Maternity, paternity and parental leave and rights are how we can achieve both aims, so when you hear someone talking about it as a 'burden', call them out on it.

- **BANG TO RIGHTS:** Employment rights against discrimination are vitally important, yet often under threat and difficult to enforce. You can support charities like Maternity Action that provide advice and support on workplace rights, join a trade union, or contact your MP urging them to protect existing rights and pressure the government to play more of a leadership role on these matters.

- **TRANSITIONS IN AND OUT:** Smoother paths in and out of work are needed, not just for women (and increasingly men) returning from periods of parental leave, but also for people caring for adults or taking a sabbatical. Structured returnships can build confidence and refresh knowledge, and communication during periods of leave is also important.

- **INVEST IN WOMEN:** One way to see more female leaders of companies is to invest in them. Recognising women entrepreneurs are underinvested in and as such generally outperform, it makes sense for venture capital funds to set aside money specifically to support women founders. If you have money to invest yourself, why not get involved with Angel Academe?

- **BENCHMARK 50:50:** Stop the self-congratulatory rhetoric about getting to 25 per cent women, and remind people you're aiming for 50 per cent. If you're on a board – of a charity, a residents' association, a school parent council, or any team in fact – look at the composition and be proactive about what you need to do to change the gender balance to 50:50.

6

CULTURE:
The Space Race

On 15 December 2015, the country was gripped with excitement and awe as Major Tim Peake prepared to blast off into space. Like for the Olympics or historical anniversaries such as Shakespeare 400, we wrapped ourselves up in a combination of national pride and amazement at what the best of humanity could achieve. These moments in history are truly special and deserve our attention. Tim Peake's six-month stay on the International Space Station was shared through social media videos and science experiments,[1] with schools and television producers capitalising on the opportunity to inspire a new generation with the wonders of the universe. After all, who better to open the minds of children to science and broaden their horizons about what can be achieved than an astronaut?

Waking up to the news that morning, though, I was confused. Talk and commentary about the first British astronaut made no sense. Back in my schooldays, I recalled attending a Young

Enterprise conference in Glasgow with a keynote speech from the first British astronaut, Helen Sharman. She'd made her space trip back in 1991, to the Russian space station Mir, after winning a competition against 13,000 others who all responded to a radio advert that had tantalisingly said, 'Astronaut wanted. No experience necessary.'[2]

I wasn't alone in my confusion: social media was soon awash with complaints about Helen Sharman's achievement being erased, and broadcasters and newspapers began to notice their error and correct their language. Some commentators rather defensively tried to justify the slight by suggesting that her achievement didn't matter because it was a privately funded mission, so she wasn't an 'official' British astronaut.

If it had been the other way round – if Helen had been Henry and Tim had been Tina – we'd have been celebrating the first British woman astronaut. Lauding the 'first woman' to reach a milestone is common. But if a woman achieves something first, why do we not celebrate the first man to reach the same goal as the 'first man' to do so, instead of erasing the woman who did it before?[3] Do we think his endeavours are less noteworthy if a woman has already got there? In this case, was it just easier to dismiss what Helen Sharman had done so we didn't have to qualify the 'first Brit in space'[4] headline with the male gender?

The first British astronaut was a woman, but men are definitely winning the race for space in our culture. From the airwaves to art galleries, from the stage to the big screen, from the history books to the public realm, you'll see and hear a warped proportion of men to women.

Turn on the radio, whose voices do you hear? When I worked at the Yorkshire radio station Viking FM in the early 2000s, our schedule listed just one daytime show presented by a woman, Sam Heywood. Other than Sam and the contributions of our news editor Kirsty Moore and her team, it looked pretty much a man-fest. In fact, the gender balance was slightly better than we knew at the time, as our anchor breakfast presenter was Stephanie Hirst, at the time known as Simon. Since her transition in 2014, Stephanie has spoken out to tackle injustice and stigma against the trans community, and her courage is a beacon to young trans people.

Looking at radio schedules today, sadly not much has changed. There almost seems to be an unspoken quota. It's like stations recognise an all-male line-up is odd, so one of the shows will be presented by a woman – often the afternoon or drive time of course, not the flagship breakfast show with the most listeners. Sometimes they may include a woman jointly presenting with a man during breakfast. But once there is that minimal representation of women, that's it. The woman box is ticked, and they can carry on unashamedly – or unconsciously – filling the schedules with men, men, men.

The content of the news is similarly skewed towards men. The people mentioned in big news stories of the day are overwhelmingly male, and while men are much more likely to be quoted as experts, women are much more likely to be in the story as a victim.[5] In 2011, the *Today* programme gave airtime to six times more male experts than women. This statistic was part of research into the gender mix of the five major UK news programmes by Professor Lis Howell – research that sparked a campaign by *Broadcast* magazine and resulted in action from editors. Four years later, the ratio had improved to 3:1 at the *Today* programme, with Channel 4 News and Sky News also making progress. Interestingly, the two programmes that went backwards on the gender equality of contributors also saw their viewing figures fall, while those that improved saw their audiences rise.[6]

Comedy panel show producers have been handed a similar manual, it seems. They were slower to get the memo that some women were allowed onto the schedule in the first place, and even now, one is deemed to be enough. Appearances tracked across 42 different TV and radio shows revealed less than one in five guests were women.[7]

In sports coverage, women should be credited with their achievements. The 2016 Olympics provided some gems of women's success being diminished in deference to men. For example, a Chicago newspaper had to apologise for running with the headline 'WIFE OF A BEARS LINEMAN WINS A BRONZE MEDAL' instead of celebrating Corey Cogdell as a person in her own right.[8] Then there was the commentator who marked swimmer Katinka Hosszú winning gold and breaking the world record by saying 'and there's the man responsible' over a camera shot of her husband in the stands.[9]

You'd think maybe the world of the arts would be different: creativity, diversity and beautiful work are prized, and surely artistic projects are judged purely on their merits? Yet look at productions on the stage in national theatres. While around two-thirds of theatregoers are women, women make up only about a third of artistic directors, writers and actors. And women playwrights are more likely to have their work relegated to smaller venues.[10] Women musicians are less likely to be given a job in top orchestras; yet when all candidates perform behind a screen, a woman's chance of success jumps by 30 per cent, demonstrating the bias at work.[11] Despite the majority of art graduates being women, male artists are twice as likely to be displayed in London galleries.[12] In the upper echelons of the art world, the positions of power are hoarded by men. Many of our most cherished art institutions and museums have *never* had a woman in the top job: the National Gallery, the Barbican, the National Portrait Gallery and the British Museum.

A trip to the cinema is similarly dispiriting. Men are seen and heard on screen twice as much as women.[13] Men are five times more likely to be lead characters, and even when women are the lead, they do not dominate the film visually and in dialogue in the way men do.[14] Even in many of the more recent Disney Princess films, men have about three times as much to say as women. Worryingly, this is much worse than the classic Disney films from many decades ago.[15] Behind the camera it is just as bad – just 23 per cent of crew members are women, and this has actually got worse in the last twenty years.[16]

But even I was surprised by the analysis of crowd scenes in family films, which showed that 83 per cent of the crowds were men.[17] Even in non-speaking roles as extras, making up the numbers as part of the backdrop to the main action, men significantly outnumber women. And the real killer is that film directors, and the viewing audience, don't see this as odd, because denying women space is so ingrained we barely see it at all. You can bet your bottom dollar that people would notice if a scene of extras was 83 per cent women.

The old justification has been that women will go to see a film about men, but men won't be interested in a film with women leads. Yet research looking at the top 100 grossing films shows those with women leads gross significantly more than those with men, and films with male and female co-leads do best of all.[18] A recent trend in Hollywood has been to remake classics with female instead of male protagonists, such as *Ocean's Eleven* or *Ghostbusters*. But while many men do in fact seem to be perfectly happy to watch good films with good leads regardless of gender, it is clear from social media backlash that there is a minority who are furious about seeing women in these roles.

The vicious response to the *Ghostbusters* remake in 2016 was most concentrated on Leslie Jones, the black comic actor who plays subway-worker-turned-Ghostbuster Patty Tolan. Leslie was initially hounded off Twitter by misogynistic and racist abuse,[19] in part facilitated by a self-styled antagonist blogger who has tried to make a career out of being a dick (and who was himself finally removed from Twitter for his part in this abuse).[20] Later she was the victim of a cyber-attack where her personal files were hacked, and intimate images and her contact details were posted widely online.[21] I have no doubt she was targeted for her role in the film, and because she had committed the double 'sin' of daring to act in a film remake of *Ghostbusters* while being both a woman and black. The message is clear: when women, and especially women of colour, take up space in culture and step outside the bounds of 'acceptable' roles, they are punished.

We need women on air, on stage and on screen, because you can't be what you can't see. That was the strapline of the powerful film *Miss Representation*,[22] which I organised to be screened in the Houses of Parliament in 2012. As well as uncovering quite how unequal Hollywood is, both in front of and behind the camera, it made the link between our cultural reference points and our aspirations. At primary school, similar numbers of American boys and girls put their hands up when asked the question 'who wants to be President when they grow up?' By the age of 11, there is a huge gender divide. That tells us not just about interest in politics, but also whether girls can see themselves in leadership roles. If the television and films they watch constantly cast women in supporting roles, and their plotlines revolve around men, then it is no wonder girls imagining their future do not cast themselves in the role of the entrepreneur, the leader or the hero.

The media and entertainment industries are hugely influential, and we should be concerned with the steady stream of sexist output and the consequences for the next generation. In government I was frustrated when our plans for a high-profile review into media sexism were blocked by the Conservative side of the coalition, who were afraid of upsetting their media backers.[23] Yet again, the power dynamics had swung into action to preserve the status quo.

The Pen Has Been in Men's Hands

One of my favourite places to luxuriate in time and learning is a bookshop: there are few experiences more delightful than a leisurely forage around Waterstones in Piccadilly, with its six floors of wonder. It's not pin-drop quiet, just a lovely low murmur of snatched conversation about suggested reads, with the efficient sounds of footsteps across carpet to place books on shelves with a satisfying papery thud. I particularly love the tables full of books face-up, clumps of ideas tempting you to 'pick me, pick me!' and inevitably resulting in me choosing several. Recently I was musing over one of these tables, and I started to notice the books on it were almost all by men. I counted. There were 47 books on the table, and going by the names, only two were written by women.[24] A casual look around the rest of the bookshop confirmed the skewed percentage, as does a quick look at bookseller catalogues or the *Sunday Times* bestseller list. Are women less good at writing books? What's going on?

In centuries gone by, women writers felt that they had to hide their gender to be taken seriously. The Brontë sisters had 'a vague impression that authoresses are liable to be looked on with prejudice', so Charlotte, Emily and Anne initially published under the names Currer, Ellis and Acton Bell. George Eliot, author of the masterpiece *Middlemarch*, was actually Mary Ann Evans. Even today, bestselling women authors Joanne Rowling and Erika Mitchell publish under the gender-ambiguous J.K. Rowling and E.L. James, and even the male pseudonym Robert Galbraith.[25] It's perhaps less surprising when you consider research by author Catherine Nichols, who experimented with sending her book proposal to agents and publishers under her own name and also under the name of George Leyer. She had *eight times* more interest in her book when she was George not Catherine – for the exact same proposal.[26]

Jane Austen published under her own name but her work

was little regarded during her lifetime. She is now judged to be one of our country's great writers. Shortly before her death in 1817, she beautifully summed up the dominance of men in our collective storytelling in a passage in *Persuasion*: 'Men have had every advantage of us in telling their own story. Education has been theirs in so much higher a degree; the pen has been in their hands.'

Even our history books are incomplete. Just 0.5 per cent of recorded history chronicles the experiences and achievements of women, and men have been the ones telling it.[27] The first time a female historian presented a significant history series on the BBC was the year 2000, with Bettany Hughes's *Breaking the Seal*. A few years later she pitched an idea for a series about the powerful women in history. The idea was rejected out of hand and she was told 'it'll just be a parade of Kings' mistresses'. Thankfully in 2015 the BBC did eventually broadcast a compelling series about women throughout history, Amanda Foreman's *The Ascent of Woman*.

Shakespeare and Austen were both right – the pen is mightier than the sword, and men have been holding the pen. It was true in 1817 and it is still true now.

In cities, towns and villages all across our country there are statues, works of art and memorials commemorating and celebrating past achievements. The vast majority of these are representing men, with a ratio of about 16:1.[28] Thank goodness for Queen Victoria, or it would be even worse. As one correspondent to *The Times* put it, 'Would it be mere piety to suggest that if and when new statues are ordered our famous women of the past should not be forgotten?'[29] That letter was published in 1952 – just think how our public spaces might look today had that advice been followed . . .

It's not too late.

The Creators of Culture

Who decides what news you need to hear, what comedy will make you laugh, what books will make you think, what art will move you to tears? The newspaper editors, festival producers, literary critics and artistic directors are now, and have always been, predominantly white men, sitting God-like in judgement with their myriad decisions that, taken together, create our society's culture in their own image. They're not bad people, they're just too much the same sort of people, so they reach the same sort of judgements in a cultural groupthink that sets the benchmark for the rest of us. Anything different is seen as a risky deviation, and the edges of what is commonly regarded as acceptable act more like a constraint than a frontier to be expanded.

The *Sunday Times* is produced from a glass-fronted building towering above London Bridge. Eleanor Mills, the editorial director of the paper's magazine and chair of the Women in Journalism campaigning group, took me on an impromptu tour of the offices. The picture was striking as we swept round the different sections. Banks of desks of white male journalists peppered with the occasional Asian man and a few women – except in the men's worlds of business and sport, obviously. Foreign affairs and money seemed a bit more balanced. Then suddenly it all changed, there was a flash of pink carpet and we were in a man-free zone: we'd reached the Style section. Yes, pink carpet – really. Then on to the central hub, where it all happens – the big decisions about what stories to lead with, what the headlines will say, and which pictures will grab our attention from the newsstands. Here it is not sufficient to be a white man, you have to be of a certain age as well. This was just one newsroom, but in its lack of diversity the *Sunday Times* is far from unique. Across newspapers, the proportion of male bylines ranges from 75 to 90 per cent,[30] and the only serious national daily newspaper to have a woman editor-in-chief is the *Guardian*, with Katharine Viner. This means the news is generally seen and communicated through a male lens: at best, more weight is given to the issues and angles men think are important; and at worst, women are portrayed in an objectified, sexualised and trivialised way,[31] or simply excluded.

My own newspaper of preference is *The Week*, which is a weekly magazine that summarises the best bits of the UK and world news and comment. They have a section for obituaries, typically featuring two recently departed individuals, and also a smaller list entitled 'Farewell' mentioning four or five people who have died. It bodes well for me, as women almost never die in *The Week*. To give you a flavour, looking at five random editions (basically ones I hadn't finished reading before the new one arrived), there were 9 full obituaries, all men, and just 3 women listed out of 23 on the Farewell lists. The 2015 end-of-year edition looked back at who had died that year: of the 73 listed, just 12 were women.[32] We all have the same chance of dying – it's 100 per cent. The fact that we look back and so disproportionately celebrate the lives of men is one of the glaring signs that women are undervalued, underreported and underrated. And the suggestion that today's

The *Sun* front page, 10 February 2014

Daily Mail front page, 28 March 2017

obituaries are a reflection on position in society decades ago is insulting to the amazing women in their seventies, eighties, nineties and beyond who lived fascinating lives and achieved great things, often against the odds, and whose obituaries would be every bit as interesting to read as those of the men who take their place on the page instead. These words are being written today, there is no need to apply 1950s sexism.

Internet technology has the potential to open up the creation of our culture to everyone, instead of the hoarding of access to information and influence by the old boys' club. In the early days of computing, women played vital roles. Ada Lovelace was the founder of the concept of computer programming with her pivotal work exploring an 'analytical engine' back in 1842.[33] As the first computing machines were built around the world in the 1940s, women were often key software engineers; indeed three-quarters of the workers at Bletchley Park were women.[34] As commercial applications for computers increased in the 1960s, Dame Stephanie Shirley recruited an army of thousands of women programmers and built a successful business to solve difficult coding problems,[35] though she found it advantageous in her early career to call herself 'Steve' to get taken seriously. Today, however, the technology sector is one of the few where representation of women is going backwards. Women make up a smaller percentage of computer science graduates than in the early 1980s,[36] and the figures for women in leadership roles in tech are stubbornly static, at between one in ten and one in six depending where you are in the world.[37]

Martha Lane Fox is determined to change that. Martha co-founded lastminute.com in 1998, and now sits on the board of

Twitter as well as in the House of Lords as a baroness. In 2015 she set up Doteveryone, a think tank campaigning to open up the Internet to people right across society.[38] When we met, we sat on leather sofas in a House of Lords bar, surrounded by red flock wallpaper and dark oil paintings of men. 'Ninety-six per cent of the Internet is written by men,' she told me. It bears repeating: *96 per cent of the Internet is written by men.* The engine of modern life, reaching right across every aspect of society, increasingly the means by which we interact with the world, and it is even more dominated by men than politics, business or the media.

While in some areas of technology women might make up as much as one in six of the workforce, the coding itself is the most male part of an already male industry. As Martha says, 'The sharp edge of the tech stuff is where money, power and influence lies in the tech world.' So Martha encourages women to learn basic coding, and runs programmes to help people better understand tech and stop being 'scared of digital'. With refreshing candour, she also told me about her own experience of being on boards, including Marks & Spencer and Channel 4, and how despite her huge success as an entrepreneur, she had to learn to quieten that inner critic that told her: 'I shouldn't be here . . . I don't have a valid set of experience.'

The online world can be hugely empowering: it has given voice to marginalised groups, and connected people far apart, like people diagnosed with a rare medical condition, people who are fighting discrimination, those who are geographically remote or people who have limited physical mobility. But the Internet can also be hugely empowering for dispersed groups that are best left unconnected or marginalised, like people promoting self-harm, plotting terrorism or organising the rape of children.

At the extreme end of these atrocities, the authorities can use criminal law to intervene and prosecute. The difficulties of trying to organise cooperation between different countries and companies can just about be overcome when the issue is as serious as child pornography. But part of the problem is that the Internet is young and immature, and in too many places the playground bullies rule the roost. He who shouts loudest gets heard, and the voices of a tiny minority – often racist, misogynistic, homophobic – have a disproportionate impact. Journalists are used to receiving abuse – of course they received it in pre-Internet days, too – but now people with nothing better to do than hurl insults at other human beings don't even need to bother hunting for a green pen to send their bile. The *Guardian* undertook a fascinating analysis of the abusive comments posted on their articles, and found that it was significantly gendered and racist. Of the ten journalists who attracted the most abuse, not one was a white man.[39] I applaud the journalists who carry on and rightly refuse to be silenced, finding ways to cope with the hate. But let's not kid ourselves: it takes its toll, no matter how much you know it is rubbish and not worthy of response. Worse still, an environment where the price for women and people of colour who speak up in public debate is to be subjected to a barrage of hate undoubtedly puts others off and reinforces the existing under-representation.

Online hate is not just reserved for those who put their head above the parapet. Just participating as a woman in the online world is enough to attract abuse. The courtesies of the physical world have not been mirrored online. Anyone who walked into a coffee shop and yelled 'YOU FUCKING BITCH!' in someone's face would be swiftly ejected by the management, and if a mob of them ganged up to do it, the police would be called. Online, this kind of abuse is happening continually and only a few high-profile cases are dealt with.

One study found that posting in chatrooms with a username that is clearly female results in 25 times as many malicious messages as with a username that is male or ambiguous.[40] Of course, this leads to a perception gap between men and women, and even between different groups of women, exacerbated by the fact that online abuse tends to be targeted and not automatically seen by others.

Men do also receive online abuse, but at a much lower rate than women, and the content is generally less sexually threatening. It is easy for them to assume that they know what women are talking about, and then prescribe solutions like 'just block trolls'. Yet when I have retweeted abuse received I have often been struck by how many men are shocked by it, in the same way that high-profile cases such as the rape threats to feminist campaigner Caroline Criado-Perez and MP Stella Creasy captured public attention. Women in the public eye were also appalled, but generally less shocked. In a similar vein, I got used to regular Twitter abuse from nationalist supporters in the run-up to Scotland's independence referendum and beyond, and when English politicians made a contribution to the debate they were often taken aback by the instancy and ferocity of the abuse that followed from the so-called 'cybernats'.

And, in turn, as a white humanist woman I was shocked when I spoke out against Nigel Farage's comments that migrants were rapists and my Twitter notifications suddenly gave me a window into the world of Islamophobic abuse, with people rushing to defend Farage and his assertion that Muslims are more likely to commit rape.[41] Oddly enough, these trolls, who were so incensed at the thought of all the future rapes that they claimed would happen as a result of EU membership, were rather less bothered by the actual appalling facts about the existing epidemic of domestic and sexual violence in this country. Most of these crimes are committed by people already known to the victim, so attempting to pin the blame on some external group is not only racist, it also detracts from what actually needs to be done to address the problem of rape and sexual assault.

I worked alongside Labour MP Yvette Cooper and a range of cross-party politicians and civil society organisations to launch the Reclaim the Internet campaign in 2016.[42] It draws its name and inspiration from the Reclaim the Night movement in the late 1970s, when women took to the streets to protest after they were told to stay in after dark to stay safe from harassment and violence. In both cases, the solution isn't to isolate and silence people so they can avoid abuse, it's to put a stop to the abusive environment.

Reclaim the Internet is working to tackle different elements of the online environment that are so corrosive to equality. Police, the law and judicial systems need to improve their responses. Employers, organisations and the education system have a role to play in shaping norms online. Social media platforms can and must do more to create and enforce clear guidelines for acceptable behaviour, for everyone's benefit. And individuals can play their part, too, by giving moral and practical support to victims of online abuse, calling out perpetrators and reinforcing a positive online culture where vibrant debate is conducted with respect.

Naturally, such a movement attracts a huge amount of trolling, often from individuals hiding behind the Internet's cloak of anonymity. There are also some genuinely held concerns about freedom of speech, which as a liberal I take seriously. Of course freedom of speech is the cornerstone of a liberal society. But for good reasons we also accept some limits on the freedom of speech – for example, by law people are not allowed to incite violence or threaten others, though this is certainly not always upheld when it comes to online abuse, and a better police response is needed. We have protection against harassment and malicious communications: you can't stand outside someone's house every day and yell insults at them as they leave for work, and restraining orders can be granted if you develop a pattern of stalking someone. These protections are important when balancing people's freedoms – the Universal Declaration of Human Rights[43] recognises that some limitations on freedoms can be necessary to ensure the freedoms of others. So to my fellow liberals I would gently ask: do you think the current climate of misogynistic, racist and homophobic abuse online is a sign that freedom of speech is alive and well? Or is it an obstacle to freedom of speech for the groups whose voices we hear least?

Freedom to do something is not only defined by the absence of a law preventing it. If the price of speaking out is to receive threats and abuse, that is not true freedom of speech. If the price of speaking out is paid disproportionately by different groups, then those who do not pay that price need to recognise that they are privileged to enjoy greater and easier access to freedom of speech than others, and should work to extend that freedom to everyone in society.

Journalist Jamie Nesbitt Golden took part in an experiment where she, and other women of colour, swapped their online avatars with white tweeters. In Jamie's case she became a white hipster guy with a beard.[44] They all experienced the same sharp drop in trolling and were treated much more reasonably; as she put it, 'It was like I was a new person.' Meanwhile the white people in the experiment suddenly received racist insults and more aggressive engagement. If you want to get a taste of how others are treated online, then you could similarly change your photo for a week or so and see what happens.

Look at your social media timelines and consider what range of views you are seeing. Most people are attracted to others like them, so they naturally gravitate to following like-minded people from much the same background. This is how the echo chamber is created, where people of similar views end up talking to each other and becoming cut off from wider opinion in society. It's part of how so many people in Scotland in 2014 couldn't understand that Scotland voted to stay in the UK, as online comment on social media was dominated by independence supporters, and dissenting voices were not heard or shared among that movement. In 2016, so many people were shocked that the UK voted to leave the EU, as everyone they knew was voting Remain. In some areas of the country there were big majorities for Remain, but even in Scotland and London, around four in ten people voted to leave.

Research shows men tend to have more followers on Twitter,[45] and that both men and women disproportionately follow men, despite the fact that there are more women on Twitter overall. The bias from the real world that we all absorb – telling us that what men have to say is more important – translates online. But what if we made an effort to notice and to amplify unheard voices? That's exactly what Anil Dash did for a year in 2013. He has a large Twitter following of more than half a million people, and had been retweeting men about 80 per cent of the time, so he made a New Year's resolution to only retweet women and see what happened.[46] It was actually fairly 'effortless', he says, apart from a few very male-dominated conversations around new tech gadgets, but even then he was able to find women whose contribution he wanted to retweet. He also noted unexpected benefits – more engagement with women online, especially women of colour, and seeing a wider range of content, issues and controversies. Since I read about this experiment I've thought about my own social media use. It's easy to thoughtlessly retweet prominent people instead of unknown voices. My online world, I realised, was much whiter than the society we live in, but by thinking a little more and delving into the timelines of black and Asian women I follow, I've found many more brilliant accounts to follow, enriched my experience and now see a broader range of viewpoints.

The Sex Factor

So those mainly white men with the power to shape and influence our culture, both online and offline, have created a situation where women are vastly under-represented. In order to 'earn' the right to occupy the small portion of space allotted to women,

women also have to pass the Sex Factor test. The days of products being advertised with a bikini-clad woman randomly attached to them may be largely (though not quite)[47] over, but the old adage that sex sells is alive, well, and naturally gendered. Hunky men in trunks have never been used to the same degree as a marketing tool, and let's be clear, the Equal Power I'm seeking is not a world where women and men are sexually objectified in equal measure. Finding examples where men are given this treatment does not justify the sustained and constant presentation of women as objects whose main value lies in satisfying the sexual urges of men whether they want to or not.

It doesn't matter what the arena is, sexual attractiveness is the lowest common denominator on which women are judged. So Olympic medallists are trolled with abuse,[48] and despite their amazing physical achievements are judged on their appearance.[49] And a Wimbledon champion is criticised by a BBC commentator for not being a 'looker'.[50] In films, female characters are twice as likely as male characters to be shown in sexually revealing attire, or partially or fully naked.[51]

Donald Trump criticised his Republican rival Carly Fiorina for her appearance,[52] and then thought the way to repair the damage was still to focus on her appearance, but to compliment her instead.[53] Barack Obama famously stuck to the same suit on the basis that cutting out unnecessary daily decisions on what to wear freed up his precious brain time for the big issues he had to consider.[54] Women don't have that luxury, as Australian TV anchors Lisa Wilkinson and Karl Stefanovic demonstrated. Lisa regularly received criticism for what she wore and how she looked, while her co-presenter Karl undertook an experiment where he wore the same suit on TV every day for a year to see if any viewers would notice or comment. They didn't. The reality is that in order to get a hearing, to justify being a woman in the public sphere and be treated well, you need to pass the Sex Factor test, regardless of your skill or achievement as a businesswoman, politician, singer, actor, journalist, sportswoman or scientist.

If you're not convinced, just think for a moment about TV journalists who read the news and present programmes. The women tend to be more conventionally attractive than you'd see walking down your local high street. The men, not so much. Coincidence? While we're on the subject, ever noticed that when there's a man-woman duo presenting a news programme, the bloke is always on the left of the screen? No, neither had I, until in 2016 the long-standing presenter of the BBC's flagship breakfast programme, Bill Turnbull, retired. His co-presenter, Louise Minchin, had apparently hoped to inherit his side of the sofa, with its unspoken aura of seniority, but her new co-host Dan Walker was allocated that spot.[55] In the Western world we read left to right, so we intuitively look first at the left of the screen, seeing that space as more important. You can – and people did – argue about whether it matters who sits where[56] – the BBC's defence for placing Dan Walker on the left was that they needed to achieve the 'best camera shot', though what exactly makes the shot 'best' when the man is on the left went undefined. Either way, though, what's undeniable is the ubiquitous placing of the male host on the left and their female counterpart on the right, and once you've noticed it, you see it everywhere. That's not random chance, so some decision-makers in TV programming think it does matter.

The only physical attribute that is applied fairly equally to men and woman elevated to visible positions in our culture is they're generally not allowed to be fat, although the weight of women celebrities is still more avidly policed by cultural outlets. Despite the nation's growing obesity crisis, we seem to have a collective aversion to larger sizes being seen.

There's also a much wider age range for the men. In this Sex Factor world, youth and perfection are prized characteristics for women. Hair must be coiffed and faces must be made up. Clothes must be carefully thought through, hitting the right side of the line between attractive and too sexy, and of course that line will change depending on the time of day, the channel, the programme audience and so on. And you really have to be younger than the bloke you're with.

The actor Maggie Gyllenhaal was turned down for a role opposite a 55-year-old man because she was 'too old' to play his partner. She was 37.[57] From James Bond films to news anchor partnerships, the older man/younger woman dynamic is pervasive, and out of sync with the reality of most relationships. We lose the wisdom and energy of older women from our culture, and while we accept the ageing process for men, the invisibility of it for women leads us to have warped ideas about what older women should look like. I remember organising a campaign to complain about excessive retouching in adverts, and one particular focus was an ad for Olay anti-ageing cream which used a hideously airbrushed picture of 1960s icon Twiggy. It was truly ridiculous – the digital editing made her look about 30, and the Advertising Standards Authority rightly banned it as misleading.[58] Yet when this hit the media, I read comments on the image claiming that was what 60 looked like – because we are so unused to actually seeing it. Frankly, Twiggy looks fabulous at 60; why can't we celebrate these faces and their lines which tell stories of past smiles and laughter? It's no wonder that cosmetic surgery is a boom industry, with more than 50,000 procedures now performed each year[59] – doubling over the last decade.[60] People are spending hard-earned money to get some 'work done', as if part of the maintenance required for the human face is cutting it open with a knife or injecting poison. I'll just use moisturiser and some toothpaste, thanks.

Yet there is an unspoken conflict here about how we tackle this. In achieving positions of power in our culture, women learn they have to play the game. Top sportswomen do magazine photoshoots in glamorous dresses. Actors eat a diet of steamed fish and pureed kale to keep their weight unnaturally low, and wear Spanx on the red carpet for good measure. Women in political life choose their clothes with great care. TV anchors spend extra time in hair and make-up every day to look the part. Singers succumb to the raunch factor. For all that these women sometimes enjoy eating fish, wearing nice clothes and make-up, or feeling sexy, the point is that their choices are constrained: the penalties for not acting in this way are real. All of this reinforces the image of how women need to look to be accepted in our public culture, and underlines that attractiveness is part and parcel of whatever your actual job is.

Periodically, outrage is sparked when women are told how to behave and look, such as the Clifford Chance memo with 150 tips from 'breathe' to 'don't tilt your head' and wear only 'understated jewellery'.[61] It originated from a session where a senior woman executive had given advice to younger women in the firm about achieving success. I simultaneously hate it and feel sympathy. In the political sphere there is often derision and criticism of training sessions for women candidates about how to dress.[62] I've experienced this training both as a participant and as someone imparting advice. I'd love it if we could just ditch these sessions, but I'm not convinced we're there yet. I spent my early twenties trying to look thirty and be taken seriously as a candidate, and came up against significant ageism, amplified by my gender. The advice about always wearing a suit and make-up and the tips for accessorising may have been irritating, but following them provided some armour to lessen the prejudice and discrimination that I faced.

Maybe this conflict is simply a reflection of the fact that positions of power are often pretty precarious for women. It's understandable that women choose to conform when the price of doing differently is severe. Perhaps the constraints society places on women's appearance is just decades behind in the curve of change compared to other areas where more progress has been made. In the workplace, women used to have to act like men in order to get to the top. While there's a huge mountain still to climb in terms of numbers in senior roles, there is now more appreciation for a feminine approach. Will we look back on the days when women had to wear make-up and heels to be taken seriously and shudder? I hope so.

I remember being especially anxious one morning as I was interviewed on breakfast television. There had been a mix-up with the transport and I'd arrived at the studio too late for the make-up artist to work her wonders, so there I was with just a touch of foundation, no eye make-up, no lipstick, no blusher. Ironically I was discussing body image, and I was up against a reality TV star who looked immaculate. I knew that what I said would be judged differently while I was looking as I naturally do when the alarm has gone off before 5 a.m. – which let's just say is not my most perky – instead of conforming to the usual TV standard. There was nothing I could really do but brazen it out, and do you know what? The sky didn't fall in, and it actually felt quite empowering.

I love the series of Hillary Clinton hair 'gaffes' – hair pulled back in a scrunchie or a clip at a major international crisis summit or the UN General Assembly. Parts of the media are enthralled by judging Hillary's hair[63] – for me, I think it's wonderful that she thought as Secretary of State she had more important things to do than arrange for a hairdresser to give her the perfect blow-dry.[64]

So maybe we should look for opportunities to dial back the Sex Factor requirement. You don't need to suddenly go bare-faced and rip up the look rulebook all the time, but when circumstances mean the usual whole shebang of appearance management isn't easily feasible, why not embrace it? All women can find ways to do this; and in those little moments of defiance, other women can also breathe a sigh of relief, and see that there is a way to chip away at the double standard of the Sex Factor.

There is another contradiction, which is about sexual empowerment. The advent of the pill in the 1960s facilitated a revolution where women's means of controlling their fertility was not largely confined to abstaining from sex. We rightly celebrate women's control over their own sexuality, and can see women portraying themselves in a sexual way as liberating. But at the same time, there is only a narrow range of roles generally permitted for women in cultural expression: mother, temptress, victim, beauty. So is it always genuinely liberating when women adopt an overtly sexual persona?

In my early twenties I was a big fan of the soap opera *Hollyoaks*, set largely around a Chester further education college. Most of the lead characters are in their late teens or early twenties, and plotlines revolve around friendships, romantic relationships, and various crimes and dramatic twists. The cast would famously pose each year for calendars in their underwear or swimwear. I remember arguing about this with a male friend who'd bought the calendar featuring the girls. He couldn't see the problem, especially as a separate calendar was produced of the blokes. As a liberal, if a woman or a man wants to take their clothes off and pose for photos and make money out of doing so, who am I to complain?

But it niggled at me. My main objection was whether there was real choice. Given that almost all of the young people in the cast took part, I couldn't quite believe that it was genuinely voluntary. Whether explicitly written into the contract or not, there would surely be huge pressure to join in. If you're an actor and the basic deal of landing a job in a soap opera is that you also have to pose in your underwear for the implicit purpose of - let's face it - people imagining having sex with you while they masturbate, that's not really okay. And when the people posing may still be teenagers, then there's also a real issue about us inviting others to consider them in a sexual way.

More recently, there was much furore about the transformation of pop star Miley Cyrus from clean-cut Disney child actor in *Hannah*

Montana to a shocking and raunchy young woman, straddling a demolition ball naked, simulating fellatio and twerking onstage at a music awards ceremony with a man nearly twice her age[65] to the annoyingly catchy but fundamentally rapey tune 'Blurred Lines' (which includes such charming lyrics as 'I'll give you something big enough to tear your ass in two'). Sinead O'Connor wrote an open letter to Miley about her choices.[66] Miley responded with some cruel tweets about Sinead's previous mental health problems.[67] The media were delighted. Now they could write about a catfight – oh, they love a catfight – while endlessly publishing titillating photos of a barely clothed young woman simulating anal sex with a guy almost old enough to be her dad.

Where to start? Firstly, in all the furore about the twerking, why was there so little criticism levelled at Robin Thicke, the 36-year-old married father-of-one who was every bit as responsible for the performance? He did not need to grind his crotch up against a 20-year-old's bottom, yet received scant opprobrium for his part, instead eliciting a collective shrug with a knowing 'well, who wouldn't?' from the male-dominated media. Secondly, the odds are absolutely stacked against women in the music industry who eschew a sexy look, so the big issue here isn't Miley Cyrus, it's the screwed-up power dynamics in an industry which, like every other, is run by men. There are a few women of amazing talent who break through without conforming to the Sex Factor – think Amy Winehouse or Adele – but in the main, women making music need to show a whole lot more flesh than blokes to achieve the same success.

Without sounding too Mary Whitehouse, it was all rather tamer in my youth. I grew up listening to Kylie and Jason, New

Kids on the Block, Take That and the Spice Girls. I loved the Spice Girls – what teenage girl wouldn't? They're still fabulous today: their performance atop London black cabs in the 2012 Olympics opening ceremony was memorable, glamorous and typically kick-ass. When Geri Halliwell (or Ginger Spice, as we all called her) wore a tiny Union Jack dress made out of a tea towel to the Brit Awards in 1997 it sparked controversy, and the performance was voted one of the most memorable at the Brits across 30 years.[68] Look back at those images through the lens of today, and while it is still a strong and iconic visual, it's hard to imagine the furore created by a pop star showing her knickers.

Britney Spears shot to fame in 1998 with 'Baby One More Time', and while it is certainly a brilliant pop tune, its huge success was also linked to the rise of music TV airplay. The video – which shows 16-year-old Britney in school uniform, with marabou-feather-topped bunches, and a pristine white blouse tied around her midriff exposing a hint of her bra – became the most requested of all time.

Part of the point of art is to test, push and extend the limits of what we find acceptable, of course, so in one sense it isn't surprising that standards of what is risqué have changed over time. But it is no coincidence that this hugely successful Britney video reflected a common theme of pornography: the schoolgirl fantasy. Our culture rightly abhors the atrocity of child sexual abuse, though revelations of historic crimes that have come to light suggest there was an appalling attitude and turning of blind eyes in some institutions in the past. Yet even as we rail against paedophiles preying on 15-year-olds and younger, major newspapers,[69] adverts[70] and music videos present older teenage girls as luscious temptresses aching with unquenched lust, offered up on a plate for the viewer's consumption.

In advertising, images are often arranged so that all we see of a woman is a particular body part.[71] Heads are cut off the page, which dehumanises the subjects, and poses can hint of violence. This is standard fare in edgy ads for fashion brands or perfumes, but it is so pervasive that it filters down. A flimsy catalogue for Asda plopped onto my doormat and I flicked through it over lunch. A double-page spread advertising jeans caught my eye and I couldn't quite believe it. Four pictures of women modelling different jeans, and four of men. All of the men were full length, with their jeans described as 'stylish' and 'durable'. All of the women had the image cut off just above the neck, showing their headless bodies in various poses, including one presenting her bum to the camera. The photos were accompanied by text and little yellow lines with arrows overlaid on the waist and thighs, showing how the jeans 'hold you in', 'enhance' and 'uplift' your bottom. And to top it all, the women's jeans were double the price. I don't think the people at Asda HQ putting together that piece of marketing communication were thinking about how to objectify or patronise women. Maybe someone was thinking about how to fleece them by charging them double. But it is so ingrained that this is what normal imagery of women looks like, it just becomes the default setting, so that unless you sit there in a corporate HQ paying attention and thinking about how you ensure you *don't* objectify or patronise women, you absolutely run the risk of doing so inadvertently.

Men are also four times more likely to be in adverts at all, and seven times more likely to be in a speaking role.[72] Then there are the stereotypes in the portrayals, with men more typically presented as intelligent and in work scenarios, and women in the kitchen. Notable exceptions to these trends can mask the overall picture, but worryingly the data shows these portrayals haven't changed in the last decade. When I spent time in an advisory role with the Advertising Standards Authority, I was delighted to feed into a ground-breaking project that looked at gender stereotyping in advertising and proposed changes to the advertising codes to drive different behaviour from advertisers. This is still a work in progress, but an excellent report signposting a way forward was published in 2017.[73]

The pornification of culture has mirrored the growth of the Internet and the easy availability of hardcore porn. Music videos and lyrics have increasingly glamorised rape and violence against women, and fetishised and degraded black women in particular. It's a kind of arms race of porn, with each video competing to be more extreme and shocking than the last one.

Is this sexual empowerment of women? Sometimes, maybe, when women are genuinely in control. But more often the imagery is stuck firmly in the groove of women as objects for the gratification of men. Some women may feel in control using their sexuality and desirability as power to achieve success. In a sense, good luck to them. But if that's the only source of power they can access, and the avenues to success for women are limited, then the titillated men are still in control, having their cake and eating it, too.

The pervasiveness of porn culture was highlighted by the #FBrape campaign,[74] when it took a group of campaigners in 2013 a shocking amount of time to get Facebook to remove offensive images of violence against women, and even then they did so only after several advertisers announced they would pull their adverts from the site.[75] Images like a photo of a woman with her head in a pool of blood captioned 'I like her for her brains'; a picture of a woman gagged with her legs and arms bound together behind her, captioned, 'It's not rape, if she really didn't want to, she'd have said something'; and a woman's crumpled body at the bottom of a flight of stairs with the words 'Next time, don't get pregnant'. The screenshots of these and many more are still preserved on the Women Action Media website.[76] They make for sickening and disturbing viewing, but if you need any further convincing, then just go and have a look. And while of course it turns your stomach to think that anyone created these images and shared them in the first place, the most shocking thing to me is that a public company with billions of users could have moderators look at these pictures and deem them acceptable. But while Facebook needs to take responsibility for its actions here, let me be clear – this is not only a problem with Facebook. That the moderators making judgements on these images thought they were fine shows how immune we have become to seeing violence against women.

It is sadly ironic that while images of women in sexual servitude are hard to remove, women's bodies in their natural, beautiful, naked form are quickly deemed offensive and deleted. At the same time Facebook was waving through images promoting rape, it was taking down images of mothers breastfeeding their babies. It was only a year after the #FBrape campaign that it changed its policy to allow nipples to be seen – if they were in the context of breastfeeding. The no-nipple policy is still in force more widely, with an undercurrent that there is something intrinsically offensive about women's bodies in their natural state.[77]

Male nipples are absolutely fine, of course – but, oh, save my eyes from seeing a hint of female nipplage! Courtney Demone undertook a fascinating project as she transitioned from being a man to a woman, taking regular photos and posting them on Facebook to see exactly where the line would be drawn between fine and causing offence, under the hashtag #DoIHaveBoobsNow.[78] It did not end well. Facebook was unbothered by the photos uploaded, until the *Guardian* newspaper got interested in the campaign and asked it about its policy.[79] Shortly after this, the photos of topless Courtney were removed, and a few months later Facebook closed Courtney's account[80] after deleting a previously approved image on her page which contained a female nipple.

In 2016 Facebook was mired in controversy again, this time for censoring the iconic and famous photo 'The Terror of War', which shows a nine-year-old girl running in fear from napalm bombing in the Vietnam War. She is naked, having torn off her burning clothes. They even removed a post from Norway's prime minister, Erna Solberg, about the image and its importance.[81] Not being able to tell the difference between depiction of child sexual abuse and powerful imagery showing the terrible cost of war, confusing celebration of women's bodies with sexual depravity – it's messed up.

Algorithms and data only get you so far, and if the vast majority of images out there containing women's nipples are pornographic, maybe a big media company thinks a uniform rule is easier and less messy. But what message does that send? What defeat is that, to say that because it's a bit difficult to separate out the context, we should just censor women's bodies? Is it really so different to cultural practices that are rightly criticised, where women are forced to cover their heads, their ankles, their faces? Is one of the reasons big tech companies struggle to get this right that they are stuck in an echo chamber, where more than three-quarters of their leaders and more than 85 per cent of their staff are men?[82]

This culture that views women primarily through the lens of sexual attractiveness contributes to economic inequality, violence and warped power dynamics.

Accessory or Agency?

The Bechdel test for gender equality in films was popularised by Alison Bechdel in a comic strip in 1985,[83] exploring an idea from her friend Liz Wallace. It's a pretty low bar. To pass the test, at some point in the film there must be a conversation between two female characters about something other than a man. It is, however, shocking just how few films actually pass.[84] Looking back at films from the 1960s, about half passed the test. Things have improved little in the intervening half-century, with only just over six in ten films passing now.[85]

It highlights how the portrayal of women in film is still largely confined to a role defined by supporting others: as sidekick, love interest, or mother, even when she is the main character. And there's another test which is even more depressing – the Sexy Lamp test. It checks whether the role of a woman in a scene could have instead been played by a decorative lamp.

The concept that you have women around to 'brighten the place up a bit' is the ultimate conclusion of assigning women value according to how they look.

Fixing the under-representation of women across our visual culture is important but not sufficient: we also need to see women with agency – a crucial part of the story, heard as well as seen, and important in their own right, not in terms of their relationship to a man.

Oscar-nominated actors should be celebrated for their skill and talent more than their ability to look good on the red carpet. The media's emphasis on the latter led to the #AskHerMore hashtag, which urges journalists to go beyond the bland and boring question doled out to so many: 'Who designed the dress you are wearing?'

Even the way men and women are encouraged to pose for the camera reinforces the accessory/agency divide. I remember doing a photoshoot for a magazine and being asked to stand with my feet together, crossed over at the ankles. I thought it was a bit ridiculous, as I'd never deliberately stand like that. One of the things you learn when public speaking is that your posture has a real impact on your voice and how to project authority. And apart from the visual cues your body language sends, there are physical consequences, too. Slouching makes it harder to fill your lungs to speak at a confident volume, and standing with your feet together makes it harder to balance. For making a speech, the ideal foot placement is shoulder-width apart, giving you a firm foundation to feel balanced and in control. Try it out – stand with your feet together and get a friend to push you, then try it with feet shoulder-width apart. Your body language and posture can literally make you more of a pushover. Yet the imagery of women around us is often meek, looking shyly away from the camera, displaying a lack of confidence and uncertainty, or overly sexualised. Men get to do the power poses. A graphic parody of *The Avengers* created by Kevin Bolk swapped the poses of the male and female characters, and brilliantly made the point about sexualisation, even of cartoon characters. The Incredible Hulk caressing his booty is something to be seen.[86]

Contrast that with the imagery for a film like *Wonder Woman*, which has both a power pose, and powerful words: *Wonder. Power. Courage.*

Harness the Power of Culture to Drive Change

While the culture that surrounds us frequently reinforces the power imbalance between men and women in society – both explicitly and in myriad subtler ways – there is a huge potential for these channels to catalyse change. Baking bread is a good metaphor here. Legislation and regulation are the flour, butter and water: necessary ingredients for the guaranteeing of rights or standards. Cultural touchstones to win over hearts and minds, creating an emotional reaction and motivator for change, are the essential yeast, which helps your straightforward ingredients rise into a proper loaf – or real and lasting change in attitudes and people's experiences in society.

Take drink-driving laws. The blood-alcohol limit was introduced in the Road Safety Act of 1967, which resulted in a swift drop in road deaths due to alcohol. However, after a few years, rates started to rise again. It was only with sustained public information and advertising campaigns that drink driving became seen as socially unacceptable, and the numbers killed or seriously injured went on a firm downward trajectory, from around 10,000 in 1979 to 1,500 in 2009.[87]

I remember the controversy around a storyline in the soap opera *Brookside* that saw character Beth Jordache kiss her best friend Margaret, in a ground-breaking television moment.[88] I recall the trip to the cinema with my dad and sister to see

Philadelphia back in 1993, and the long, heated discussion we had after it about HIV, AIDS, homosexuality and stigma.[89] When my dad was growing up, homosexuality was illegal – something we think is horrendous where it occurs in foreign countries today, yet we easily forget that it's still within living memory for millions of people in the UK. While he was never homophobic, my dad would be the first to say his views on LGBT+ issues have changed significantly over the decades. He spent several years working in Romania in the early 2000s, and his business partner came out as gay then went on to set up one of the only gay clubs in Bucharest. I recall a phone call with my dad one evening as he told me about the fascinating conversation he'd just been having at the club with a transvestite. Attitudes really can change, and changing them is just as important – and less straightforward – than changing the law.

To Kill a Mockingbird shone a spotlight on racism in the American South, and in the UK, Malorie Blackman's *Noughts & Crosses* told a powerful story about racism in our society, set in a world where black 'crosses' are seen as superior to the white 'noughts'.

One of the major characters in TV series *Orange is the New Black* is Sophia, a black trans woman played by trans actor Laverne Cox,[90] an important step for trans visibility and acceptance. When Cerrie Burnell started presenting on children's TV channel CBeebies in 2009, some parents complained that her short arm might scare their children. However, most parents reacted positively and embraced the on-screen diversity of the channel, and Cerrie became a firm favourite with her young audience.[91] The 2012 Paralympics launched the hugely successful Channel 4 comedy show *The Last Leg*, combining disability, current affairs and comedy, and it is now on its twelfth series. BBC Radio 4 soap opera *The Archers* explored the complex issue of domestic violence, including emotional abuse, over the course of several years with its storyline about Helen Archer and Rob Titchener.[92] Not only did this result in campaigns to raise thousands of pounds for charities supporting domestic violence victims, the storyline became a major talking point and lots of listeners spoke about how it had helped them to understand the issue better.

Of course, none of these problems are solved: hundreds of people still die each year due to drink driving; racism, disability discrimination, homophobia and transphobia are still rife; and violence against women is endemic in society. But these examples of progress show how art and culture can challenge the status quo and make people think differently about difference.

That's why it is so important that this power is harnessed in a positive way – to promote equality instead of reinforcing inequality – and why you need to help make that happen. Here's how.

- **CELEBRATE WOMEN'S STORIES:** If you're in a book group, choose a book to learn about the life of a less well-known woman from history. Look in your own family – arrange to go and chat to your great-aunt or grandmother about their lives, and pass on their stories. Develop ideas for how your school or community group can mark Women's History Month in March each year – and celebrate these stories all year round.
- **MAKE WOMEN VISIBLE:** Check out if there's a local history group in your area – who are the women who shaped your community? Who are the women commemorated in your

local schools and churches, with plaques, memorials, prizes and school house names? If it's currently all men, suggest a change. Write to your local councillor and local newspapers asking for women to be included in monuments, artworks and street names in your area. Support the invisiblewomen.org.uk campaign by giving information about who is on the plinths in your civic space, suggesting women who could be honoured in statues and raising the issue with your MP.

- **CHEER WHEN YOU HEAR:** Send positive feedback to broadcasters, brands and publishers that include a fair mix of men and women, and a representative mix of women in terms of age, race, sexuality, background, disability and so on - especially when they promote images of women with agency that resist tired stereotypes and objectification.

- **AMPLIFY:** Follow Anil Dash's example and make a conscious effort to notice who you share and retweet, and correct bias. You don't need to retweet only women for a year, but if your networks on social media are predominantly white or male, seek out other views and voices so you hear from a wide variety of women and men from all backgrounds. Just expanding your feed brings a whole new set of ideas and perspectives, and of course then you're regularly seeing a wider range of voices you can then amplify.

- **COMPLAIN ABOUT ADS:** Back in 2010 I challenged the idealised and flawless portrayal of women in adverts by making complaints about individual adverts to the Advertising Standards Authority (ASA), which is the regulator for the advertising industry. I had to complain on the grounds they were misleading consumers about the product - so I targeted ads for anti-wrinkle cream and foundation, but sadly had no traction against perfume ads objectifying women. Nevertheless, I succeeded in getting the issue onto the regulator's agenda, they changed their guidance on digital retouching of images, and the publicity helped brands to think differently. Over the years, the ASA have become much more confident about banning adverts on the grounds of irresponsibility for showcasing models looking unhealthily thin, and in 2017 they published proposals to change advertising rules to tackle gender stereotyping. Making a complaint is a simple way to keep the pressure up – and even more so if you share on social media and encourage others to follow suit. It takes just five minutes to make a complaint online at www.asa.org.uk, and just one complaint can trigger an investigation.

- **GIVE FEEDBACK TO THE MEDIA:** When journalist Kira Cochrane confronted the editor of BBC Radio 4's flagship *Today* programme about the lack of women contributors to the show in 2011, he replied with warm words but also emphasised how listeners didn't raise the lack of women as an issue.[93] The people making the media assume we're okay with it unless we say so, so get out your typing fingers and make yourself heard. Better still, do some counting and get the figures out there; they're hard to argue with. Choose your favourite programme, log the mix over a period of time and share the results. The research has not all been done already – and once it is, it can often attract media attention and be a catalyst for change.

- **OPEN UP ONLINE:** If you have ideas about opening up the online world to everyone, connect with Martha Lane Fox's Doteveryone initiative, who support the testing of innovative projects to find what works. Reclaim the Internet is one campaign you can support that tackles trolling, and there's also TrollBusters, founded by former journalist Michelle Ferrier, which sends messages of support and solidarity to victims of trolling attacks.[94] Not being a bystander is important – if you witness online harassment, speak up in support of the victim so they know they are not alone. You can also offer practical help by reporting abuse, and calling out others for unacceptable behaviour.

- **SUPPORT WOMEN IN CULTURE:** By buying tickets to see women comedians, choosing books by women authors, visiting exhibitions by women artists and seeing plays written or directed by women, you are demonstrating there is a market and helping to knock down one of the excuses made for denying women space in our culture.

- **BREAK THE MOULD:** If you work in the media, advertising or arts industries, then look for ways to break the mould. Introduce new characters, commission new types of programme, depict women in a non-stereotypical way, and use the huge power of cultural creativity to forge new and exciting role models and messages.

7

SPORT:
The Gender Play Gap

Throughout history, women's physical activity has been constrained by a combination of social norms and medical quackery. For centuries, the notion that it was 'unladylike' for women to ride astride a horse forced women to ride side-saddle, even though this meant the rider had less control and was at greater risk of being crushed under the horse in an accident.[1] In the late nineteenth century, women who wore bloomers as practical clothing for cycling attracted outrage, with even medical professionals declaring it an 'abomination'.[2]

Despite Stamata Revithi completing the 1896 Olympic marathon, her result was unofficial as the rules didn't allow her to compete,[3] and the view prevailed that running such a distance would damage a woman's fragile health. Women were not allowed to run the Olympic marathon until 1984.

Women ski jumpers had to wait even longer, till 2014. Explaining why women were excluded, the International Ski

Federation's president, Gian-Franco Kasper, said in 2005 it 'seems not to be appropriate from a medical point of view'.[4] Yes, those ovaries just fall out if you're not careful.

Boxing was slow to let women take part officially, though women have been boxing since the 1700s. The Amateur Boxing Association of England only lifted their 116-year-old ban on women's boxing in 1996.[5] In 1998, the British Boxing Board of Control argued that women should not fight because periods made them emotional.[6]

In cycling, Le Tour Entier was set up to campaign for a women's race alongside the iconic Tour de France.[7] In 2014 it achieved some success when cycling's governing body, the UCI, launched La Course, a one-day women's race scheduled prior to the final stage of the men's race. In further progress, the 2017 La Course expanded to become a two-stage race covering 90 km. By comparison, however, the men competed over 3,540 km in 21 stages. Old assumptions about women's stamina are baked into international cycling rules, which forbid women's races to exceed eight stages and any single stage to be more than 130 km.[8]

Men even dominate sports where any difference between the sexes in physical strength is irrelevant. The outrageous 'justifications' that are given for the lack of women sound like something out of a period drama, but worryingly are currently held views. In 2013, former motor-racing driver Sir Stirling Moss argued women lacked the aptitude for Formula One, stating: 'The mental stress I think would be pretty difficult for a lady to deal with.'[9]

In trying to explain the paucity of women at the highest levels in chess, Grandmaster Nigel Short opined that men's and women's brains are just 'hard-wired very differently' and 'rather than fretting about inequality, perhaps we should just gracefully accept it as a fact'.[10] But Oxford academic research actually shows the success of men at the top of the game is almost entirely explained by the greater numbers of men playing chess in the first place, rather than any kind of biological difference.[11] When women in the game complained about the implicit sexism in Short's remarks, he hit back: 'the feminist lobby has become so tyrannical in its shrill orthodoxy, harping on about nurture over nature.'[12] This from the same man who in 2012 wrote about the 'sheer volume of totty' among the teenage Filipina hostesses with whom 'liaisons were struck up' during a chess tournament in Manila.[13]

Power in sport is still concentrated in the hands of men – whether it's the financial power of prize money, the power of media coverage, or the decision-making power of sport's governing bodies and brand owners choosing where to put their sponsorship cash. Even at the grassroots level there is power in numbers: greater participation by men than women, driven by a combination of historical factors and contemporary pressures.

Thankfully, history is peppered with people who have taken on the dinosaurs and proved that women and girls can and should do sport, including competing at the highest levels.

Nineteen-year-old student Kathrine Switzer entered the men-only Boston Marathon in 1967, and caused uproar. A race official used physical force to try to stop her while she was running, but she got away and completed the course. Reflecting on the experience later in the race (marathons give you lots of time to think), she mused: 'The reason there are no intercollegiate sports for women at big universities, no scholarships, prize money, or any races longer than 800 metres is because women don't have the opportunities to prove they want those things. If they could just take part, they'd feel the power and accomplishment and the situation would change. After what happened today, I felt responsible to create those opportunities. I felt elated, like I'd made a great discovery. In fact, I had.'[14] She went on to launch a series of women's running events for more than a million women in 27 countries,[15] and has become a key advocate for women in sport.

Ski jumpers Lindsey Van and Jessica Jerome filed a lawsuit to sue the 2010 Vancouver Olympics for not letting women compete. This was instrumental in the International Olympic Committee reversing their decision for the 2014 Games. Jessica's father, Peter, who was involved in campaigning for the change, summed up the challenge: 'It's just an old boys' club making decisions. That's why it takes so long for everything.'[16]

In 1991 Susan Polgár became the first woman to earn a chess Grandmaster title. Later that year, her younger sister Judit followed suit, breaking Bobby Fischer's record and becoming the youngest-ever Grandmaster, at the age of 15.[17] Rather than 'gracefully accepting' women's inferiority at chess, Judit proved more than a match for teenage-Filipino-admiring Nigel Short, beating him eight games to three with five draws over her career.

Arsenal FC championed women's football early on, and in 1987 set up Arsenal Ladies, who have gone on to win 43 trophies to date. In their 30th-anniversary year, they took the decision to drop the 'Ladies' and refer to the team simply as Arsenal, in a 'statement of intent, support and unity [between the Arsenal men's and women's teams]'.[18]

One of the key lessons from these trailblazers is the importance of not accepting things the way they are, and believing that change is possible. The good news is you don't have to be an Olympic ski jumper or chess Grandmaster to make a difference. Increasingly the appetite is there for change, as shown by teams, clubs and organisations – like Arsenal – who recognise that women's sport should now be in the mainstream.

Why Does It Matter?

Some people might argue that it doesn't really matter if sport remains a male domain – it's only a game, after all. Actually, it does matter. Sport plays an important role in our national life, it brings people together, it showcases excellence, and it currently does all of this while reflecting back restrictions and limitations for women and girls.

There are also important physical and mental health reasons for wanting to see women and girls participating in sport and physical activity as much as men and boys – and, indeed, for the overall levels of activity for everyone to increase.

Earlier on we explored the impossibility of beauty and how the relationship between girls and their bodies is in a critical state. Rising rates of eating disorders and self-harm are causing huge damage to young people – with incidence much higher among girls than boys. Body dissatisfaction is a risk factor for these conditions. At the heart of body image issues is the disproportionate priority placed on how a body looks, compared to what a body can do. Sport helps individuals to focus instead on what their body can achieve – distance, times, technical skills, speed, precision. Valuing the body in this intrinsic way gives girls confidence and power, instead of putting that power in the eye of the beholder. So the sharp drop in sport participation rates when girls reach their teenage years is doubly bad – hitting both physical health and self-esteem.

And on top of this there is another, less obvious, consequence of women's limited presence in the world of sport.

Dr Jane Dennehy led research in 2010 which identified the positive impact of sports participation on competitive behaviour in the workplace. She found competitive sport was 'a good framework to learn about winning and losing in an environment governed by rules . . . there was this unspoken language about how to work together as a team and how to divide up work.' Her study found that men's greater propensity to indulge in social competition gave them an advantage at work: 'Culture has gone from the sports field into the workplace. Many of the women I interviewed couldn't understand how men could be fiercely competitive at work, then go off to the pub and talk about something totally different over a beer. They learn to play hard on the field, and then move on.'[19]

While not all aspects of sports culture should be welcomed in the workplace – especially if Trump's 'grab 'em by the pussy' comments really are how men talk in locker rooms – playing sport certainly helps develop many skills and behaviours important for success in leadership roles.[20] Whether it is for reasons of health or self-esteem, or to practise how to compete in the workplace, the benefits of sport are equally important for men and women.

It's the Taking Part That Counts

I didn't really like PE at school, and didn't consider myself to be sporty. I wasn't great at hockey and never managed to do very well at jumping or throwing things. While I was a bit better at cross-country, for some reason this was always scheduled for January. Pounding the hard, frosty ground in shorts and a T-shirt didn't really appeal, and it was only years later that I realised running could actually be enjoyable, especially with the right kit for all weathers.

I dropped out of hockey when I was 15. Only in my twenties did I discover genuine enthusiasm for exercise, first through working out at the gym and later entering a 5 km Race for Life event with my mum. I got the running bug and moved on to 10Ks, a half-marathon, and then the Loch Ness Marathon when I was 27. Four years later I ran the London Marathon in under 4 hours, and in 2017 secured a PB:PB (post-birth personal best – my invention but it should be a thing!) in the inaugural Stirling Scottish Marathon. Not bad for someone not 'sporty'! Actually, I just needed to find the activity I enjoyed.

Not only do I feel healthier and physically fitter when I'm running regularly, my mind is calmer, too. Many a time I've used a run to think through issues and problems. Once I'd had the idea to write this book, I was searching for weeks for the right title – it finally came to me while I was running down the Old Kent Road. Sometimes I enjoy just switching off and letting my mind wander, or really noticing the beauty all around, whether it's the urban energy of central London or the lush greenery of the west of Scotland. Running has become my new dancing. My nightclub days are long gone, so apart from the occasional wedding, I no longer experience the joyous abandon of the dancefloor. But with my earphones in and my heart rate up, Madonna or the Black Eyed Peas can spur me on up the hill. I love running to connect with a place: scoping out my new surroundings when I've moved house, or to experience a less touristy side of somewhere I'm visiting. I've laced up my trainers and headed out for runs all over the world: round Sydney Opera House at 6 a.m., through a bustling maze of colourful Mumbai streets, marvelling at the abundance of birdlife on the banks of the Danube Delta. Running has dealt me tears of frustration and highs of elation. Sometimes I've run lots; sometimes work, pregnancy or campaigning have made it impossible. Yet, like a friend, running is still there for me to come back to: a space to be myself, to challenge myself, to be inspired by what my body can do. My running is someone else's rock climbing, netball, golf, badminton, archery or swimming . . . there's all sorts of activities it could be.

Too few women and girls have been encouraged to stick at exercise or sport – or to try something new – in order to find what they love to do, which is a huge shame. As early as eight years old, girls' participation in sport begins to drop off. This continues into the teenage years, meaning that by the age of 14 girls are only half as likely as boys to meet the recommended levels of physical activity.[21] The picture is even starker when you look at competitive sport – boys are three times more likely than girls to play in a sports team outside of school.[22] There are 1.73 million fewer women than men playing sport.[23]

There are lots of reasons for this, some of which are easier to address than others. Girls cite many factors: limited choice of PE activities, concerns about how their body looks (especially as it changes through puberty), a perception that getting sweaty is unfeminine, inadequate changing facilities, and a lack of safe transport routes to and from the activity.

Family support is really important. More than a third of active girls point to having an active mother as a role model.[24] If you're a woman, the girls in your life can be inspired by what you do – whether they're daughters, nieces, pupils, neighbours, or girls you've never met who happen to see you cycling past their house. So being active yourself is a good place to start. Encourage the girls (and women) you know to try out new sports and experiences, and to discover what types of physical activity they like best.

The 'This Girl Can' advertising campaign by Sport England has been hugely successful in changing behaviour, with 2.8 million women under the age of 40 saying they have taken action as a result.[25] When I first saw the advert, I got goosebumps and wanted to go for a run. Previously, the sanitised media representation of women's fitness offered up was as formulaic as it was unrealistic: long-haired, slim, twenty-something woman in a gym environment with perfect make-up and not a hair out of place. Breaking the mould, the This Girl Can clips show women *actually* exercising. Women of different ages, skin colours and body shapes loving their sport, giving every last inch of effort – red-faced, out of breath, sweat-covered, make-up smudged, body jiggling. The soundtrack is uplifting. Text flashes up: 'Sweating like a pig . . . feeling like a fox'. It takes one of the biggest barriers for women – *what will I look like?* – and moves the focus to the amazing feeling of putting your all into physical activity, whatever your level, whatever your chosen sport. These women look powerful, and that power looks beautiful – in a direct challenge to society's ridiculous norms. If you haven't seen it, look it up online, and share the inspiration with your friends and family. Then why not decide on a new activity to try together, and sign up for a local class or taster session.[26]

Schools can make a huge difference, too. If you're a parent or a teacher, ask what the school is doing to increase participation, and point them towards the Youth Sport Trust resources[27] and Women in Sport toolkit for schools.[28] Have they asked girls what they want from PE? Are they highlighting sportswomen as positive role models? Do they connect with local sport clubs? Are the PE teachers mainly men, and if so, what are their recruitment plans next time they have a vacancy? Have they addressed any simple barriers to participation, such as a lack of hairdryers, or sports kit that girls feel self-conscious in? You could even volunteer to help the school develop a plan of action.

When there isn't provision for girls in a given sport or a given area, parents and sport officials can be powerful advocates for change. In her retirement statement, Olympic cycling gold medallist Nicole Cooke spoke about the battles she and her father fought in the early days to enable her to ride competitively at all: 'There were no British Championship events for girls. My father and I worked very hard with British Cycling, formerly the British Cycling Federation (BCF). We strived to convince them to hold events for girls and to provide the necessary support to help them progress . . . I was expressly forbidden by the BCF from riding in the senior women's championship event. I had received a 3 page letter telling me all the reasons why I could not compete!'

On that occasion, a race official intervened and let the 14-year-old schoolgirl ride anyway: 'Worth far more than any medal was the applause of the crowd of cycling enthusiasts as I crossed the line first . . . My father wrote to the official who had ruled I could not ride and asked for championships to be established for girls. The result was that the following year, the BCF put on a superb set of British track championships.'[29]

There are initiatives, large and small, aimed at getting girls to take more exercise or to try out and master specific sports. If you're already involved in a sport, you might be able to volunteer to help an existing programme, or start your own.

Masha Gordon got into mountaineering in her thirties, and kept challenging herself with one new ambition after another, culminating in an attempt to be the fastest woman to complete the Explorers Grand Slam, which involves expeditions to both the North and South Poles and climbing the highest peak on each of the seven continents. Reflecting on the way mountaineering develops resilience and discipline, she set up Grit&Rock – an initiative to train inner-city teenage girls how to climb, developing their mental strength at the same time.[30] Meanwhile former racing driver Susie Wolff launched Dare to be Different, a series of events to encourage girls to explore the world of motorsports.[31] But you don't need to be climbing Everest or a Formula One driver to do this.

Right across the country, people are changing the old world of sport to make it accessible to a new generation of women and girls. People like Sarah Ginn, who started playing cricket when her brother's team were short on players. When she went to Cardiff University, she wanted to play but there was no women's team – so she started one. 'I just thought, well there's no point complaining that there's not one, you may as well go and set one up . . . We managed to get 12 or 13 regulars who came and trained and played, and the year after we got about 20, so it did grow.'[32] Sarah is now head of women's cricket at Berkswell Cricket Club, having set up the first women's team in its 122-year history.

Large organisations can also play an important role in increasing sports participation by women and girls. Race for Life began back in 1994, when 750 women completed 5 km in Battersea Park, raising £48,000 for cancer research. Since then, more than 7 million people have taken part, raising more than £550 million for Cancer Research UK. The events are designed for women – deliberately uplifting and accessible, focusing on the atmosphere, memory of lost loved ones, and on collective achievement rather than individual times. Participants can run, walk or both.

Through corporate sponsorship, big employers can provide the money to make these events possible, and encourage employees to take part themselves, increasing activity at the same time as building team morale. Backing from media partners and key sports or TV personalities helps to publicise and celebrate participation. It's not just running, there are cycling challenges, midnight city-hikes, swimming in the Serpentine – all sorts of different ways to engage people in physical activity for a good cause, which might also lead to new, more active habits.

Role Models

'Our #Lionesses go back to being mothers, partners and daughters today, but they have taken on another title – heroes.'[33]

That was the official tweet sent by the Football Association in 2015, welcoming home the England women's team after they achieved the country's best World Cup result in half a century – since the men's team won in 1966. Patronising in the extreme, it failed to recognise that the sports stars were in fact going back to their jobs as professional footballers, and defined them by their family relationships in a way that would never have happened with the men's team.

Only men do sport. That's the overwhelming impression you get from reading the sports pages of newspapers. Only about 3 per cent of newspaper sports coverage is about women's sport.[34] The journalists are overwhelmingly men, too – in a list of the top 50 sports journalists in 2012, just two women featured.[35] Flicking through the sports pages of any newspaper confirms what a bastion of male dominance it is. Broadcasting is marginally better, with 5 per cent of radio coverage and 10 per cent of TV coverage dedicated to women's sport.[36]

Back in 2011, the BBC announced their shortlist for Sports Personality of the Year – with not a single woman included. Along with three other MPs, I wrote to the BBC to complain, and to question their shortlisting process.[37] At the time, it involved a group of sports editors (men, naturally) voting on which sportspeople should make it onto the list. Bizarrely, the editors of *Nuts* and *Zoo* were included in this process, despite being men's magazines mainly focused on pictures of boobs. (Shortly after I was first elected as an MP, *Zoo* magazine actually asked me to pose for a 'tasteful' photoshoot to give me the 'chance to talk about my policies'. I declined the 'opportunity'.) Thankfully, neither publication is still with us – though this may be less a victory for women's equality and more down to the ubiquity of much more hard-core porn on the Internet. Anyway, we met with the BBC, and they devised new guidelines for choosing the Sports Personality of the Year shortlist.[38] Since then, a third of the shortlisted sports personalities have been women – not equality, but a big improvement.

Partly spurred on by some of these public failures, the BBC has made significant progress on sporting coverage, too, with women's sport now making up almost 30 per cent of their sports coverage.[39]

When women do get a look in, however, don't expect that it will all be about the sport. Boris Johnson described athletes as 'semi-naked women . . . glistening like wet otters' in the run-up to the 2012 Olympics, while he was London mayor.[40] That man is now the UK Foreign Secretary, at the time of writing at any rate. Or remember when John Inverdale described the new Wimbledon champion Marion Bartoli as 'never going to be a looker'? Gold-medal-winning 800m runner Caster Semenya, meanwhile, has been the target of vicious media commentary denying her very womanhood, despite the extensive and invasive gender testing she has endured.[41]

While being interviewed live on air by sports reporter Mel McLaughlin in 2016, cricketer Chris Gayle invited her out for a drink and added, 'Don't blush, baby.'[42] And BT Sport's football presenter Lynsey Hipgrave was bombarded with sexualised abuse online for tweeting an opinion about a penalty: '. . . this is why we don't hire any females unless we need our dicks sucked or our food cooked', 'fuck off you fucking titbag we need sandwiches not opinions you slag'.[43] Top tennis players Serena

Williams and Eugenie Bouchard were asked to 'give us a twirl' by a male reporter at the 2015 Australian Open.[44]

It all sounds a bit stuck in the middle of the last century, like these blokes haven't quite noticed the world has moved on. And, of course, they're less likely to notice in a world that remains stubbornly dominated by men. The macho culture and 'banter' mean disrespectful behaviour to women can more easily go unchallenged.

It doesn't have to be like this. Seeing the coverage of the 2012 Olympics was the catalyst for Jo Bostock and her partner, the top martial arts athlete Tammy Parlour, to found the Women's Sport Trust. As Jo explained it to me: 'A broad range of diverse, powerful female role models – different shapes, different sizes, different sports, and being valued for what they were capable of rather than what they looked like on a red carpet . . . You've seen some sort of tantalising glimpse of nirvana, and then what happens either side of these slightly artificial Olympic spikes, you've very aware of some of the systemic imbalances that lead to that . . . it was very much sitting round the kitchen table thinking "What small thing can we do?"'

The Women's Sport Trust campaigns to change the game, and to increase media coverage and funding for women's sport. From their #BeAGameChanger Awards to projects getting men involved in change, they are already having a real impact.

So what can you do to start demolishing outdated norms? Lots. Calling out nonsense is always a good start, as hundreds of people did in response to the condescending tweet about the Lionesses. The Football Association deleted the tweet and revised the article it linked to. Drawing attention to gender double standards like this creates awareness, and encourages those who don't see the problem to reflect on the issue.

Andy Murray brilliantly and matter-of-factly corrects journalists when they pose inaccurate questions that erase women's achievements in the sport. In 2016, John Inverdale (he has form) said Andy was the first person ever to win two Olympic gold medals in tennis. Andy shot back: 'I think Venus and Serena have about four each.' In 2017, a journalist asked Andy about Sam Querrey being the 'first American player' to reach a Grand Slam semi-final since 2009. Deadpan, Andy corrected him – 'male player' – winning deserved praise from Serena Williams. It is powerful when men roll their sleeves up and get stuck into the work of dismantling gender prejudice, one question at a time.

You can also look at the newspapers you read – national, regional or local. Are they giving due prominence to women's and girls' sport? Do they treat the women they feature with respect rather than trivialising or sexualising them? If not, then – rather than silently fuming about it – let them know. Writing a letter to the editor about the issue will not only prompt them to think about it, but if they print it you'll reach a wider audience. You can do the same with radio and TV, sending an email or social media message to give them feedback. They do need to take heed of what their readers and viewers think.

But one of the simplest – and most effective – ways you can help things to change is to watch women's sport. Tune in, buy tickets, support the teams and athletes. The greater the audience, the harder it is for media owners to ignore. You can find out news and information about upcoming women's sport events on sites like Sportsister and Women's SportsNet. And audiences are growing. In 2017, 1.1 million people in the UK watched England win the cricket World Cup, which is more than the number who tune in to the average Premier League game.[45]

You can also help encourage the next generation of sportswomen and sports journalists. Dr Carrie Dunn is a university lecturer and sports journalist who has written on her research about women in football.[46] She makes a big effort to encourage girls to sign up to her sports journalism course at the University of East London, changing the open days to make them less formal and making a point of seeking out the girls for a chat. When she arrived, just 7 per cent of the students were women. The following year, the new intake had 21 per cent women.

Money, Money, Money

If you follow the money in sport, you see an even greater dominance of men. Research by Women in Sport in 2009 found that just 0.4 per cent of sponsorship revenues went to women's sport, compared to two-thirds going to men's and 32 per cent to mixed events.[47] Up-to-date figures are hard to come by. There are signs of progress, with some high-profile deals such as SSE sponsoring the women's FA Cup, but there is a long way to go.[48]

Of the top-earning 100 sportspeople, there is only one woman, Serena Williams – and despite her record-breaking dominance of modern tennis,[49] she earns the least of the six tennis players on the list.[50] Indeed, it's hard to understand the sponsorship figures for Serena Williams without considering the interplay of race as well as gender stereotypes. Until 2016, Maria Sharapova – an undoubtedly talented, but significantly less successful tennis player than Williams – was the top-earning sportswoman for 11 years running.[51] Viewed through the sponsors' eyes, the conventionally glamorous, white-skinned, blonde-haired player was more valuable than one of the most brilliant athletes of all time, who happens to be a black woman.

In the US, there are 52 male basketball players who *each* earn more than the *combined* salaries of the women players in all 12 teams in the WNBA.[52] The prize for winning the men's football Premier League in 2016 was £38 million – the winning team in the women's Super League gets nothing.[53]

Even in mixed events, prize money is not equal between men and women. In 2007, Wimbledon became the final tennis Grand Slam to equalise winnings for men and women (though their attitude to equality doesn't extend to ticket prices – they charge over 20 per cent more for the men's final than the women's final).[54] Outside of the Grand Slams, a pay gap persists in tennis, which means women players lower down the rankings earn only two-thirds of what similarly ranked men do.[55]

The naysayers who proclaim different prize money is acceptable because men and women play different numbers of sets overlook the fact that this outdated differential is imposed by the tennis authorities, and many women players would be happy to play five sets.[56] In any event, what makes sport most exciting is the skill and competition between brilliant athletes, not the arbitrary length of the encounter. No one suggests Usain Bolt is an inferior athlete because his race is over in the blink of an eye.

And tennis is actually at the forefront of equality in sport. It is no coincidence that the top-earning sportswomen are tennis players. Women have participated in Wimbledon since 1880, and the US Open equalised prize money between men and women back in 1973.[57] Women's tennis owes a huge amount to the pioneering legacy of Billie Jean King. Not only did she convincingly beat self-confessed male chauvinist pig Bobby Riggs in the infamous Battle of the Sexes match in 1973, but her activism created the year-round women's professional tennis circuit.[58] As a result, women's tennis has enjoyed significant media coverage for many years – Wimbledon fortnight in June and July is one of the few times you'll see lots of coverage of sportswomen in the back pages of the newspapers. Media profile builds audiences for broadcast coverage or physical ticket sales and creates role models, which encourages participation and leads to greater funding and sponsorship. Put together, these create a virtuous circle that improves the quality of the sport.

Progress has taken more than a century in tennis. For the sports that have only relatively recently allowed elite women to compete at all, they will need a catalyst.

Money is one such catalyst. In many sports, even elite women athletes have to fit training around a day job to pay the bills. It was only *after* winning the Ashes twice that England's women's cricket team landed sponsorship from Kia which enabled them to be given professional, paid full-time contracts.[59]

This attitude to money and women's sport filters all the way down. A friend of mine told me about a charity event where Team GB signed hockey sticks from the 2016 Olympics – sticks from the men's and women's hockey teams were up for auction. The women's team had won gold, while the men's team came home without a medal. But guess which one sold for more? Depressingly, it was not the stick used by the gold medallists.

Buying tickets to women's sporting events and watching them on TV is one way to demonstrate the audience, which helps the funds to flow. But you can also use your money to donate to charities that are championing the cause, like Women in Sport, the Women's Sport Trust, or specific initiatives that support getting more women into a particular sport. Organisations that campaign for change can have a real impact. Back in 2009, Women in Sport raised the issue of the lack of women on the boards and executive teams of sport's governing bodies. Their efforts over six years, coupled with support from the government and Sport England, have helped to drive numbers up from 21 to 40 per cent women in executive teams, and from 21 to 30 per cent women on sports boards.[60]

Corporate sponsorship often defaults to men's sport without any thought, as co-founder of the Women's Sport Trust Jo Bostock explains, creating an incongruence for the business: 'One part of the corporate brain is focused on aspirations for gender progression, [the talent] pipeline, board representation, the 30% Club and so on . . . and then the other part of the corporate brain chooses to sponsor exclusively men's rugby.'

Former CEO of Newton Investment Management Helena Morrissey used sponsorship to transform the Oxford and Cambridge Boat Race, which in 2015 for the first time included the Women's Boat Race on the same day.[61] Before the sponsorship began in 2011, the women rowers had to buy their own kit and pay for all their own transport, while the men had significant funding.

If you're in a senior position like Helena, use your influence. If not, then you can still ask questions about your company's strategy for sports sponsorship. You can also follow Clare Balding's advice to look at which brands are backing women's sport, and tell the companies you use what you think: 'If your bank doesn't support any women's sport, but continues to fund men's, then write to them to ask why. Do the same for your energy suppliers, retailers and phone companies . . . It's the job of all of us to make it happen and create the change.'[62]

Male domination of the sporting world matters. Not only do lower participation rates by women and girls have knock-on impacts on fitness, health and confidence, but sport also has a powerful place in other worlds. Many a business deal is done on the golf course, or through corporate hospitality at a sporting event – most often with exclusively male participants. The backdrop for any negotiations in these venues is men in charge.

Sport itself is big business, with the top players becoming high-profile role models in our society. The way sportswomen are portrayed and the disproportionate focus on sportsmen reinforces the attitude that it is men who are strong, powerful and physically skilled, whereas women are best-appreciated for how they look.

Imbalance in sport can lead to a testosterone-fuelled environment with a macho culture, where women are dis-respected and homophobia goes unchallenged: of nearly 15,000 athletes in the 2012 Olympics, only 23 were openly gay.[63] That's an astonishingly small number. It's fairly obvious why countries with archaic laws banning homosexuality will lack out gay athletes, but we really need to look at what this says about the UK. It's half a century since England and Wales repealed the laws criminalising gay sex (though this didn't happen in Scotland and Northern Ireland until the early 1980s), and we pride ourselves on being one of the first countries to allow same-sex marriage. Yet sporting culture is so heteronormative that it is incredibly difficult for many gay athletes to come out.

Sport holds a special place in a nation's psyche, bringing people together in shared cultural experience. The icons we look up to and celebrate in these moments matter.

There's a long way to go to reach Equal Power in sport, but think back to the world where women weren't allowed to run marathons and doctors railed against the abomination of bloomer-wearing women cyclists.

The changes that have happened have been down to individuals doing things differently. The list below recaps some of the ideas from this chapter for changing the world of sport. Have a look and decide what you can do.

- **BE ACTIVE:** Setting an example yourself is one of the simplest ways to encourage participation, and if you are a woman it helps create powerful role models for girls growing up.
- **THIS GIRL CAN:** Spread the word, and use the This Girl Can campaign to inspire and encourage girls and women you know to try new sports or activities.
- **CHANGE PE:** Help your school develop an action plan to improve girls' participation and target the danger points where activity rates for girls drop off a cliff. Encourage your local school to recruit a mix of people as PE teachers. If they're looking

for gender-specific teachers, challenge them to explain their reasoning.

- **VOLUNTEER:** Contact a local sports club and offer to volunteer – and make sure they cater for all children. UK Coaching are keen to get more people, especially women, working at all levels – from activating young people to coaching elite athletes.
- **CHALLENGE:** Question, and push for change when authorities have rules in place that you feel exclude people on the basis of gender in a way that is arbitrary or unjust, Kathrine Switzer-style.
- **IF IT AIN'T THERE, SET IT UP:** If there is a gender gap in your local sports club, why not set up a new team yourself, like Sarah Ginn did.
- **FAN ACTIVISM:** Hold your sports team to account for performances 'off the pitch', not just on it. Perpetuating gender stereotypes should be called out, and adopting a healthier approach to gender equality should be recognised.
- **DIVERSIFY ROLE MODELS:** Use your social media to follow and highlight athletes who are women, people of colour, Paralympians, LGBTQ or any combination of these.
- **COMPLAIN:** Tell media outlets that give women's sport scant coverage or focus on sportswomen's looks that it is not on and you're not happy.
- **CONSUMER POWER:** Tell your bank, energy providers and other companies that you want them to support women's sport, not just men's. And shout about the good stuff some brands are doing to support a broader range of sport; magnifying the halo effect for the sponsors that do break new ground and back women's sport makes it more attractive for others to follow suit.

- **GO WATCH:** Buy tickets to women's sporting events, and tune in when they are on TV. Sit back, relax and enjoy.
- **CALL OUT THE CRAP:** Challenge outdated attitudes about women and sport, whether on social media or in conversations with friends and family.

8

VIOLENCE

It's about 10.30 p.m. I'm travelling back from the Liberty Human Rights Awards at the Southbank Centre – an inspiring evening celebrating remarkable campaigners, many with devastating personal stories. I get off the bus and walk home. This final part of the journey only takes about eight minutes, but I've recently moved house, and haven't walked this way at night before. I turn off the main road and notice a group of young men on bikes, loitering on the corner. My route goes straight past them. My mind is on alert, trying to calculate what they are doing – are they a threat? Closer, I realise they're probably young teenagers. I see the shop light on next to them, the only place still open. This is probably just where they hang out, where a bar of chocolate or packet of crisps is never far away. They let me pass without comment. Now I'm on a quieter road, hardly a soul in sight. I curse my high heels. In the silence, they send out a loud 'clip-clop', like an audio neon arrow pointing to me when I'd rather be unnoticed. I make a mental note to pack flat shoes for the walk home in future. A car door opens ahead of me; a man gets out. Quick risk assessment. He shows no sign of menace. It'll be fine. Probably. Should I cross the road anyway, to the side where there are no cars parked, no surprises? Nearly home. I can see the light on, and get out my key. Through the front door with a sense of relief.

This is not a remarkable story. Most women reading this have had countless similar experiences. Sadly, too many have also experienced so much worse. Harassment of and violence against women and girls is commonplace – at school, on campus, at work, on public transport, in the street, online, and even where you should feel safest, at home.

I tell it, because it needs to be told. I realise that these everyday experiences for women are often invisible to men. If worries about your own personal safety don't cross your mind when you're walking down a dark and quiet street, then you are probably a man. If you never yourself leer and shout 'bouncy, bouncy' or 'nice tits' out of your car window at a woman out for a run, or no strangers yell at you when you're exercising, you probably don't realise this everyday intrusion happens to others. If you don't use emotional and physical pressure to coerce a girlfriend into having sex then you might not understand that men who commit rape are not just faceless villains attacking women in dark alleys; they are also partners or acquaintances who don't respect the need for consent.

One obstacle to men understanding the impact of their behaviour on women in these situations is that they tend to extrapolate their own actions and behaviour to other men. If you know you are respectful of women and would not contemplate acting violently, it's hard to see yourself as a threat. But the woman walking home on a dark street a few paces ahead of you doesn't know that. All she is judging is the pace of your steps, whether the distance is decreasing, trying to assess the risk.

Violence – and the threat of violence – is one of the ways some men have exerted control over women for centuries. At the heart of this fundamental power dynamic between men and women is biology. Men's greater physical strength is exploited to force women into submission.

While anthropologists can argue about how prehistoric societies were organised because of the natural advantages bestowed on men, in the 21st century there is simply no good argument for violence being the source of power in any civilised modern society. Yet in countries around the world, in all age groups and walks of life, gender-based violence remains a significant barrier to equal power-sharing between men and women.

Young People and Education

The concept of consent is fundamental to loving, trusting, healthy relationships, yet there are worrying signs about a disregard for consent by many teens. The sending of sexually explicit messages and photos – so-called sexting – is increasingly common, and already more than a quarter of teenage girls in England say they have felt pressurised into sending these messages. The rise of 'revenge porn', where intimate images taken consensually in a relationship are then shared publicly without consent, often after a relationship breaks down, has seen the UK government change the law to make it easier to prosecute.[1] Forty per cent of teenage girls in the UK have been pressured into sex, and one in five teen relationships include physical violence.[2]

Most young women aged 13-21 will experience sexual harassment in school or at college.[3] One in five of them experience unwanted touching, and this is also a problem for younger girls, with one in ten 7-12-year-olds reporting unwanted touching. That's a significant proportion of primary school children, for heaven's sake.

In this climate, it is ridiculous that until 2017 there was no legal requirement for all schools in England and Wales to provide sex and relationships education,[4] including exploring the concept of consent. Some universities now include consent classes for new undergraduates, a move that sparked a backlash in some quarters, underlining the very nature of the problem. Warwick University student George Lawlor protested against the classes and illustrated his rant by holding up a sign saying 'This is not what a rapist looks like'.[5] But the myth that intelligent, courteous, clean-cut young men never commit rape is a dangerous one – you can't tell how someone will behave in an intimate situation just by looking at them. My own university experience included an occasion where saying no and putting up physical resistance was not sufficient to stop a 'nice young man' – the only thing that did was actually using the R-word: 'No, I don't want to and if you make me, that's rape.' And that's hardly an unusual experience.

One in four women studying at university have suffered unwanted physical sexual advances, defined as 'inappropriate touching or groping'.[6] The prevalence of rape culture creates a hostile environment for female students, documented extensively in NUS research interviews,[7] and the government is urging Universities UK to take action[8] to tackle the problem.

*

'The phrase "I'm going to put you in half" (that's "fuck you 'til you can't walk", for anyone not in touch with lad language) was a phrase constantly shouted at female sports teams, whether it was during one of our matches whilst trying to concentrate on a game of sport or on a night out accompanied by a boob grab.'

'I was on a bus once . . . a lot of lads started making quite horrific rape jokes . . . they were like "wahaay blah blah!" like firing them off. And someone made a particularly horrible one . . . and there was kind of like a mood change and one of the guys was like, "Don't worry ladies, none of us have been convicted yet!" and . . . [it was] like, "You guys just can't take the banter." And it's not banter, it's people's real lives.'[9]

Sexual assault is no laughing matter. One in ten women have been made to have sex against their will, which is seven times higher than the figure for men.[10] The impact of rape and sexual assault goes beyond the crime itself. Sara Roebuck, a student and blogger, wrote movingly about her experience in an open letter to the man who tried to rape her, published shortly after he was sentenced. Her blogpost went viral and was covered by media across the globe, from the *Huffington Post* to the *Daily Mail* (who chose to illustrate their story with a holiday snap of Sara in a bikini). Sara's powerful words are a searing insight into the relentless sexual objectification of young women in particular, and I encourage you to read her post in full on Medium.[11] I met up with Sara a few months after she wrote her piece. Over a pot of tea in the blazing spring sunshine, she explained the frustration of the 'instant stigma' she experienced, and the pressure and judgement she faced from some colleagues and friends: 'We stereotype people who are attacked.' Her advice for loved ones or colleagues supporting survivors of sexual abuse is to be calm, listen and ask how they are, and jettison any predefined expectations of how the person should react to having been attacked.

Public Spaces

Even just walking down the street in broad daylight can mean running the gauntlet of yelled 'compliments' - unsolicited assessments of various parts of your body and descriptions of what some random bloke would like to do to you sexually. And how are women expected to respond? Meeting such 'banter' with anything other than demure, 'flattered' silence can often bring a rapidly hostile exchange.

What is going through the minds of the guys shouting this? Are they really, as they often insist if challenged, meaning to pay a compliment? If so, why do they consider that, out of the blue as you're going about your business, a stranger interrupting you to say they find your body arousing and suggesting they'd like to have sex with you will be seen as welcome, not creepy and threatening? And why, once they realise that the effect has been to cause intrusion rather than leave the woman feeling good, do they go on the offensive rather than apologise?

A handy tip for anyone trying to work out whether their greeting or unsolicited comment to a woman is likely to be acceptable is to apply the test of whether you'd make a similar comment to a guy you didn't know in the same circumstances. Elon James White started the #DudesGreetingDudes hashtag, making the point eloquently on Twitter: 'You see a dude in a nice suit, just roll up on him like, "Damn. You wearing that suit. Hmm Hmm!"'

But street harassment merely underscores the wider societal problem of seeing women's value as inextricably bound up in their appearance. In itself it can range from being mildly annoying to causing significant distress, with girls or women dreading walking particular routes or even feeling compelled to change their journey. It is also invasive, because it represents a potential threat of physical violence. How does the woman know that the group of lads will stop at comments? They don't always stop there.

Poppy Smart was sick and tired of her walk to work in Worcester being interrupted by catcalls and whistles from a particular building site. One man from the site even deliberately physically blocked her route. After enduring this every day for a month, she took matters to the police and complained about harassment. Writing on her blog, she summed it up brilliantly: 'I wouldn't put up with harassment in my workplace – I'd tell my boss. I wouldn't put up with someone on the other side of a restaurant shouting over at me whilst I was trying to have some food with my family, I'd ask the staff to ask them [to] stop. So why should I put up with it in the street every day?'[12]

The police asked the builders to stop, and they did. However the media managed to whip up a firestorm, with predictable, sensationalist headlines like 'BAN WHISTLING AND YOU'LL HAVE TO

STOP GIRLS OGLING POLDARK ACTOR AND BECKHAM'[13] and 'POPPY, BE SMART AND QUIETLY SAVOUR CHEEKY FLATTERY WHILE YOU CAN'.[14] These were complemented by dinosaur quotes, like the one from Tory MP Philip Davies saying: 'I would have thought the police have better things to do. I don't know how many burglaries there are to investigate in Worcester, but there are probably quite a few. I'm sure the public would feel safer if police devoted more time to investigating them.'[15] So no need for the police to help women to feel safe on their way to work, Philip?

One of the 'lads' from the building site gave an interview where he explained that women who receive wolf whistles are 'lucky', and said of Poppy: 'I don't know why she complained, she must be thinking things above her station.'[16]

Those words 'above her station' speak volumes about the mindset at play here – that women can be judged by men for their appearance, and 'complimented' by yelling across a building site, but heaven forbid they might actually express an opinion or take control of the situation.

People's responses to the behaviour will vary, from ignoring it to pointing out that it is unacceptable. Stop Street Harassment's website lists a range of possible assertive replies. I have to say I laughed with the brilliance of one of them, which may not be applicable in all circumstances but I can think of times when it would be worth a try:

Tell the harasser that you are conducting a street harassment research project or survey. Take out a notebook and start asking them questions such as, 'How often do you do this?' or 'How do you choose which people to harass?' or 'Are you more likely to

do this when you are alone or when you're with other people?'
or 'Do you discuss people you harass with your mother, sister, or
female friends?'

Different women experience harassment differently. White, straight, cis women experience less harassment and violence than their sisters who are gay, trans, disabled or women of colour.[17] Our layered identities, visible and otherwise, play into what is said, who says it, and how we feel about it. A combination of homophobia and the appropriation by the porn industry of sex between women for the purpose of straight male stimulation often leads to particular types of abuse hurled at gay women. Trans women report street harassment turning into physical violence when catcallers recognise they are trans.[18] Our country's shameful history of slavery still reverberates today, in the racism still embedded in culture and institutions. Black women face a toxic combination of sexism laced with racism in their everyday life, including just walking down the street.

Writer and activist Feminista Jones started the hashtag #YouOKSis to highlight the problem of harassment and show a way to offer solidarity, after she intervened to support a young mother pushing a buggy who was being harassed, by simply saying, 'You okay, sis?' Such a small gesture can make a huge difference to someone being harassed. It doesn't even need to be a direct challenge to the harasser; a distraction can be just as effective, as Feminista explains: 'You can ask her for the time . . . And just by putting yourself in that space, you make the harasser aware that somebody is watching, that somebody is paying attention, that someone is conscious.'[19]

The fact that it is seen as controversial to call out street harassment shows quite how ingrained such behaviour is, in countries around the world. In 2015, Cornell University published the results of an extensive survey of more than 16,000 women in 22 countries. It found that most women first experience harassment during their teenage years. Two-thirds of German women reported being fondled or groped. Nearly nine in ten Italian women say they take a different route to their home or destination because of harassment. Four in five Canadian women reported being followed by a man or group of men.

Movements to call out and change this behaviour are growing. Hollaback! was founded in New York in 2005 by Emily May and six other young people to highlight the problem of street harassment through sharing experiences on a blog. The campaign is now active in 84 cities across 31 countries – and there's a waiting list of people wanting to receive support and training to set up groups and Hollaback! sites in many more places. As well as raising awareness and providing advice, location data is used to map incidents and inform policy-makers about the prevalence of street harassment in different areas.

Online

Harassment continues online, and is often amplified by the cloak of anonymity. I'm pretty sure many online abusers would never articulate their vile threats face to face, but a random Twitter handle, 12 followers and an egg avatar seem to be all they need to give them virtual bravado.

Dealing with online misogyny is part of the daily experience for women in the public eye – whether sportswomen, journalists, politicians, actors, academics or campaigners – and indeed for anyone who dares to put their head above the parapet and advocate equality.

Australian campaigner Coralie Alison came under fire for objecting to a forthcoming tour by US rapper Tyler, The Creator, whose misogynistic lyrics include: 'Keep that bitch locked up in my storage/Rape her and record it,' and, 'You call this shit rape but I think that rape's fun . . . I just got one request, stop breathin'.'

Coralie wrote to the Immigration Minister to revoke the rapper's visa. Before any decision was made on the visa, Tyler, The Creator tweeted his then 2.5 million followers to say he had been banned, and blamed Coralie Alison. The abuse flooded in.[20]

@CoralieAlison Take a thick rope and put it around your neck and go for a 1080 suicide off the Golden Gate Bridge . . .
@CoralieAlison drink bleach and die slut
@CoralieAlison I want you to put a toothpick in your vagina, then thrust a wall as hard as you can.

People sent more than 2,000 abusive tweets in this vein to Coralie, over 48 hours. When she tweeted that Twitter were now taking action,[21] she was accused of attention seeking and some said she deserved the abuse: 'You literally deserve every bit and more. Censorship is never okay.'

This is no isolated incident. In January 2014, Isabella Sorley and John Nimmo were jailed for tweeting abuse and rape threats to Caroline Criado-Perez, for daring to campaign for Jane Austen to appear on UK banknotes.[22] On a happier note, Caroline's campaign was successful, with the Jane Austen tenner first appearing in 2017.

In 2015, at a meeting of Parliament's Backbench Business Committee, MP Jess Phillips expressed her view that Parliament did not need to hold a special debate for International Men's Day. Sickening online abuse followed. One online commenter wrote: 'He should have asked her to kindly shut the fuck up or he'd rape her in front of everyone', while another continued: 'You know what would be funny. Pouring molten iron down this cunt's cunt until she starts vomiting . . . [people like her] deserve to be bound up in a basement and repeatedly raped. I think watching her spirit die . . . would be a really rewarding experience. Remove the eyes last.'[23]

Diane Abbott has spoken out about the truly shocking and horrific level of abuse she receives, in emails and letters – sometimes including vile images and swastikas. One example she gave was: 'Pathetic useless fat black piece of shit Abbott. Just a piece of pig shit pond slime who should be fucking hung (if they could find a tree big enough to take the fat bitch's weight).'[24] One of her staff has said that what surprised them most about the job was how often they have to read the N-word.

Amnesty International research found that Diane Abbott receives almost a third of all abuse sent to women MPs – and on average was getting more than 50 abusive tweets a day in the run-up to the last general election. Black and Asian women MPs receive 35 per cent more online abuse than their white women colleagues.[25]

Although the stories that make the headlines often relate to high-profile politicians or celebrities, abuse is common across the Internet against women from all walks of life. Having an opinion is enough to make you a target. Yet the online anonymity cloak and lack of police resources mean that online harassers rarely face judicial consequences.

Public Spaces

Just catching the bus or train to and from work or school can have consequences for women's safety. Major cities all around the world have this problem. A survey of nearly 1,800 New York subway users found that, overall, more than nine in ten women had experienced sexual harassment on the subway system.[26] And a disturbing new trend has seen men AirDrop penis pictures directly onto the phones of unsuspecting women in the same carriage.[27]

Complaints led transport authorities in Boston to run anti-groping advertisements, with the strapline 'Rub against me and I'll expose you', and the initiative was later expanded to other cities, including Chicago, Washington DC and New York.

The Toronto-based Metropolitan Action Committee on Violence Against Women and Children pioneered the Safety Audit process, now much more widely used, for tapping into the experiences of local women to identify what physical changes could be made to improve safety in their area.

In 2004, Transport for London published a Women's Action Plan, with a range of steps to improve safety, from installing Help Points in stations, to CCTV on buses, and real-time arrival information on electronic displays at thousands of bus stops that is also available online, by text and on free apps.

In 2015, the French government launched a plan of action to tackle harassment on public transport, including easier reporting, an awareness campaign about the potential £75,000 fine and prison sentences for harassers, a crackdown on sexist advertising, and allowing buses to drop passengers between stops so they are closer to their home.[28]

Women-only transit has been another response to the problem – for example, in cities in Japan, India and Mexico –[29] though it is rather an admission of defeat about what can be expected in the other carriages. When UK Labour party leader Jeremy Corbyn raised the suggestion during 2015 that he would look into the idea of women-only train carriages, there was a public outcry. The journalist Fleet Street Fox nailed the basic problem with the approach:

> If you have one carriage which is just for women, in order to protect them, then any women who sit on the rest of the train are by definition inviting attack. It would take the medieval and ridiculous idea that women are somehow 'asking for it' when they are assaulted to a new, state-endorsed level of silly. Where do women go when the women-only carriage is full? What happens in rush hour? What if they don't want to be segregated, or naively expect most male passengers not to rape them?[30]

It is an appalling state of affairs when some women feel the only way to feel safe is to withdraw from general public space and restrict where they go. If separate carriages are seen as the only way to stop women being groped, harassed and sexually assaulted on public transport, the message is clear – men own the public space.

The savage gang rape and murder of an Indian student on a Delhi bus in December 2012 shocked the world.[31] Jyoti Singh was travelling home one evening from the cinema with a male friend. A group of six men beat the 23-year-old and took turns to rape her, then violently assaulted her internally with a rusted iron bar. They attacked her friend and knocked him unconscious when he tried to intervene. Jyoti Singh later died from her horrific injuries in hospital. Protestors took to the streets in their thousands to demand change. Six new fast-track courts were introduced to hear rape cases, and new laws were passed against sexual harassment and stalking. Jyoti Singh's attackers were arrested and convicted,[32] but this is very much the exception – of the 706 rape cases filed in New Delhi in 2012, this was the only one to result in a conviction.[33] Speaking two years after the attack, the victim's father said, 'Nothing in India has changed.'[34]

Documentary-maker Leslee Udwin interviewed some of the attackers, and her findings were chilling. One of the men convicted of this rape and murder, Mukesh Singh, said, 'A decent girl won't roam around at nine o'clock at night. A girl is far more responsible for rape than a boy … Housework and housekeeping is for girls, not roaming in discos and bars at night doing wrong things, wearing wrong clothes. About 20 per cent of girls are good … When being raped, she shouldn't fight back. She should just be silent and allow the rape.'[35]

It's easy to sit in Europe or the United States and think this kind of problem is foreign - something horrific that happens elsewhere, not here. Yet the per capita reported incidence of rape is more than ten times higher in the US than India.[36] Even taking into account differences in the likelihood of reporting such crimes in different countries, there is no room for complacency anywhere. One in 20 women in the UK have been raped.[37]

In the Home

Our intimate relationships are where we should feel safest; our home should be a place of sanctuary. For too many, abuse in these relationships means the home is a place of fear. Controlling and coercive behaviour was finally recognised as abuse in England and Wales in 2015. This crime covers a range of ways in which someone may control their partner: financial control, isolating them from friends, controlling where they go and who they can see, monitoring their communications, threats, and damaging their property.[38] Early prosecution[39] and police investigation data shows the problem is disproportionately one of men controlling women.[40]

Across the UK, around 100 women are killed each year by their partner or ex-partner.[41, 42] That's two women a week - a shocking figure. Globally, three in ten women will experience sexual or physical violence by their partner.[43] While the rates do vary in different parts of the world, in no region is it less than one in four women: in the words of Dr Margaret Chan, Director-General of the World Health Organization, 'Violence against women is a global health problem of epidemic proportions.'[44]

Children are also impacted - often present in the same

or next room as the violent acts, and themselves directly harmed in a majority of households where domestic violence is happening. The psychological effects can be severe, and can last a lifetime, contributing to a cycle of yet more violence in the home.

Reporting of partner violence is low, not surprising when the response from public authorities has been so patchy. Not that long ago, police would trivialise abuse within the home as 'just a domestic', or see it as something where public services should not interfere. It has been estimated that women will endure on average 35 episodes of violence from their partner before reporting it.[45]

Disabled women can find their condition used against them in abuse, and are more likely to experience sexual violence and financial abuse. A lack of accessible refuge spaces and support services can make it much harder to escape. As one such victim said of her ordeal: 'Oh yes, he would drag me along the floor because I couldn't walk or get away – that was how it would start, the way it always went. He'd insult me with all those names, "you spassy" and so on, "who'd want to marry you?" And he smashed me against the wall, shouting insults, "you cripple", all that sort of thing.'[46]

Meanwhile Asian and Muslim women can find cultural expectations that they should suffer in silence, and when they seek advice from family they may be told that they are to blame for the problem, or they should patiently wait for it to improve. They may be at greater risk of forced marriage or 'honour-based' violence, and also experience greater social stigma or taboos in speaking up about these crimes.[47] More than 11,000 so-called honour-based crimes – an oxymoron if ever there was one; as family members beat, imprison or even kill their daughter or sister for some 'transgression' – took place across the UK in 2010–14.[48]

In the UK, the Forced Marriage Unit was set up to support people at risk; it deals with more than 1,400 cases a year. Four in five of those are women, from right across the length and breadth of the country. Almost one in ten of these relate to people with learning disabilities.[49]

Behind the statistics of domestic violence, of course, are the individual lives destroyed. In 2009, 36-year-old Clare Wood was raped, strangled and set on fire by her former partner George Appleton. He had a history of violence and harassment, and had kidnapped a former girlfriend at knifepoint. The case was not only tragic, it was preventable. Clare's devastated father, Michael Brown, campaigned to change the law. He kindly agreed to speak to me about his experience:

> I don't know if it was the timing of my daughter's death, the manner of my daughter's death, or the publicity my daughter's death got, but it was like a snowball rolling down the hill. It just gathered momentum. I was handed a baton I couldn't put down . . . If I had said no, all I was doing was condemning other parents to experience exactly what I did. I didn't think I could be hurt that way . . . It just put me in a spiral of depression. When I came out of that, I realised that for every girl that was killed, there was two like me – parents. And that was without brothers and sisters, or uncles and aunties, grandmas and grandads . . . It was like dropping a pebble into the water, the rings just touched everybody . . . I got to the age of 67 before domestic violence showed its face in my life. When you find out how prevalent it

is, when I found out what was going on in this country, as a man I was really appalled. For the police to tell you there's anything between 25,000 and 50,000 well-known predators on the national database ... these people aren't just harming the partner if they're in a family circumstance, they're harming the kids as well. And it goes on and on, and it costs the country billions.

His campaign took almost three years, building support from the coroner, police, Parliament and the Home Secretary. The result is 'Clare's Law', which came into force in England and Wales in 2014, and in Scotland in 2015. People can now ask police if their partner has a history of domestic violence. In the case of vulnerable people, police have a duty to inform them proactively about a partner's violent record.

State-sanctioned Violence

Safety within intimate relationships cannot be taken for granted. It should not be controversial to say that consent is a vitally important element of any sexual relationship, yet until relatively recently, laws in many countries meant that no offence was committed when a husband raped his wife. Some countries explicitly outlawed marital rape more than 50 years ago – for example, Poland in 1932, the Soviet Union in 1960, Sweden in 1965. Some parts of Europe were much later – Scotland in 1989, England and Wales in 1991, Finland in 1994, and Germany not until 1997. Nearly 20 other African states have followed the lead of South Africa,[50] where a law was passed in 1993 making clear that husbands could be convicted of the rape of their wife.

However, Nigeria, Ethiopia and Kenya still have an exemption for husbands and there are many countries where marital rape is legal. Singapore and India both have a specific legal immunity for husbands who rape their wives.[51]

In the developing world, a third of girls are married before their 18th birthday, and more than one in ten are married under the age of 15.[52] In countries like Niger and Bangladesh, as many as three in four girls are married before they are 18. Child marriage often leads to reduced education opportunities, sexual abuse, and complications in childbirth for girls whose bodies are not ready for labour. In developing countries, complications in childbirth are the leading cause of death for young women aged 15–19.[53]

Gender-based violence within the home environment goes beyond rape and domestic abuse, and extends to daughters as well as wives and partners. Around the world each year, three million young girls are at risk of being cut – that is, parts of their labia and/or clitoris being removed in a distressing and barbaric procedure, often conducted without anaesthetic, which causes pain, leaves girls prone to infection and can result in complications for menstruation, urination, sexual intercourse and childbirth. This practice is known as female genital mutilation, or FGM. Here is how Waris Dirie describes her experience in her book, *Desert Flower*:

I peered between my legs and saw the gypsy. The old woman looked at me sternly, a dead look in her eyes, then foraged through an old carpet-bag. She reached inside with her long fingers and fished out a broken razor blade. I saw dried blood on the jagged edge. She spit on it and wiped it on her dress. While she was scrubbing, my world went dark as Mama tied a blindfold over my eyes.

The next thing I felt was my flesh being cut away. I heard the blade sawing back and forth through my skin. The feeling was indescribable. I didn't move, telling myself the more I did, the longer the torture would take. Unfortunately, my legs began to quiver and shake uncontrollably of their own accord, and I prayed, Please, God, let it be over quickly. Soon it was, because I passed out.

When I woke up, my blindfold was off and I saw the gypsy woman had piled a stack of thorns from an acacia tree next to her. She used these to puncture holes in my skin, then poked a strong white thread through the holes to sew me up. My legs were completely numb, but the pain between them was so intense that I wished I would die.

My memory ends at that instant, until I opened my eyes and the woman was gone. My legs had been tied together with strips of cloth binding me from my ankles to my hips so I couldn't move. I turned my head toward the rock; it was drenched with blood as if an animal had been slaughtered there. Pieces of my flesh lay on top, drying in the sun. [54]

In 2012, the UN General Assembly passed a resolution to intensify global efforts to stamp out FGM, urging countries to enact and enforce laws against it, to protect girls and take measures to change cultural attitudes that tolerate the practice.[55] Nevertheless, it is still practised in countries including Yemen, Iraq and Indonesia.[56] Even in countries with strong measures in place to combat FGM, girls are at risk of being taken abroad to be cut.

At the age of seven, Nimco Ali was taken from Manchester to Djibouti on holiday, where she was cut. Now 34, she is using her experience to protect girls of the next generation. She co-founded the charity Daughters of Eve, and told her story publicly at the Women of the World Festival at London's Southbank Centre. Her campaigning work helped to catapult the issue up the political agenda: International Development Minister Lynne Featherstone unveiled significant resources for research and programmes to end FGM within a generation,[57] and the UK hosted the Girl Summit in 2014, which secured international commitments to tackle the issue. Importantly, Nimco has also succeeded in breaking the cycle in her own family – her niece and cousin, aged six and nine, will not be cut.

The Weapon of Rape

Given the sense of entitlement over women's bodies that we see displayed openly and in public in peaceful, democratic societies where the rule of law is generally respected, it is not surprising that where order breaks down, violence against women and girls escalates. It is not only the result of men looking for sexual gratification and availing themselves of the 'spoils of war' – appalling though that is in itself. Rape and sexual assault are also used systematically as a weapon of war, to demonstrate power and control, to terrorise and humiliate a population, and as a form of ethnic cleansing. The former commander of UN peacekeeping forces in eastern Congo, Major General Patrick

Cammaert, explained the devastating impact: 'You destroy communities. You punish the men, and you punish the women, doing it in front of the men . . . It has probably become more dangerous to be a woman than a soldier in armed conflict.'[58]

I find it beyond comprehension the sickening acts one human being can inflict on another – seeing enemies as subhuman, the vile creativity of punishment. Women Under Siege is a journalism project set up to document the prevalence of rape and sexual violence against women in conflict situations, bringing together sources from media outlets like the BBC and NGOs such as Oxfam and Amnesty International. The testimonies they have collected from survivors make for difficult reading.

Sixteen-year-old Vumiliar Lukindo spoke about her rape in DR Congo: 'Four men took me. They all raped me. At that time I was nine months pregnant. They gang-raped me and pushed sticks up my vagina – that's when my baby died – they said it was better than killing me.'[59]

Perpetrators torture whole families with rape, such as the horror inflicted on this woman and her family from DR Congo: 'The soldiers arrived and brought my daughter to our house where they raped her in the presence of my husband and me. Afterwards they demanded that my husband rape my daughter but he refused so they shot him. Then they went into the other house where they found my three sons. They killed all three of my boys. After killing them, two soldiers raped me one after the other.'[60]

Children are not excluded – in fact, sometimes the opposite, as 17-year-old Miranda witnessed in a rape camp in Bosnia: 'There were women from various towns and villages. There were more than 1,000 of us. I spent more than four months in that camp.

It is a nightmare that cannot be talked about, or described, or understood . . . Sometimes I think that I will go crazy and that the nightmare will never end. Every night in my dreams I see the face of Stojan, the camp guard. He was the most ruthless among them. He even raped 10-year-old girls, as a delicacy. Most of those girls didn't survive. They murdered many girls, slaughtered them like cattle. I want to forget everything. I cannot live with these memories. I will go insane.'[61]

In many cultures, victims of rape suffer an additional sentence following the crime, as they are seen as dishonoured, or guilty, like this woman in Burma: 'The soldier grabbed me and kicked my legs until I fell to the ground. Then he grabbed my legs. I tried to escape, but he was stronger than I am. He raped me for an hour and a half. When my husband came home (after the rape), I told him what had happened. He was furious at me and beat me. The relationship between me and my husband suffered tremendously as a result of the rape. Every day, my husband and children would say, "Prostitute! If you want to sell sex, we will build you a small hut in the jungle. You can sell sex there."'[62]

The warped ideology of ISIS has even tried to construct a theological case for raping children. In 2014, the attack on the Yazidi population at Sinjar bore signs of a chilling planned bureaucracy which captured thousands of women and forced them to become sex slaves - in the process, boosting ISIS coffers. Buses were laid on to transport the women and girls to huge processing centres, where details were taken and information logged about each individual before they were sent to slave auctions to be sold.[63]

One 34-year-old Yazidi woman, who was captured and raped by a Saudi fighter in Syria, described the horrors inflicted on a

12-year-old girl slave in the same household who was raped for days on end despite heavy bleeding and infection: 'I said to him, "She's just a little girl." And he answered: "No. She's not a little girl. She's a slave. And she knows exactly how to have sex. And having sex with her pleases God."'[64]

These women – and millions more like them – have endured almost inconceivable horrors. But while the scale and intensity of these crimes is massive, they share a common foundation with the daily domestic abuse and violence against women in societies which are not torn apart by war. The fundamental lack of respect for women in societies right across the world is the core issue, encapsulated in the words this Colombian woman heard from the man who raped her: 'He threatened to kill me if I resisted. He took off my clothes, he covered my mouth and he forced himself on me. He raped me. Afterward he told me to get dressed and then he said: "Nothing happened here. That, after all, is what women are for."'[65]

As long as women are viewed as sexual objects whose role is subservient to the pleasure of men; as long as women are judged and valued for how they look instead of what they do; then women will be abused, including in some of the worst ways imaginable.

Modern Slavery

Exploiting women sexually is used as a route to power – whether social or economic. The vile modern slave trade is big business, with forced labour estimated as a $150 billion industry worldwide.[66] The United Nations estimates that 21 million people are victims of modern slavery at any one time. Over half of the victims are women or girls, and more than a quarter are children.[67] Ninety-eight per cent of those forced into sexual exploitation are women.[68]

Modern slavery victims are also brutalised with physical violence and emotional manipulation. Sreypov Chan, who was sold into slavery in Cambodia as a seven-year-old girl, has told of being bound and covered in biting ants, being whipped with electric cables, and being given electric shocks if she didn't meet her 'quota' of men for the day. When she refused her first client, the pimp crushed up hot chilli peppers and pushed them into her vagina, then thrust a hot metal poker inside her.[69]

How can someone do that to anyone, let alone a seven-year-old child?

Sreypov eventually escaped after three years, and now works on a project to rescue other girls sold into sex slavery. The testimony she hears from those she helps shows that her story is all too common.

Sometimes in the West we imagine that such horrors only happen elsewhere. Yet Megan Stephens[70] wrote in her book *Bought & Sold* how as a vulnerable 14-year-old on holiday in Greece she was trafficked into the sex industry. She told the *Guardian,* 'They [the men] were queuing up outside. There were 10 to 15 rooms in the same place and it's just . . . literally, you don't stop . . . If I did 40 to 50 people, that would be nothing. It wasn't enough.' Regular violence, threats to kill her mother and emotional abuse created a dependency from which she could not escape, which was only broken when she was sectioned for three months in a Greek hospital and confided in the staff.

Thousands of women each year are trafficked from West Africa to Europe and forced into prostitution,[71] and many girls and young women are groomed or trafficked for sexual exploitation within countries like the UK and US as well. Pimps and traffickers are responsible for this misery, of course. The clients of women and children who are forced to sell their bodies are also guilty of rape, morally at least. Ignorance is no excuse. Regardless of whether money changes hands, people bear their own responsibility for ensuring that any sexual partner consents to the activity.

Using Your Power to Create Change

Researching, writing and reading about these horrors takes us to a dark place. Nowhere near as dark as for the people who are living the nightmare of course, but nonetheless, it can feel too much to process, too difficult to comprehend, too sickening to contemplate.

Violence against women and girls is not a separate problem from the challenges of economic inequality, or the warped media representation of women – it's all part of the same issue.

Men are victims of violence too, but to ignore the gendered elements of these types of violence against women is to be blind to a root cause and prevents us from understanding how to create workable solutions. Four in five victims of forced marriage are women.[72] Four in five of those killed by a partner or former partner are women.[73] Women are more likely to suffer repeated and more severe incidents of domestic abuse than men.[74] Better support should be provided for male victims, as well as for female victims. But recognising the needs of male victims should not stop us also recognising the gendered nature of these crimes against women.

Violence against women and girls is not inevitable. It can be stopped, and stopping it must be our aim. We need to recognise that the roots of this violence are in the wider power imbalance between men and women in society,[75] in the sense of male entitlement to supremacy, in the objectification of women as if they exist for the sexual gratification of men.

The abuse of women is a symptom of our unequal society, and also a cause. It is a destructive cycle: where women are beaten, raped and forced into subservience to men, their unequal status is reinforced in the minds of the next generation.

In the same way, taking steps to prevent and challenge violence against women chips away at, and starts to change, the underlying sexist attitudes about the value of women in society. There are many ways you can take action:

- **RAISE AWARENESS:** In conversations with friends, family or colleagues, and on social media, you can spread information about these issues. Drawing attention to information from campaign organisations on everything from female genital mutilation to consent within teenage relationships (check out the Disrespect Nobody campaign[76]) is a useful and practical way to increase awareness.

- **LISTEN AND SHARE EXPERIENCES**: It's important to understand the violence people endure, especially when their lived experiences are different from yours. So why not start by seeking out views online and asking questions to understand better the perspectives of others – young and old, people of colour, LGBTQ, disabled women and other marginalised groups especially. The power of your own experience is significant. Sharing this with those close to you can be one of the most effective ways of increasing awareness and understanding. If you would rather remain anonymous, there are websites like everydaysexism.com where you do not have to be named.

- **VOLUNTEER:** Give time or money to help a cause. There are large numbers of charities and campaign organisations that work to combat gendered violence, and they are usually underfunded and poorly resourced. You could look up your local domestic abuse refuge or choose one of the national organisations listed at the end of this chapter, and make a donation. You could organise a fundraising event. Or ask how you could give your time, and be creative – if you're an accountant, you could take on the role of treasurer or audit their accounts; if you have good research skills you may be able to help them evaluate the success of a project or assist with a funding bid. Refuges also welcome donations of toys, clothes, toiletries, make-up and sanitary products for the people who may arrive having fled with few possessions. For obvious reasons, they don't tend to publish their address, but if you contact them they will often have an office where donations can be dropped off.
- **PARENTAL ADVISORY:** Parents have an important role to play in shaping the views and actions of their children. As teenagers navigate their changing bodies and emotions, they need to understand the importance of consent within sexual relationships, and how to recognise abuse, whether in their own or their friends' relationships. While parents will understandably want to put in place measures to reduce the likelihood of their

children seeing pornography, it's naive to imagine that young people will not encounter it at all. Online porn is often extreme compared to what would have been easily accessible in the 20th century. Parents need to help young people understand that loving, consensual sex bears no resemblance to most of the sex depicted on the Internet. Helping children understand about consent starts from the very beginning, both in their behaviour towards other children and being able to decide about their own body – if your infant does not want to kiss Grandma, don't force them. Encourage them to blow a kiss or wave goodbye instead.[77]

- **CITIZEN POWER:** At election time, ask your candidates what they plan to do to address violence against women and girls. Look at the manifestos published by groups campaigning on the issues, with specific asks for policy-makers that you could refer to. Even when there isn't an election on, raising these issues with your MP helps keep the pressure on, and even more so if it is as part of a wider campaign, so that lots of people are raising the same subject around the same time. Local councils control many of the budgets for domestic abuse refuges, which are too often seen as an easy target when cuts need to be made. That's partly because hardly anyone contacts their local councillor about the importance of the local domestic abuse refuge, compared to an issue like potholes on the roads. You can change that, by doing something as simple as sending an email.

- **CALL IT OUT**: As friends, we can make a real difference. Listening to a friend who has experienced or is experiencing violence can help her feel supported in her decisions. Every case will be different but you can provide emotional and practical support – Women's Aid has helpful advice on how to raise the issue sensitively and provide help.[78] Peer pressure is powerful, so friends also have an important role to play in calling out and stopping harassment and violent behaviour. Instead of staying quiet if your mate shouts at a woman across the street, or makes a rape 'joke', have the courage to stand up to him and say it's not right.

- **BE A BETTER BYSTANDER:** I love the Hollaback! campaign's pledge and simple tips on this.[79] Most people feel deeply uncomfortable if they witness harassment whether in person or online, but are paralysed into inaction by uncertainty about how to intervene safely. The first principle is to check in with the person experiencing the harassment – which you could do privately if it's online – to see if they'd welcome support. Confronting the harasser by making clear their behaviour is not okay is one way to intervene, but depending on the circumstances – and always bearing in mind your own safety – there are other ways to help, too. A distraction can work well, so just asking the person being harassed for directions, or what the time is, may be enough to interrupt and stop the harassment. Or you might enlist an official or member of staff to deal with the problem, depending where you are. Even a knowing look or asking the person if they are okay after the event can make a big difference, reducing the feeling of isolation. Online assistance can include offering to screenshot and report the harassment on their behalf. If someone is receiving a lot of online abuse, another way to help is to make a Storify of all the positive comments so the person can see the support they have received without trawling through abuse.

- **EYES AND EARS:** ASC (Ask Support Care) is a training programme run for medical professionals, emergency workers, hairdressers and others, to help them spot signs of domestic abuse and feel confident offering support in the best way.[80] Taxi drivers and hotel workers can help by being informed about modern slavery and look out for signs of people at risk – as taxis and hotels are sometimes used to transport and abuse victims. Brenda, an activist in Liverpool, designed helpline stickers for cabs and information leaflets for drivers so they know what to do if they are suspicious. The local authority now issues the stickers along with taxi licences – why not ask your local council to follow suit?[81] In some areas, campaigners have organised coffee breaks for local taxi drivers to spread the word. Stephen, a London campaigner, visited his local hotels with a door-hanger information leaflet from the Stop the Traffik campaign, to encourage them to undertake staff training and raise awareness with guests to spot the signs of people at risk.[82]

- **MAKE SCHOOLS SAFE FOR EVERYONE:** Teachers and those working in the education system can check that issues of consent and abuse in relationships are explored in the curriculum, and ask whether the policies on harassment are sufficient, up-to-date and properly followed. Adults in education settings can make a difference by taking concerns seriously when they are reported – yet more than three in five secondary school girls say that teachers sometimes or always tell girls to ignore harassment behaviour at school.[83] Taking harassment seriously is obviously important for protecting young people and creating a positive environment for learning, but it has wider impact, too: young people are at a formative stage, developing their understanding of what is acceptable behaviour. If groping and harassment are treated as a 'joke' and not responded to with any sanction, then everyone will come to believe this is normal behaviour. There are many free resources to support teachers dealing with these issues – such as Hollaback!'s pack for educators on street harassment,[84] the PSHE Association's advice on teaching about consent,[85] and the Disrespect Nobody website. Teachers may spot signs of concern, or be confided in about issues of sexual violence, female genital mutilation,[86] or forced marriage[87] – being aware of the issues, listening to the young person, and using the available guidance to respond, can prevent harm and save lives.

- **EMPLOYER ACTION:** Employers have a responsibility to create a workplace where staff can get on with their jobs in safety and without threats of violence. Violence has an impact on business: domestic abuse costs UK businesses £1.9 billion a year through reduced productivity and absences.[88] Challenging sexist behaviour in the workplace is important, as is responding swiftly and seriously to allegations of harassment. It can help to have a clear policy setting out that harassment is unacceptable and how any complaints will be dealt with. Organisations like Acas provide free guidance and advice for employers on issues like this.[89] Employers should think proactively about how to support their employees who might be experiencing harassment on their journey to work,[90] or those who are dealing with a violent partner.[91]

- **REFLECT ON OUR OWN BEHAVIOUR:** Wherever we live in the world, we've all grown up and live in a society where violence against women happens with worrying regularity.

We need to be aware of how our own views, comments and behaviour impact on the problem. Use respectful language, avoid misgendering people, and don't walk intimidatingly close to others, especially if they're on their own late at night. Breaking down the victim-blaming myths is important – more than a third of people still believe that victims of sexual assault are partly responsible for the crime if they have been drinking, using drugs or flirting.[92] How many times in conversations about domestic abuse does someone ask: 'Why doesn't she just leave?' The sobering statistics about women killed by their ex-partners demonstrate one reason why, for many abused women, it isn't a simple decision. The sheer numbers of girls and women reporting some degree of pressuring or coercion into sex suggest that respect for consent is not what it should be: is the memory of sexual behaviour witnessed or practised as young men the reason why fathers are often so protective of their daughters in this regard? There are many men in our communities who are abusing their partners right now. They can change, and recognising the behaviour is wrong is the first step. The charity Respect runs programmes for perpetrators of domestic violence, which are successful in achieving a significant reduction in violence and partners feeling much safer.[93]

- **TAKE THE WHITE RIBBON PLEDGE:** The White Ribbon campaign is a global movement to end male violence against women. Men and boys are a crucial part of the solution, and so far more than 30,000 in the UK have signed up to say: 'I pledge never to commit, condone, or remain silent about men's violence against women in all its forms.' You can sign up online at whiteribbon.org.uk

- **CAMPAIGN FOR CHANGE:** Michael Brown succeeded in making Clare's Law a reality, honouring his daughter's life by protecting other women from attack. If you identify a big change you think should happen, why not build a team to campaign for it? You'll need to demonstrate the need for change, show why the specific action you propose would work, and grow support for the idea. Securing buy-in from high-profile or influential people helps – in Michael's case, his local radio station, his MP and then the Home Secretary. The media can be used positively to raise awareness and create pressure for change. It can take time, and there's no guarantees, but changes only happen when people make them happen. As Michael told me:

To get the result that we did was phenomenal, and not just to get it, to see the impact it's having. In the year it was rolled out in Manchester we saved potentially 300 women . . . We never looked back, we looked forward. We were encouraged everywhere we went . . . I didn't get where I am without Michelle Livesey [Key103 journalist], Hazel Blears [MP], Theresa May [Home Secretary] and Jennifer Leeming [coroner] at my back and encouraging me. There's lots of people who don't get the publicity that I got or my daughter's death got, who are doing wonderful jobs out there. Keep doing it. Eventually somebody's going to listen.

Further information and resources

- Hollaback! – an international campaign against harassment in public spaces http://www.ihollaback.org/
- Refuge – a charity working against domestic violence http://www.refuge.org.uk/
- Women's Aid – a UK charity campaigning against domestic violence http://www.womensaid.org.uk/
- White Ribbon Campaign – men campaigning to tackle violence against women http://www.whiteribbon.org.uk
- Rape Crisis – specialist services for women and girls who have experienced sexual violence http://rapecrisis.org.uk/ (England & Wales); http://www.rapecrisisscotland.org.uk/ (Scotland)
- Center for Relationship Abuse Awareness – a US organisation working to prevent and educate about relationship and sexual abuse http://stoprelationshipabuse.org/
- Disrespect Nobody – a UK Government campaign to tackle abuse in teen relationships https://www.disrespectnobody.co.uk
- End Violence Against Women – a coalition of organisations and individuals working to end all forms of violence against women http://www.endviolenceagainstwomen.org.uk/
- Respect – a UK charity working with perpetrators to end domestic violence http://respect.uk.net/
- Equality and Human Rights Commission – UK statutory body for challenging discrimination and promoting human rights http://www.equalityhumanrights.com/
- Stop Rape Now – UN action against sexual violence in conflict http://www.stoprapenow.org/
- Women Under Siege – US journalism project to investigate rape in conflict situations http://www.womenundersiegeproject.org/
- Stop the Traffik – an international campaign to prevent human trafficking http://www.stopthetraffik.org/

9

MEN:
Equal Power
is a Win-Win

'What about men?' is the half question, half accusation frequently flung at anyone raising the issue of women's equality. It's neatly summed up by the graph on the following page, which shows Internet searches for the phrase 'International Men's Day'. This day has been marked annually on 19 November since 1999, yet while we see small spikes in searches for the term in November, they are dwarfed by the frantic googling of the words in March, around the time of International Women's Day.

While many of these searches will be innocent random keyboard musings along the lines of 'I wonder if there's a similar day for men?', there is also a band of people who are eager to cry foul on behalf of men whenever anyone campaigns to improve the lives of women. Imagine what could be achieved if the same people poured their energy into constructive work to make progress on the important issues affecting men . . .

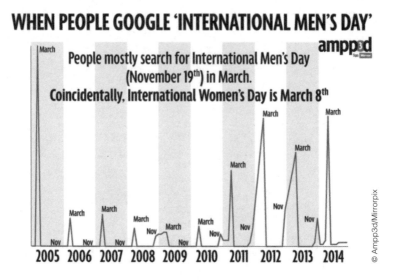

WHEN PEOPLE GOOGLE 'INTERNATIONAL MEN'S DAY'

ampp3d

People mostly search for International Men's Day (November 19th) in March.
Coincidentally, International Women's Day is March 8th

© Ampp3d/Mirrorpix

The 'battle of the sexes' rhetoric invites us to imagine that gender equality is a zero-sum game: if women achieve more power, men will have less, which will inevitably be bad for men.

I wholeheartedly disagree. A world where power is shared more equally is better for everyone. Economies do better when they tap into the skills and talents of both women and men. Concentrations of power are damaging, a magnet for corruption and oppression, and so dispersing power more widely makes for better functioning and more efficient societies. At the family level, power and responsibility often go hand in hand, so sharing power also means sharing the burden of responsibility: a productive partnership of equals.

We've explored how society's expectations of gender are harmful to women and girls – threatening their safety, taking a toll on their physical and mental health, and restricting their opportunities. These expectations also harm men and boys.

The rigid requirements of masculinity in our society present a narrow view of being a man. Not all men and boys are comfortable with stereotypical, unemotional, arrogant alpha-maleness. Yet in the absence of richer, more nuanced visions of masculinity, many laugh along with the laddish 'bants', suffer in silence when their health takes a hit, or feel self-conscious if someone else's child falls near them and needs comforting in the playpark.

As a political candidate and then MP, I became aware of one significant advantage of being a young woman. Knocking on doors, elderly people opened them without feeling physically threatened. Visiting nursery schools, I joined in playing with the infants without worrying about how it might look. When a woman cried in my advice surgery I instinctively squeezed her hand. In all of these scenarios, my male colleagues had a different calculation and mental risk assessment to make, because of society's assumptions about – and sometimes suspicion of – men.

Better Sex

'Hello, my name is Martin Daubney, and I'm a wanker.' It was certainly a memorable introduction. How very self-aware, I thought. For eight years, Martin edited *Loaded* magazine, known for its titillating photoshoots of scantily clad models, its sensationalist cover stories about sex ('My missus beds seven men a day', 'I'm shagging twins') and its encouragement of blokes to be wankers in all senses of the word.[1] I was on a mission to understand the lad culture that causes such damage to young women, and so – in the name of research – I had arranged to meet Martin for a chat.

I confess I was surprised by him during our discussion in All Bar One on Regent Street. We had rescheduled the time and location as Martin had been doing an interview at the BBC about research that showed men want to spend more time with their children. Looking dapper in his TV outfit of a three-piece suit, talking passionately about the perils of porn and the delights of fatherhood, he seemed a far cry from the boorish loafer dubbed 'King of the Lads', whose magazine had fostered such disrespect for women in the noughties.[2] Like many provocateurs, he manages to be way more reasonable in real life over a cup of tea than his Twitter persona suggests. He has certainly been on a journey, prompted by his desire to become a dad and accelerated by researching a Channel 4 documentary on porn.

Listening to young people talk about the impact of porn on their lives had clearly shocked and moved Martin. He told me what he'd heard. The young woman who said, 'If I get another guy who doesn't do foreplay and goes straight for my arse, and wants to come in my face, I'm gonna scream.' The young men 'reared on porn' who had messed up their exams, or lost their job, or had a relationship meltdown through their addiction to watching porn. Or the young men who thought watching porn would make them great in bed, and instead found themselves unable to get a hard-on because of physical insecurities, and the real world not living up to their porn fantasy. He told me about the time he was in the car with a porn addict, who saw a girl in tight shorts and suddenly had to stop driving and go and masturbate in the toilets of a pub.

I wanted to understand this perspective better. I'd been well aware of how the ubiquity of wham-bam-don't-care-if-you-want-it-ma'am sex in porn is damaging for young women, but I hadn't fully considered quite how negative it is for young men, too. From the body image pressure to look like male porn stars, to difficulties enjoying real sex in the context of a loving relationship, the porn industry is doing no favours to men either. And of course, at the end of the day, it's all about money, and what Daubney calls the 'cynical manipulation of young men' to turn them into paying customers, either through webcam sex or links with escort agencies and prostitution in the offline world.

While almost half of young men say porn helps them learn about sex, young women overwhelmingly disagree. Seven in ten young people think porn can damage their view of sex and relationships.[3] With a gaping hole in our education system where good-quality, up-to-date and relevant sex and relationships education should be, we are letting down all young people.

The Dangerous Constraints of Masculinity

Comedian Jake Mills struggled for years with the idea of 'being a man'. You could hear a pin drop at the Southbank Centre when he talked of his battle with depression: years of not feeling manly enough; drinking to mask his unhappiness, leading to anger and aggression; trying to prove himself; and eventually a suicide attempt. His recovery made him reassess notions of masculinity and become a firm advocate for gender equality. He has since founded a charity, Chasing the Stigma, to help people experiencing mental illness to find support.

Kenny Mammarella D'Cruz has been convening 'men's groups' for more than a decade, providing space for small groups of up to nine men to meet and together explore their thoughts and experiences. Kenny leads the conversation with a starter question to encourage everyone to give their own perspective, and the discussion can get very deep. It sounds a bit like a men's version of the 1970s feminist consciousness-raising groups Susie Orbach told me about, but what's striking is how unusual it is for a group of men to delve into emotional discussions in this way. As we chatted in the coffee bar of a Mayfair office block, Kenny told me that a one-to-one, face-to-face conversation can feel confrontational for men, and that it's often easier for discussions to take place when men are side by side, focusing on something else in the distance. I smiled when I heard this, reminded that many of the best conversations I've had with my husband have been on long walks together, or during car journeys. Kenny's conclusion is that men haven't been 'shown how to talk, how to listen', with negative consequences for their relationships and emotional health.

In January 2017 I met social entrepreneur Josh Babarinde in a trendy coffee shop, all mismatched furniture and Lego-brick tabletop art. His initiative, Cracked It, teaches mobile-phone repair skills to marginalised young people, giving them a safe, legal and entrepreneurial way to earn a living. He sees a significant pressure on the young men he works with to be the breadwinner. He told me about boys as young as 15, feeling cast into the role of family provider with no father on the scene, turning to drug-dealing as the only way they could see to get cash, secretly slipping the money into their mum's handbag so she can pay the bills and keep the family afloat.

Conforming to the demands of masculinity starts early – think 'boys don't cry', or 'boys will be boys' – and continues to feed a series of problems. Our education system is failing boys in a similar way to how our workplaces are failing women. The educational-attainment gender gap is significant and growing – and magnified in particular groups, such as white boys from low-income backgrounds, fewer than one in ten of whom go on to university.[4] If current trends were to continue, by 2034 our university intake would be 75 per cent female.[5] I think it's no coincidence that the education system, at primary level in particular, is a female-dominated space; 85 per cent of primary school teachers are women,[6] and 98 per cent of nursery staff.[7] Not only does this reduce the number of role models for boys in the educational setting, it also means the norms of the institutions are gendered. It is just as skewed as the male-dominated workplace.

While men as a group tend to have the upper hand at work, the structures and norms that favour alpha male behaviour are not only damaging to women's prospects. Many men have no interest in the destructively competitive one-upmanship of workplace politics, and would also benefit from being judged more fairly on what they contribute. Men who for whatever reason don't conform to the stereotypical alpha male mould – through their socio-economic background, religion, disability, age, sexuality, personality type or skin colour – would also do better in a system that valued people as individuals instead of being designed to favour one narrow group.

Men's concentration in more dangerous sectors also means that they are much more likely to be killed at work.[8] In the last five years, men have accounted for 96 per cent of the 743 workplace deaths in the UK. Agricultural work carries the highest risk of fatal injury, whether being killed by a vehicle, livestock or machinery.

Construction accounts for the greatest overall number of deaths, with around 42 people losing their lives in site accidents each year.[9] While the long-term trend is positive, with an 85 per cent drop in workplace fatalities since 1974, the fact remains that on average two men die at work each week, so measures to improve health and safety are hugely important – and particularly so for men.

Society places an expectation on men to be strong: the provider, the protector. So when men are victims of abuse themselves, it can be even harder to speak out. More than 700,000 men experience domestic abuse each year, compared to more than 1.2 million women. Yet almost four in ten of them told no one.[10] It's true there are differences in the violence and abuse men and women experience – women, for example, are five times more likely to be sexually abused than men,[11] and women are more likely to experience sustained campaigns of abuse, whereas men more typically experience a single incident.[12] Four times more women than men are killed by their partner or ex-partner each year.[13] Women who suffer abuse are let down by the system, with too few refuge places and helplines. Men who suffer abuse are also let down, with even sparser provision of support.

Men's important role as fathers has been consistently belittled and ignored by our public services, legal system, employers and culture. We have hospitals which kick men out of the door and separate them from their new baby just a few hours after birth. We have workplace cultures that assume men don't miss their children or want to be home for bedtime, or that if they do that's tough, as sacrifices have to be made. We have a legal system that consistently places less value on fatherhood than motherhood.

How many men avoid going to the doctor? And why do we blithely roll our eyes and silently tut – *huh, men* – rather than considering this a significant public health problem that needs to be addressed as a matter of urgency? Heart disease and strokes kill many more men than women. Cancer claims the lives of almost 87,000 men in the UK each year,[14] and they are 37 per cent more likely to die from it than women.[15] Suicide is the biggest killer of men under the age of 35, and more than three in four suicides are men.[16] 12 men a day are driven to kill themselves.

'Man up'? It's society that needs to wake up to this disaster.

How Did We Get Here?

Our awareness of these challenges of masculinity, these problems faced specifically by men and boys, is decades behind the campaigns to address gender issues for women. Why?

Some keyboard warriors would have you believe this is because feminists hate men and are glad to see boys flounder at school and men die prematurely.

Obviously that level of debate shines no light on what's really happening. The answer is more subtle. It's about invisibility of gender, and solving this goes to the heart of how we can genuinely achieve Equal Power.

For many men (and women too, for that matter), gender issues are invisible until something happens to bring them into sharp relief. The chief executive who does a gender pay audit and is appalled that, contrary to his values and intentions, men and women are being paid differently. The film fan who was appalled at the racist and sexist slurs and hacking attack doled out to Leslie Jones, having never seen that type or level of abuse before.

The husband and new dad supporting his wife as she fights the downgrading of her job and a salary cut on her return to work after maternity leave. Or Michael Brown, heartbroken and grieving after the murder of his daughter Clare, suddenly confronting the terrifying reality of domestic violence.

Until that point, it is easy to believe the myth that men and women have equal opportunities. You can recognise the inequalities and injustices of the past, but today – if it's even noticed – there's always the explanation that gender difference in positions of power is probably just down to men and women making different choices. As a man, you may not consider the advantages you have as a result of being male. It's not a pleasant concept to reflect on, after all, that some of what you've achieved isn't entirely because of your own inimitable brilliance.

This rejection or blindness to privilege isn't confined to gender. I recall, in my university days, a conversation I had with an American student, where we were discussing social mobility. I pointed out that while I had certainly worked hard to secure my place at the London School of Economics, luck had also played a part. After all, I had been born in a middle-class suburb of Glasgow with excellent comprehensive schools, to parents with a passion for education who always encouraged me to make the world my oyster. I mused that while I might still have got to LSE had I been born into a low-income family on a council estate in Liverpool, the chances would certainly have been lower – even with exactly the same personal aptitude and potential. With an astonishing lack of self-awareness, my fellow student – who had benefitted from a top-class private education in the richest country in the world – asserted that he had got where he had entirely on his own merits.

There's a parallel with race. It's easy for white women to focus on the challenges they experience as white women, and yet ignore the multilayered disadvantage that women of colour face. We all see the world through the lens of our own life, but we need to be proactive about viewing the world from the perspective of others.

So just as white women can totally miss the toxic combination of racism and sexism – dubbed 'misogynoir' – directed at their black sisters, many men don't see gender at all. In fact, I know men who proclaim this as a virtue, proud that they are oblivious to someone's gender when assessing them for a job opportunity or promotion. The problem is that, in not seeing that the world we have created is gendered, we all embody expectations about gender, and we are all biased to varying degrees.

Gender ≠ Women

We need to see it to change it. Frustratingly, when we do see gender, all too often we fall into the trap of thinking 'gender = women'. It's one consequence of seeing male as the default: rather than considering everyone has a gender, it's seen as a different characteristic. You might remember the children's game Guess Who? – where players guess which of 24 characters their opponent has selected by asking yes or no questions about their characteristics. There are only five female characters. When a six-year-old girl wrote to Hasbro to complain – 'it's not fair to only have 5 girls in Guess Who and 19 boys' – the astonishing reply came that there were 'five of any given characteristics' in the game.[17] This complete blindness to male gender being a 'characteristic' – while female gender being viewed exactly as such – brilliantly demonstrates the problem of the assumption that gender = women.

The field of gender analysis ends up dominated by women,[18] which reinforces the association of the words 'gender' and 'women' being almost interchangeable.

There is one common catalyst that opens men's eyes to the ubiquity of gender norms and expectations: having a daughter. Nothing helps you see the world through someone else's eyes in quite the direct way that having a child does. From a baby's first cries, their parents are constantly scanning their environment for dangers, and predicting their needs. The form of assistance changes as the child grows and gains independence, but the parental instinct to protect their child remains. Fathers of daughters suddenly have a bird's-eye view of the challenges of being a girl, and can be horrified by what they see.

I remember back in 2009 when I was presenting my policy paper, Real Women, to Liberal Democrat colleagues. Among the recommendations on pensions and the workplace, we also included policies on body image. It was ground-breaking at the time to consider this a political issue, and I anticipated some pushback from the ranks of mainly middle-aged or older men who needed to approve the paper before it was debated at the party conference. But some of the strongest advocates for including the body image policies were fathers of daughters. One told of how his seven-year-old daughter had turned to him and said, 'Daddy, do I look fat in this?', which stopped him in his tracks and made him realise there was a huge problem.

There is even evidence that people who have daughters become more liberal and left-wing politically,[19] and that CEOs with daughters invest more in and score more highly on corporate social responsibility issues.[20]

So it does have an impact, though we also shouldn't overstate the link – sometimes I hear people talk about how amazing changes will happen as a result of men in positions of power having daughters, and that it will drive equality. All very well, but men have been fathering daughters – and loving them very much – since the dawn of our species, and yet we still have this unbalanced, unequal power dynamic, so let's not pretend this is the holy grail solution to gender inequality.

But while fathers of daughters often stumble into feminism and have their eyes opened to gender inequality, it is every bit as important for fathers (and mothers) of sons to be engaged with these issues.

We have a false sense of security that everything will be all right for little boys as they grow and become men, given the overall advantages that men enjoy in society. Yet gender issues for men and boys are underexplored, despite – or perhaps because of – the prevalence of men in positions of power.

The House of Commons has held an annual debate to celebrate International Women's Day for many years, yet only had such a debate about International Men's Day for the first time in 2016. The gender inequalities that affect men are important and rightly should be discussed in Parliament. But while 19 MPs spoke in the debate on the issues affecting women,[21] just 8 MPs made a speech to discuss challenges for men and boys – and 6 of those were women.[22] It probably didn't help that the men's debate was convened by Philip Davies MP, who is not known among his colleagues for his ability to win friends and influence people, and often approaches equality issues in a combative manner, as if men and women need to be pitched against each other. But nonetheless, the facts here beg a key question. When 70 per cent of MPs are men, how can issues specifically affecting men go unraised for so long? It sums up the invisibility of gender, for men in particular.

Do You Feel Powerful?

Even those in positions of power often don't feel powerful, so it's not surprising that people working further down in organisations feel disempowered. When facing redundancy, or shifts being cut, or bureaucratic public services, or romantic rejection, or just the daily grind of making ends meet, most people feel powerless. And it's hard for disempowered individuals to see and feel the collective power and privilege they enjoy as part of a group in society – this power is not evenly distributed and it is mostly not wielded consciously.

When we feel powerless, we simultaneously feel that therefore we're not – we surely can't be – part of the problem; and equally, that we have no agency to be part of the solution.

As an opposition MP when I was first elected, I used to watch government ministers coming to the House of Commons to set out their policies and plans. When they obscured details and evaded questions about timescales, I imagined they were keeping their powder dry for some precisely coordinated and polished launch event, to secure maximum fanfare. The calm projection of authority is almost graceful, like a swan swimming across a lake. But as a government minister myself I saw the furious kicking underneath the water, and realised how there is much more cock-up than conspiracy. The image of a well-oiled, professional machine, with everything following a predetermined plan, was entirely wrong. There was the time I was due to speak on a bill, and the government position I needed to outline on a controversial issue was only agreed minutes beforehand. There were the mad rushes to submit amendments to bills, with the clock ticking as we waited for official government 'clearance' to go ahead – which meant a civil servant loitering in the dusty Commons corridors waiting for a confirmatory text message that meant they could dash in with the relevant piece of paper before the Public Bill Office shut up shop for the night. Despite committed and excellent civil servants, the realities of resource constraints, external events, competing priorities and the art of the politically possible means government is much more about finding a path through the maze as you go.

There was a story about how people would arrive in government and often expect to find a locked room somewhere containing a cadre of highly qualified experts beavering away – the ones who were really in charge and had everything under control. I never found that room, because it doesn't exist. The truth is more mundane: government, like any organisation, is a bunch of human beings doing their best – sometimes brilliantly, but often making mistakes along the way.

Even government ministers and CEOs feel powerless at times, when they want to achieve something and the levers to do so seem out of their grasp.

And if as a man you already feel powerless, then it's easy to see why moves to ensure that power is shared more equally between men and women can feel like a threat.

Fearing Feminism

'Don't underestimate how much men feel afraid,' one senior executive from a professional services firm told me. He described how men coming up through the ranks view more equal numbers of men and women being promoted as a reduction in opportunities for them, even if they don't feel that they can articulate this. This was epitomised in 2017 in the now-infamous Google diversity memo,[23] penned by a disgruntled (now ex-) employee who objected to diversity programmes in the company. He cited 'biological differences' as being the reason why, in his view, men were better coders – and therefore how the 80 per cent male skew of Google's tech workforce was not something which needed to be tackled. His arguments were roundly debunked, not least by senior figures in tech who argued that he had fundamentally misunderstood what skills were needed in software engineering, such as collaboration, creativity and teamwork.[24]

Online, under the cloak of anonymity, the fear is palpable. Language used to describe women who are feminists not only denigrates in typical gendered ways – 'shrill', 'harpy', 'bitch', 'whore' – but also paints a picture of aggression and oppression: 'man-hating', 'would you rather your child had feminism or cancer?',[25] 'feminazi'.[26]

The intense social media backlash against feminism is a manifestation of this fear. It is striking in its precision targeting, in its volume and vitriol and in its attempts to attack individuals instead of ideas. From time to time, the most extreme elements make the headlines when violence is threatened against high-profile people, but day-to-day it just rages on. Little mobs of harassers unleashing misery on everyone from youth workers to schoolgirls – all because they have dared to voice an opinion – the ebbing and flowing perhaps according to some dark threads in the corners of the Internet flagging up who is to be singled out next for the 'treatment'.

Some of these people are MRAs – so-called men's rights activists. Others define as anti-feminists. There are crossovers with other types of hate and division: anti-Semitic, neo-Nazi, Islamophobic. When, on Sky News, I challenged Nigel Farage's disgusting comments saying if we didn't vote for Brexit then women would be at risk from 'mass sex attacks',[27] I found a nasty little stream of Islamophobic tweets in my timeline,[28] linking to horrendous websites equating Islam with rape. These keyboard warriors were not interested in the facts or how to actually protect women from violence – or that for nine out of ten women who are raped or sexually assaulted, the perpetrator is someone they already know.[29] Engaging proved fruitless – these accounts with weird, cartoon-like avatars and pseudonym usernames, some of which have since been suspended or deleted, seemed locked in their echo chamber of the truth as they see it, with no regard for any conflicting information.

Similarly, when I joined forces with MPs Yvette Cooper, Maria Miller and Jess Phillips to launch the Reclaim the Internet campaign, there was a predictable onslaught of trolling: 'Homophobic, misogynistic, racist abuse, & intimidation online is freedom of speech in practice', one keyboard warrior proclaimed.[30]

I became embroiled in a conversation with one user called EyeISBloke, who seemed obsessed with Jess Phillips and her past experience with a nasty group of trolls who decided it would be funny to tweet her about how they wouldn't rape her. She turned on her phone to find more than 600 notifications in this thread – pretty vile stuff. One of the worst things about Twitter mob abuse is that, typically, among it are occasional comments or questions from constituents totally unrelated to the mob, who just by chance sent their tweets around the same time. And in order to find and respond to those, you have to scroll through and see the bile. That's why all these exhortations to just ignore it, or to block people (by that stage you've already seen their abuse at least once), don't really solve the issue.

For some reason this EyeISBloke account was trying to nitpick what Jess had written about her experience, and took issue with a headline that referred to 'hundreds' of rape threats. In our Twitter exchange I pointed out that she didn't write the headline nor claim that every single notification was a threat. He seemed to think politicians have a lot more control over the media than is actually the case, but did seem to accept some of my argument, which was unusual.

So I decided to reach out to have a chat with this blogger, whose website includes an article titled 'Is the gender pay gap good for business?' Some online searching revealed that he was not an entirely anonymous account, and though he clearly kept his persona out of it, he did have a name: Alex.

I offered to meet Alex in person over a cuppa, but he said he'd rather Skype. Just before our scheduled call, he messaged to say it would be audio only, which I was disappointed about, but I respected his choice.

I always think it's easier to have a proper conversation if you know someone's name and are face-to-face, making a human connection in place of the distant insulation of the online world. In more than ten years as an MP, I have spent many hours engaged in intense conversations with people discussing our disagreements – from constituents to campaign groups, political opponents and, on occasion, even party colleagues. It's usually possible to have a respectful, civilised dialogue, and even find some points of agreement.

Alex/EyeISBloke was no different in this respect. We were able to agree that the gender pay gap exists, and that media reporting of it is often simplistic. We agreed there are other issues of inequality that are also important, like runaway executive pay and socio-economic disadvantage – I defended the principle that it is possible to care about multiple injustices at once, something often forgotten when online debates descend into 'whataboutery'. He told me he agreed with most of my TEDx talk about the importance of involved fatherhood. We agreed that sexual harassment is clearly a problem. We both thought the focus on getting girls into science, technology, engineering and mathematics ought to be matched with greater efforts to get boys into caring careers, and more men into primary schools. His concern about the title 'Minister for Women and Equalities' was interesting – while the Government Equalities Office does undertake work on issues where men are disadvantaged, the very words in that title can seem exclusive.

EyeISBloke distanced himself from the 'men's rights activist' label. Yet he simultaneously felt comfortable calling himself an 'anti-feminist', while claiming to be a 'gender equality champion'. His perception of feminists was deeply cynical – painting them as playing the 'victim card' or becoming 'extremely aggressive'. I winced when in our discussion about the abuse high-profile women receive, he talked about how the language they use 'might invite' the abuse – a classic technique to belittle or dismiss an injustice, by insinuating the victim was asking for it. The same logic blames rape victims for their attack, based on their clothes. Denying women the opportunity to dress, speak and debate as they choose – or else run the risk of sexual abuse – is an assault on freedom of expression that somehow doesn't register as problematic with defenders of trolling who claim to be in favour of freedom of speech.

Even EyeISBloke's recognition of the existence of sexual harassment betrayed a blindness to the scale of the problem. Saying it was only a 'small proportion of men' responsible doesn't mean only a small proportion of women are on the receiving end. Arguing that sexual harassment is 'rarely out-and-out horrific assaults' denies the importance of people having autonomy over their own bodies on an everyday basis – not just the absence of attacks at knifepoint, or gang rape. Considering that 'women are disadvantaged by biology' made me feel queasy, again framing the issue as some kind of problem with women's bodies rather than with society's assumptions, culture and the structures around reproduction.

It was hard to reconcile a self-described 'gender equality champion' with the writer of a blog that seeks to take down feminism and targets individuals based on the premise that they're lying, aimed at catching them out on a technicality such as considering whether a comment about raping you is actually a threat. I couldn't quite understand spending hours trying to disprove that Laura Kuenssberg receives lots of sexist abuse, or quibbling over how nasty gendered abuse had to be before it could be deemed sexist, or dismissing the possibility that some trolls had later covered their tracks by deleting their abusive tweets. It's a microcosm of that perennial problem of victims of abuse not being believed by authorities which has led to so many preventable crimes being committed. Not to mention that this approach also misses the bigger, gendered picture about which high-profile individuals are targeted for abuse in the first place: with women, men of colour, trans, disabled and gay people much more likely to be on the receiving end than white, cis, straight men.

And that bigger picture is exactly what's missing. At the heart of fearing feminism is the feeling it has gone too far, that men and women have pretty much equal opportunities now, apart from a few issues of violence or pay at the periphery. The consequence of this view is the assumption that the massive disparity in power that remains between men and women must be the product of choice, and is therefore okay.

There is a need for perspective. When I asked Martin Daubney what he was worried about in terms of gender inequality for his son and his daughter, he spoke eloquently and at length about the issues for boys, from educational inequality to how boys and men can be labelled as a problem. But he had misplaced optimism when it came to the prospects for girls. Apart from recognising issues around sexual harassment, he professed not to be worried about much for this generation of young women. I almost choked on my tea when he said he expected to see a complete inversion of the gender pay gap in 'five to seven years'. It is absolutely right to broaden the gender equality debate to include men and boys, as it is to explore gender in non-binary terms, but let's not kid ourselves that the problems facing women and girls specifically are almost solved.

That's why feminism is still relevant.

Why are we all so afraid of this F-word? I don't agree with every other feminist about everything, but the definition is clear: 'the belief and aim that women should have the same rights, power, and opportunities as men'.[31]

I am a proud feminist. Yet when writing this book, I decided that the word 'feminism' would not grace the front cover. I didn't want to put people off – people for whom the word is loaded and carries negative connotations, or people who think that the idea isn't relevant to them.

When Prime Minister David Cameron was interviewed by *Red* magazine in 2013, he floundered over the question 'Are you a feminist?'[32] In researching this chapter, I surveyed dozens of men in my life about their views and experiences. While they overwhelmingly agreed that women should have equal rights and opportunities, almost half said they were not feminists, rising to two-thirds among older men.

There is a fear of feminism. Fear of change, fear of rocking the boat, fear of going too far, fear of women in power. A fear that it is about women taking over the world, instead of sharing power and responsibility with men. But this fear is not confined to men. Plenty of women reject the feminist label, too.

The Battle of the Sexes is a Myth

The biggest myth about feminism is that it is about women versus men, some kind of epic clash where only one gender can emerge victorious. But the battle is not between the sexes; we're attacking the wrong enemy if we fight each other. The battle is against sexism and all its negative impacts on everyone – and to win, we need to work together.

In discussing his book, *How Not To Be a Boy*, comedian Robert Webb recounted a pearl of wisdom from his six-year-old daughter, who had summarised the problem of the patriarchy with a child's beautiful simplicity – it 'makes men sad, and women get rubbish jobs'.

The way the world works - or more accurately doesn't work - in terms of gender structures harms us all, in many ways: men, women, and those who identify as neither.

Instead of women v men, it needs to be women + men + everyone else. Together, we can create a world where there is Equal Power, and all reap the rewards. Here are some ideas for action.

- **SUPPORT ORGANISATIONS THAT SUPPORT MEN AND BOYS:** The Men & Boys Coalition is an umbrella group that brings together all sorts of research and support groups, and there may also be local organisations you can give time or money to.
- **BOYS DO CRY:** We must stop making boys feel like they are inadequate when they cry, forcing them to bottle up their

feelings. When they are hurt, scared or upset, they have just as much right to cry and be comforted as their sisters.

- **JOIN A TRADE UNION:** Unions have a vital role in promoting health and safety in the workplace, and this campaigning work must continue to make workplaces ever safer and prevent avoidable accidents and deaths.
- **DON'T PATRONISE DADS:** They know what they're doing, and it's not babysitting.
- **IT'S GOOD TO TALK:** Make time and non-judgemental space for men you know to talk about problems they may be having.
- **ENCOURAGE BOYS AND MEN TO CONSIDER CARING AS A CAREER:** Breaking down the barriers for men in teaching, childcare and nursing is every bit as vital as supporting women in science, construction and engineering.

I also asked the men in my survey what actions they would suggest that men could do, and here's what they said:

Nick – NEVER use the word 'babysitting' to describe what we do – always speak with quiet gratitude about the privilege of being a parent.

Jim – Be aware that if you're a middle-aged man employing young women, you're the boss and not a future husband, i.e. behave professionally and respectfully.

Adair – Try the gender-based Harvard implicit association tests [https://implicit.harvard.edu/implicit/] which can often reveal underlying prejudices that a person may not be aware of.

Tim – Challenge wherever you see inequality. Even just saying 'I'm not comfortable with you referring to x like that' can help someone else reconsider their position. Ensure you have explicit consent for any sexual activity. Talk about your feelings.

Austin – Realise that as smart and hard working as we all are, whatever degree of success we have had in life is *at least in part* down to the fact that we have a penis. I'm smart, and I work hard, but if I were a woman I would, on average, have progressed less than I have. That's just a fact, and we need to stop being offended by it.

Mark – Make sure employers place the same emphasis on parental leave for men AND women.

Gavin – Remember that whoever is shouting loudest or pushing themselves forward the most – whether that be a man or a woman – is not necessarily the best person for a job.

Chris – Tell women to apply for the promotion (even when they only meet 5/10 of the criteria).

Giles – A conscious effort is needed to keep in touch with female alumni [of your organisation], so that when more senior, head-hunted positions arise, the go-to people aren't all male.

Ross – Share housework equally (or do more than 50 per cent). Raise boys and girls the same way.

Richard – When I'm in a meeting and a woman has a suggestion that promptly gets ignored (which, y'know, happens all the time), I make a point of repeating her point and giving her credit. If you don't give credit, then men walk away thinking it's your idea, and women walk away thinking you're stealing the credit.

Alistair – When chairing any meeting, don't pick the people to ask questions according to who puts their hand up first. Wait for several hands to go up and then pick a woman as the first questioner.

Geoff – Be prepared to step in and take action. I volunteered in my local Sunday school because there were no men at all amongst the teachers and helpers.

Jon – Encourage men to call out incidents of sexism. Encourage high-profile men in powerful positions to call out such incidents more often.

Neil – Look at your team and ask yourself: 'Is my team diverse or is it lots of me?'

Rory – Understand that we have a stake in it. Just 'not being sexist' isn't nearly enough – we should seek out and oppose sources of inequality because they are bad for all of us.

Steve – Intervene when you see a friend or another male act in a way that is discriminatory or derogatory towards women.

David – Positively support male work colleagues who decide to look after young children or elderly relatives.

Rob – Consciously promote gender equality. For instance, a colleague has just turned down an invitation to a conference in Athens because it was 80 per cent men last year. Instead, he's hunted out an excellent woman as an alternative – and nominated her.

Steve – Listen. Listen. Listen.

CONCLUSION: Towards Equal Power

In October 2016 I gave a speech to a women's network in London. It was just a few weeks before the US Presidential election, and Hillary Clinton had finally secured a commanding lead in the opinion polls. I warned that a by-product of her Presidency would be cultural complacency about gender equality. Too many voices would rail that with a woman in the White House, what more did feminists want? I pointed out, too, the depressing fact that it was only when her patently unqualified opponent had been caught on tape admitting to sexual assault that she had managed to open up a clear lead, and this spoke volumes about residual sexism.

As a politician, I had not recently had a happy experience of elections. In May 2015, my party was shaken by a catastrophic result, down from 57 seats in Parliament to just 8, resulting in both my husband and I losing our jobs on the same day. In June

2016, I took my two-year-old son to the polling station with me as I voted to Remain in the European Union. By the early hours of the next morning the future of my country seemed to me in tatters, and liberal values themselves under threat.

So on the evening of 8 November 2016, it was with much-needed optimism that I bought some prosecco on the way home and settled down to watch the US election results. I vividly remember that night. My son had a cough, and each time I settled him, he would wake a few minutes later. Eventually I decided a bit of being upright would do him good and he snuggled next to me on the sofa for a while as we watched results come in from different states. But, in a depressingly familiar pattern, it all started to go wrong. States that should have been dead-certs were too close to call. The electoral college votes started piling up for Trump.

It was heart-breaking to see Hillary Clinton's concession speech the next day. Hot tears flowed as I listened:

We have still not shattered that highest and hardest glass ceiling, but someday someone will...to all of the little girls who are watching this, never doubt that you are valuable and powerful and deserving of every chance and opportunity in the world to pursue and achieve your own dreams.[1]

It wasn't my party, my campaign, or even my country, but the message of that US election was so devastating to women and girls across the world. An immensely qualified woman beaten by a man who had neither the experience nor the temperament to do the job well, a man who wanted to ban all Muslims from entering the US, who denounced Mexicans as rapists, who insulted the family of US soldiers killed in the line of duty, who mocked people with disabilities, who admitted sexual assault. Any one of these things ought to have seen him roundly defeated.

The only silver lining is that this should shake us out of our collective complacency. The election of President Trump shatters the myth that I have tried to debunk in this book: that progress on gender inequality is inevitable. It is not.

The risk of going backwards should stiffen our resolve to keep pushing forwards – in all different parts of society and walks of life – to create a world of Equal Power.

Listen and Learn

We should do this with humility, openness and in a spirit of inquiry. Gender equality can't be pursued in a vacuum. It overlaps with movements for race equality, against religious intolerance, to combat prejudice against LGBT+ and disabled people, and to tackle entrenched economic disadvantage. Some of these areas you may know a lot about, others less so. I, for one, am certainly still learning. I understand gender equality so much better than when I first took up government responsibility for the matter as Minister for Women. I feel I am at a much earlier stage in truly understanding racism, for example, and the invisible protection and advantages my white skin gives me. Renni Eddo-Lodge's brilliant book *Why I'm No Longer Talking (to White People) About Race* was enlightening about the historical foundations of race discrimination in the UK and how that impacts society today. It made me aware of how little I really knew about the sometimes horrendous experiences black people face in my country.

I find there are often two flawed responses to these equality issues from people who mean well. One is the paternalistic, knight-to-the-rescue, solve-the-problem attitude, implementing a few new Key Performance Indicators and declaring that this will be resolved in five years. Targets and initiatives can help, but something is lost if it is not recognised that these entrenched biases are more complex and harder to fix than the problem of how to increase efficiency on a production line, or how to segment the perfect audience for an advertising campaign. Another common response is to fear saying the wrong thing or making a faux pas, and consequently withdraw from the debate, leaving it to the women, or the ethnic minorities, or the LGBT+ group to sort out.

Then there is the less well-meaning 'Not All Men' response, where the description of a gender equality problem is interpreted as a personal attack and that person goes on the defensive, pointing out that not all men act that way. The main outcome of this is less attention on the actual problem and how it might be solved.

The harder route, but the better one, is to recognise what we don't know, and seek to fill those gaps by listening to others, asking questions sensitively where necessary. Be proactive about finding a wide range of less-heard voices to follow on social media. Don't just pick up the same newspaper every day. Read articles and books written from perspectives you understand less well. Take the opportunity to broaden your horizons not just in terms of gender, but ethnicity, class, age, sexual orientation, race and religion.

We all make mistakes: inadvertently causing offence, not recognising the seriousness of an issue, making false assumptions.

More important than any pretence at perfection is the way we respond when we do get it wrong. Don't immediately put the defences up and justify why you must be right. Take time to listen, understand and learn.

Speak Out and Support Others

A culture where people try to understand one another instead of rushing to belittle, criticise or shout others down makes it easier for people to speak out. In late 2017, prompted by the Harvey Weinstein scandal, actor Alyssa Milano urged people to share their experiences of sexual assault or harassment using the hashtag #MeToo[2], building on a campaign started more than a decade ago by black activist Tarana Burke. Millions responded, and this flood of responses made the scale of the problem impossible to ignore. The power of that movement, of the solidarity, the greater safety in numbers, was significant. Yet even as people opened up about their experiences, others opined in the media about how a man's career could be ruined by multiple women coming forward with such allegations 'even if it was just touching'.[3] That's why it is so important that when people do take the brave step of sharing their personal experiences, the voices of support overwhelm those who will inevitably take aim and try to shoot the messenger, instead of tackle the underlying problem.

Sexism is everywhere around us. We need to name it, to call it out, to share our anecdotes and stories with those friends and loved ones who might not otherwise see it. The intergenerational conversations we have are especially important when it comes to changing minds. And we need to support others when they speak out. This can be backing someone up in a meeting when they raise a pertinent point about inequality, or amplifying a message on social media, or offering moral support to people challenging the power imbalance.

Dr Michael Kimmel, sociologist and author of *Angry White Men*, talked in 2016 at the Women of the World Festival about the importance of men speaking out when they witness unacceptable behaviour, and the barriers they experience in doing so.

> *Men's silence is taken as assent, it gives the illusion that all other men agree with it… our silence is what keeps this system going. We are also scared shitless of other men and we are scared of breaking that silence because we know they'll come after us… the way to do it, is not to do it alone. I can't speak up unless I have him with me. If he sees what I see, I can speak up, because he'll have my back, so the conversation that has to be taking place is between men and other men: I will support you when you speak out against racism and sexism and homophobia.*[4]

Whether you are a man, a woman, or identify as neither, it is easier to speak out when others stand with you. We are stronger together.

Your Power to Create Change

It is easy to feel powerless: to scream at the television in frustration, to lament the direction society is heading in, to despair that the United States elected a sexual predator as President. The day after Trump's inauguration, Women's Marches were held around the world. The crowds far surpassed the numbers from the day before. I joined the march in London with my husband and our three-year-old son. It was a crisp, clear winter day, the sun glinting off windows of tall buildings. The atmosphere was warm and welcoming, and the mood was one of positive, proactive defiance. It was like - and at the same time unlike - any protest march I had been on before. The familiar notes of the ubiquitous samba band lifted spirits and got people moving. But where mass-produced hard-left placards usually dominated, instead here was a multitude of home-made, colourful, witty and inspiring signs: 'Grab 'em by the policy', 'This will be a peaceful protest. Unless we are all on our periods, of course', 'I can't believe we still have to protest this shit', and simply 'Feminism is for everyone'.

Feminism is for everyone, whether you like the word or not. It is a movement to create a world free of gender prejudice, stereotypes and discrimination, a world where the entrenched bias of the default male is painstakingly unpicked, and a world where the power currently concentrated in the hands of the rich, white men is spread and shared - and not just with rich, white women. Too often different strands of feminist thought are pitted against one another, divisions created, energy wasted fighting internal battles. I prefer the approach of the late MP Jo Cox, who, when asked what kind of feminist she was, simply replied 'a massive one'.[5]

What matters most, however, is not whether you want to call yourself a feminist or not, it's what you *do*. Throughout this book are examples of people of all ages, genders, ethnicities, religions and backgrounds who have challenged the status quo of gender inequality. You can do it too.

As you've read these chapters, you've seen dozens of ideas for action. You might have already tried some out. These are a springboard for inspiration, not an exhaustive list. There is no limit to the innovative and new ways we need to find to challenge the gendered concentration of power in our society.

You can start small, if you like. Change a conversation, sign a petition, pass this book on to someone else you think should read it. Or you can dive straight in to begin a campaign against an injustice that has been bugging you.

The most important thing is to take action. Whatever power you have - as a friend, as a voter, as a consumer, as a parent, as a person with an opinion and a voice - use it. Then congratulations - you're part of the movement to create Equal Power.

Time to take action!

Use the hashtag #EqualPower to share your stories,
ideas and personal commitments for building a
society with gender equality at its heart.

Acknowledgements

The idea to write *Equal Power* came to me in May 2015, so this project has been nearly three years in the making. Researching and writing a book has felt to me a bit like training for and running a marathon, or the experience of pregnancy and then childbirth. It is a lengthy and often painful endeavour; there are many moments of wondering why on earth you signed up for this, and ultimately no one else can do it for you. I am optimistic that this analogy will extend to it all feeling worthwhile, pain all forgotten, when I finally hold my completed book baby in my hands.

I owe a huge amount to so many people who have helped me along the way: as book midwives, writing coaches and spectators shouting encouragement on the way to the finish line.

My agent, Rowan Lawton, believed in this book from the start and helped find it a home. My editors, Margaret Stead and then Clare Drysdale, guided me and encouraged me throughout with patience and understanding, not least when a General Election was called 12 days before my original deadline. Kirsty Doole and the rest of the Atlantic Books team have been superb in making sure we can spread the Equal Power message far and wide.

Gemma Wain was a fantastic copyeditor, and I am grateful to Sarah-Jane Forder for the proofreading. Any errors which remain are mine and mine alone.

I am indebted to those who gave me their time, whether for interviews, commenting on text or giving me advice: Nimco Ali, Vinous Ali, Coralie Alison, Ross Allen, Sara Allen, Maggie Aderin-Pocock, Roma Agrawal, Marie Anderson, Hannah Azieb Pool, Josh Babarinde, Tracy Barker, Kirsty Bashforth, Sam Barratt, Andrew Beddard, Jo Bostock, Nic Bottomley, Juliette Bottomley, Charlie Brinkhurst-Cuff, Belinda Brooks-Gordon, Michael Brown, Sarah Brown, Chris Calland, Laura Carstensen, Sarah Childs, Martin Daubney, Sarah Davies, Natalie Davis, Carrie Dunn, June Eric-Udorie, Alex Feakes, Daniele Fiandaca, Sarah Ginn, Dan Godsell, Katy Gordon, Masha Gordon, Chris Green, Sally Greengross, Abigail Herron, Stephanie Hirst, Bettany Hughes, Nicky Hutchinson, Antony Jenkins, Tara Kaufmann, Sean Kemp, David Lammy, Martha Lane Fox, Clare Laxton, Marianne Legato, Corrine Leon, Caron Lindsay, Polly Mackenzie, Sabrina Mahfouz, Kenny Mammarella D'Cruz, Emily May, Jessy McCabe, Andrew McCarthy, James Millar, Eleanor Mills, Jake Mills, Alex Moog, Jon Neal, Sally Neal, Sue O'Brien, Susie Orbach, Geoff Payne, Lauren Pemberton-Nelson, Vanessa Pine, Kate Polling, Therese Procter, Simon Ragoonanan, Nav Rai, Claire Rannard, Austin Rathe, Ben Rathe, Phil Reilly, Adair Richards, Elena Rossini, Alex Runswick, Neil Sherlock, Ella Smillie, Cilla Snowball,. Peter Swinson, Karen Teago, Nicola Teece, Laura Thomas, Fionna Tod, Dipa Vaya, Steve Waygood, Shirley Williams, Thea Willis and Zoe Young. Additionally, more than a hundred of my male friends, colleagues and acquaintances completed my online survey to help me understand their perspective better – thank you all.

Huge thanks go to my husband, Duncan, for his constant encouragement and support, and our son Andrew, for cheerful distraction whenever I needed it.

And finally, thanks to you, the reader, for picking up this book and investing your time in it. Every action you take as a result will get us one step closer to Equal Power.

Endnotes

Introduction

1 http://www.newstatesman.
com/lifestyle/2014/04/kimberl-
crenshaw-intersectionality-
i-wanted-come-everyday-
metaphor-anyone-could

1. POLITICS

1 http://www.nationalarchives.
gov.uk/pathways/firstworldwar/
document_packs/women.htm
2 http://www.parliament.uk/about/
living-heritage/transforming
society/electionsvoting/
womenvote/overview/thevote/
3 http://www.parliament.uk/
briefing-papers/sn01250.pdf, p.7
4 http://news.bbc.co.uk/onthisday/
hi/dates/stories/february/7/
newsid_2738000/2738475.stm
5 http://www.bbc.co.uk/news/
world-middle-east-35075702
6 http://www.wsj.com/articles/
saudi-arabian-women-love-
bumper-cars-but-not-for-
bumping-1466445023
7 https://secondreading.uk/
elections/as-many-women-mps-
ever-as-men-now/

8 https://www.institutefor
government.org.uk/blog/
government-reshuffle-eight-charts
9 https://www.theguardian.com/
world/2016/apr/27/whitehall-
fewer-female-bosses-david-
cameron-tom-watson
10 www.parliament.uk/briefing-
papers/sn01250.pdf, p.11
11 https://medium.com/athena-
talks/pitiful-progress-women-
councillors-in-wales-after-the-
2017-local-elections-edbf39258c7
12 http://www.women5050.org/
13 http://www.pewresearch.org/fact-
tank/2017/03/08/women-leaders-
around-the-world/
14 http://conservativehome.blogs.
com/goldlist/2006/08/the_costs_
of_be.html
15 http://www.theconservative
foundation.co.uk/index.php?
page=who
16 http://www.huffingtonpost.co.uk/
sophiewalker/womens-equality-
party_b_8784496.html
17 http://researchbriefings.files.
parliament.uk/documents/CBP-
7483/CBP-7483.pdf
18 http://www.bbc.co.uk/news/uk-
politics-23177856

19 https://www.gov.uk/access-to-elected-office-fund/overview
20 http://researchbriefings.files.parliament.uk/documents/SN01663/SN01663.pdf
21 http://researchbriefings.parliament.uk/ResearchBriefing/Summary/SN01663
22 http://www.huffingtonpost.co.uk/dr-rosie-campbell/women-in-politics_b_4608418.html
23 http://www.bbc.co.uk/news/uk-politics-36752865
24 http://gap.hks.harvard.edu/price-power-power-seeking-and-backlash-against-female-politicians
25 'As the Prime Minister says goodbye to his fourth Tory leader, is it not also time to say goodbye to the Punch and Judy style of Prime Minister's Questions?'
26 http://news.bbc.co.uk/hi/english/static/vote2001/results_constituencies/constituencies/330.stm
27 http://www.libdemvoice.org/jo-swinson-writesbeen-there-got-the-tshirt-49772.html
28 http://www.5050parliament.co.uk/askhertostand/
29 http://www.parliamentproject.co.uk/
30 http://www.ukpolitical.info/FemaleMPs.htm
31 http://www.parliament.uk/biographies/lords/baroness-williams-of-crosby/740
32 http://news.bbc.co.uk/onthisday/hi/dates/stories/may/23/newsid_2504000/2504227.stm
33 http://www.channel4.com/news/sexual-harassment-culture-in-parliament-exposed-westminster-commons
34 http://www.stylist.co.uk/people/sexism-misogny-harassment-mp-female-political-journalists-flattered-westminster-isabel-oakeshott-hardman-cathy-newman-julia-hartley-brewer and https://www.theguardian.com/commentisfree/2016/apr/14/mp-totty-isabel-hardman and http://www.telegraph.co.uk/women/politics/i-know-what-its-like-to-be-called-totty---i-was-once-called-a-sl/
35 http://www.bristol.ac.uk/media-library/sites/news/2016/july/20%20Jul%20Prof%20Sarah%20Childs%20The%20Good%20Parliament%20report.pdf
36 Conversations on 06/09/2017 at Women's Lobby drinks.
37 http://www.huffingtonpost.co.uk/jo-swinson/childs-review-breastfeeding_b_11111012.html
38 https://constitution-unit.com/2015/05/14/uk-elects-most-diverse-parliament-ever-but-its-still-not-representative/
39 http://www.theguardian.com/politics/2008/mar/02/women.gender
40 http://leanin.org/book/
41 http://link.springer.com/article/10.1057/bp.2012.28
42 http://www.publications.parliament.uk/pa/cm201516/cmhansrd/cm151110/halltext/151110h0001.htm#15111043000435
43 http://www.libdemvoice.org/jo-swinson-writesdissolution-honours-make-the-contribution-of-women-look-invisible-47270.html

2. CHILDHOOD

1 https://www.theguardian.com/science/2007/aug/25/genderissues

Endnotes

2 http://digest.bps.org.uk/2011/09/at-what-age-do-girls-prefer-pink.html

3 http://www.standard.co.uk/news/uk/campaigners-attack-marks-and-spencer-for-gender-stereotyping-over-boys-only-dinosaur-shirts-9994891.html

4 https://www.britannica.com/science/human-development/Boys-and-girls-height-curves Height data: https://www.britannica.com/media/full/275624/147088 Weight data: https://www.britannica.com/media/full/275624/147089

5 https://letclothesbeclothes.uk/2015/11/05/ban-high-heels-and-wedges-for-children-end-of-healthnotheels/

6 https://letclothesbeclothes.uk/2016/05/22/kids-sun-safe-swimwear-exposure-to-sexism-really-is-bad-for-your-health/

7 http://www.theiet.org/policy/media/press-releases/20161206.cfm

8 http://www.popsugar.com/tech/Lego-Instructions-From-1970s-36164980

9 https://pinkstinks.wordpress.com/2010/12/05/early-learning-emergency-revisited-one-year-on/

10 http://www.lettoysbetoys.org.uk/boots-agree-to-let-toys-be-toys-in-store/

11 http://www.lettoysbetoys.org.uk/debenhams-to-remove-gendered-signage/

12 http://www.lettoysbetoys.org.uk/toys-r-us-drops-boys-and-girls-categories-from-uk-website/

13 https://www.theguardian.com/world/2017/feb/14/childrens-clothing-and-toy-retailer-gender-leave-the-stone-age-costumes

14 http://www.amightygirl.com/keepmeridabrave

15 Quotes from telephone interview, 01/04/2016.

16 https://twitter.com/HasbroNews/status/684555948959096832/photo/1?ref_src=twsrc%5Etfw

17 http://www.theiet.org/policy/media/press-releases/20161206.cfm

18 https://www.theguardian.com/money/2013/apr/30/boots-removes-gender-signs-toys

19 http://www.wes.org.uk/statistics

20 http://www.iop.org/policy/statistics/gender/page_67095.html

21 https://www.iop.org/education/higher_education/stem/outreach/file_59034.pdf, slide 10

22 http://www.ilcuk.org.uk/index.php/publications/publication_details/the_future_care_workforce

23 https://hansard.parliament.uk/Commons/2015-01-13/debates/15011342000002/CareSector?highlight=%22play%20with%20dolls%22#contribution-15011342000183 Relevant quote: 'Stereotyping is important, as are the messages we send children about the roles of men and women, and whether boys can be nurturing and caring and – yes, dare I say it? – play with dolls. We should see habits of care and nurture as being just as appropriate for boys and men as for girls and women.'

24 http://www.thesun.co.uk/sol/homepage/news/politics/6260834/boys-should-play-with-dolls-to-make-them-more-caring.html (print story had the 'Give lads a Barbie' headline)

25 http://www.bbc.co.uk/news/uk-13082946

26 http://www.idosi.org/wasj/wasj29(1)14/20.pdf
27 http://www.jstor.org/stable/42576224
28 http://www.theguardian.com/books/2011/may/06/gender-imbalance-children-s-literature
29 https://www.researchgate.net/publication/257663856_Male_and_Female_Pronoun_Use_in_US_Books_Reflects_Women%27s_Status_1900-2008
30 https://seejane.org/wp-content/uploads/key-findings-gender-disparity-family-films-2013.pdf
31 https://ukie.org.uk/research#fact_sheet
32 https://www.washingtonpost.com/posteverything/wp/2015/03/04/im-a-12-year-old-girl-why-dont-the-characters-in-my-apps-look-like-me/?utm_term=.5edd66fc88da
33 https://msu.edu/~pengwei/Mou&Peng_gender%20and%20racial%20stereotype.pdf
34 https://www.hastac.org/blogs/ezobel/2014/03/06/damsels-distress-female-representation-video-games
35 http://www.huffingtonpost.co.uk/entry/doctor-who-menbabies-jodie-whittaker-first-female_uk_596b9412e4b017418628374d
36 http://science.sciencemag.org/content/355/6323/389
37 Telephone interview with Jessy McCabe, 14/12/2015.
38 http://www.telegraph.co.uk/women/womens-life/11841976/Britain-schools-Exam-boards-must-stop-writing-women-out-of-curriculum.html
39 http://www.independent.co.uk/news/education/education-news/june-eric-udorie-feminism-to-be-taught-in-a-level-politics-curriculum-after-teenagers-campaign-a6804161.html
40 http://www.nytimes.com/2012/11/14/world/europe/swedish-school-de-emphasizes-gender-lines.html?_r=0
41 https://sweden.se/society/gender-equality-in-sweden/
42 https://www.gov.uk/government/uploads/system/uploads/attachment_data/file/533618/SFR21_2016_MainText.pdf
43 http://www.gov.scot/Publications/2016/12/9271/336278 (Table 3.4)
44 https://www.gov.uk/government/uploads/system/uploads/attachment_data/file/572290/ITT_Census_1617_SFR_Final.pdf (p. 9)
45 https://www.gov.uk/government/uploads/system/uploads/attachment_data/file/355075/SFR33_2014_Main_report.pdf (p. 128)
46 https://www.malala.org/girls-education
47 https://www.theguardian.com/society/2017/mar/17/girls-from-poorer-families-in-england-struggle-to-afford-sanitary-protection
48 http://gbc-education.org/wp-content/uploads/2015/09/The-Journey-of-a-Girl.pdf
49 https://documents-dds-ny.un.org/doc/UNDOC/GEN/N14/627/78/pdf/N1462778.pdf?OpenElement
50 https://www.washingtonpost.com/posteverything/wp/2017/02/10/why-does-the-united-states-still-let-12-year-old-girls-get-married/?utm_term=.c1ec23e03b02&wpisrc=nl_rainbow&wpmm=1
51 http://www.nytimes.com/2014/05/04/opinion/sunday/kristof-bring-back-our-girls.html?_r=0

52 https://www.hks.harvard.edu/m-rcbg/CSRI/publications/report_40_investing_in_girls.pdf (p. 3)
53 https://www.malala.org/students
54 *Neart-Tre-Eolas*, which is Gaelic for 'Strength through Knowledge'.
55 https://www.girlguiding.org.uk/social-action-advocacy-and-campaigns/research/girls-attitudes-survey/
56 https://www.theguardian.com/politics/2016/jul/05/ken-clarke-caught-camera-ridiculing-tory-leadership-candidates-theresa-may-michael-gove
57 http://www.politico.com/story/2016/10/trump-clinton-nasty-woman-debate-230047
58 https://www.youtube.com/watch?v=hK0Q8b6QhDo
59 https://nationalcareersservice.direct.gov.uk/resourceportal/Resourse%20Portal%20Doc%20Library/Your%20Daughters%20Future.pdf
60 https://www.princes-trust.org.uk/help-for-young-people/who-else/employment/careers-advice
61 https://www.malala.org/

3. BODIES

1 https://www.jsc.nasa.gov/history/oral_histories/RideSK/RideSK_10-22-02.htm
2 https://www.bustle.com/articles/198540-menstrual-huts-still-exist-and-heres-why-thats-a-problem
3 http://www.telegraph.co.uk/news/worldnews/us-election/11791693/Donald-Trump-says-Megyn-Kellys-tough-questioning-was-due-to-menstruation.html
4 http://mentalfloss.com/article/24501/not-so-famous-firsts-ads-feminine-products
5 https://www.youtube.com/watch?v=kOHCtQfFn7E
6 https://www.publications.parliament.uk/pa/cm201516/cmhansrd/cm151026/debtext/151026-0003.htm (col. 116)
7 http://jezebel.com/348766/let-it-bleed-a-look-back-at-period-related-advertising
8 https://www.youtube.com/watch?v=Bpy75q2DDow
9 https://www.youtube.com/watch?v=8Q1GVOYIcKc
10 http://www.independent.co.uk/life-style/health-and-families/menstruation-study-finds-over-5000-slang-terms-for-period-a6905021.html
11 https://www.youtube.com/watch?v=96cbK087d70
12 https://www.theguardian.com/society/2007/sep/12/health.medicineandhealth
13 http://www.stylist.co.uk/life/the-magazine-that-changed-our-life
14 http://www.telegraph.co.uk/women/sex/the-male-pill-is-coming---and-its-going-to-change-everything/
15 https://www.newscientist.com/article/2110729-male-contraceptive-injection-works-but-side-effects-halt-trial/
16 http://www.nhs.uk/Conditions/contraception-guide/Pages/combined-contraceptive-pill.aspx#Risks
17 https://www.washingtonpost.com/news/morning-mix/wp/2017/03/10/a-lawyer-named-amal-clooney-gave-a-powerful-speech-at-u-n-some-only-saw-her-baby-bump/?utm_term=.d64dbb798841
18 http://mashable.com/2017/03/10/amal-clooney-time-baby-bump/#hVk7HiMRsEqP
19 http://www.independent.co.uk/news/world/americas/us-republican-justin-humphrey-

oklahoma-abortion-law-sex-planned-parenthood-pro-choice-a7580326.html

20 http://www.dailymail.co.uk/news/article-2464452/Pregnant-minister-Jo-Swinson-forced-stand-PMQs.html

21 Quoted in http://www.salon.com/2013/10/18/is_it_sexist_to_offer_a_pregnant_woman_a_seat/

22 http://blogs.spectator.co.uk/2013/10/i-would-give-up-my-seat-for-any-pregnant-woman-except-jo-swinson/

23 https://www.ncbi.nlm.nih.gov/pubmed/3960433

24 https://www.tommys.org/our-organisation/what-we-do/our-research/miscarriage-research

25 http://www.bbc.co.uk/news/uk-scotland-scotland-politics-37270135

26 http://www.newstatesman.com/politics/2015/07/motherhood-trap

27 http://www.huffingtonpost.com/entry/for-the-record_us_57855586e4b03fc3ee4e626f

28 http://www.telegraph.co.uk/women/womens-life/10199339/Royal-baby-OK-magazines-Duchess-of-Cambridge-baby-weight-loss-cover-defies-belief.html

29 http://www.csmonitor.com/The-Culture/Family/Modern-Parenthood/2013/0723/First-glimpse-of-British-prince-brings-comments-about-mom-s-postpartum-body

30 http://everyonesbusiness.org.uk/wp-content/uploads/2014/07/Call-to-ACT.pdf

31 https://www.rcog.org.uk/en/news/campaigns-and-opinions/human-fertilisation-and-embryology-bill/rcog-opinion-the-abortion-act-40-years-on/

32 Phone interview with Dr Legato, 27/02/2017.

33 https://www.theguardian.com/society/2012/sep/01/thalidomide-scandal-timeline

34 https://www.theguardian.com/artanddesign/2015/jun/15/the-last-women-in-china-with-bound-feet

35 http://www.medicalbag.com/body-modification/neck-elongating-still-practiced-within-this-indigenous-tribe/article/472349/

36 A Vindication of the Rights of Woman, Author's Introduction (p. 1).

37 https://nyamcenterforhistory.org/2015/05/29/did-corsets-harm-womens-health/

38 https://strangeremains.com/2017/01/31/beauty-to-die-for-how-vanity-killed-an-18th-century-celebutante/

39 https://qz.com/718103/skin-lightening-is-a-10-billion-industry-and-ghana-wants-nothing-to-do-with-it/

40 https://www.parliament.uk/documents/post/postpb011_skin_lightening_treatments.pdf

41 http://www.ibtimes.co.uk/skin-lightening-beauty-industrys-ugly-billion-dollar-secret-1579218

42 http://www.gal-dem.com/illegal-skin-bleaching-south-london/

43 https://www.youtube.com/watch?v=1Flmw3T6ftE

44 https://www.youtube.com/watch?v=dDjBtRS1TP4

45 http://www.criticalmediaproject.org/cml/media/fair-and-lovely-ad/

46 http://uk.businessinsider.com/the-most-popular-plastic-surgery-in-korea-2015-10?op=1&r=US&IR=T

47 https://www.theatlantic.com/health/archive/2013/05/the-k-pop-plastic-surgery-obsession/276215/

48 http://www.stylist.co.uk/beauty/all-about-afro-hair-straightening-up-the-truth-about-chemical-hair-relaxers

49 http://www.cosmopolitan.com/uk/beauty-hair/hair/a31037/afro-hair-industry/

50 https://www.theguardian.com/commentisfree/2011/jun/17/cornrows-black-traditional-hairstyle

51 http://news.bbc.co.uk/1/hi/6251239.stm

52 http://professionalbeauty.co.uk/site/ShowNewsDetails/Hot-topic-2

53 http://www.telegraph.co.uk/beauty/skin/does-ipl-hair-removal-really-work/

54 http://www.marieclaire.com/health-fitness/a13489/celebrities-swear-by-it-but-is-waist-training-actually-healthy/

55 http://theillusionists.org/watch/

56 http://www.teenlibrariantoolbox.com/2013/04/body-image-take-iii-popular-culture-and-the-effect-on-gay-teens-and-body-image-a-guest-post/

57 http://www.dummies.com/careers/career-planning/choosing-a-career/proportions-in-fashion-drawing/

58 http://www.huffingtonpost.com/leona-palmer/fashions-night-out_b_952984.html

59 https://yougov.co.uk/news/2013/11/20/size-12-britains-ideal-dress-size/

60 http://www.telegraph.co.uk/fashion/people/14-of-models-over-a-size-12-the-stats-are-in-on-diversity-in-the/

61 https://www.theguardian.com/fashion/2013/jul/05/vogue-truth-size-zero-kirstie-clements

62 http://www.nydailynews.com/life-style/health/barbie-real-womaan-anatomically-impossible-article-1.1316533

63 Quote sourced from an article in The Week, 13/02/2016, taken from Telegraph Magazine.

64 http://www.bbc.co.uk/news/magazine-35670446.

65 http://www.allwalks.org/2012/05/timeline/

66 http://www.allwalks.org/diversity-network-launch/

67 http://www.any-body.org/

68 http://www.berealcampaign.co.uk/assets/filemanager/documents/appg_body_image_final.pdf

69 https://campaignforbodyconfidence.wordpress.com/body-confidence-awards/

70 http://www.adassoc.org.uk/wp-content/uploads/2014/09/Pretty-as-a-picture.pdf

71 http://www.adassoc.org.uk/wp-content/uploads/2016/10/The-Whole-Picture-3.pdf

72 http://www.adassoc.org.uk/wp-content/uploads/2016/08/Picture-of-health_FINAL.pdf

73 http://www.bbc.co.uk/news/magazine-25402020

74 Interview with Isabelle, 13/09/2017.

75 https://www.ft.com/content/1939f00e-1818-11e6-b197-a4af20d5575e

76 http://www.smithsonianmag.com/science-nature/how-much-is-being-attractive-worth-80414787/

77 http://gladwell.com/blink/why-do-we-love-tall-men/

78 http://www.ctpa.org.uk/content.aspx?pageid=295

79 http://www.bbc.co.uk/news/health-16391522

80 http://www.bbc.co.uk/news/health-24942981

81 https://www.change.org/p/apple-stop-plastic-surgery-apps-aimed-at-kids-surgery-is-not-a-game

82 https://www.buzzfeed.com/tabathaleggett/heres-charlotte-churchs-2013-john-peel-lecture-on-women-and?utm_term=.cf0ZNqRY1o#.msvW8Z56yE

83 http://www.bbc.co.uk/news/uk-24539514

84 http://www.bbc.co.uk/news/29596583

85 http://www.independent.co.uk/news/uk/home-news/revenge-porn-law-scotland-maximum-sentence-5-years-sharing-naked-photos-a7821856.html

86 https://www.gov.uk/government/news/revenge-porn-helpline-given-further-funding

87 http://www.bbc.co.uk/news/blogs-trending-37176299

88 http://www.dailymail.co.uk/news/article-3497932/MPs-flaunt-er-agendas-Feminists-howl-s-reason-ladies-House-parade-curves.html

89 https://www.fawcettsociety.org.uk/Handlers/Download.ashx?IDMF=fbf75b5f-aee4-4624-8df4-833ffcc1a2d7

90 http://www.billboard.com/video/madonnas-full-acceptance-speech-at-billboard-women-in-music-2016-7624369

91 https://www.dawn.com/news/1221699

92 https://www.theguardian.com/tv-and-radio/2016/aug/14/bake-off-winner-nadiya-hussain-racist-abuse-is-part-of-her-everyday-life

93 https://books.google.co.uk/books?id=9aL_vW6GOjYC&pg=PA532&lpg=PA532&dq=rumsey+body+confidence+school+attendance&source=bl&ots=0QjlDWnRN_&sig=X3XuiZwzpl3_-hfT_

jKy8ylRD6Q&hl=en&sa=X&ved=0ahUKEwj6mNqMgo3TAhVKAsAKHciUBF4Q6AEIJjAC#v=onepage&q&f=false

94 https://www.girlguiding.org.uk/globalassets/docs-and-resources/research-and-campaigns/girls-attitudes-survey-2016.pdf (p. 7)

95 https://www.childrenssociety.org.uk/what-we-do/resources-and-publications/the-good-childhood-report-2016

96 http://pediatrics.aappublications.org/content/early/2016/02/24/peds.2015-3223

97 https://www.b-eat.co.uk/support-us/donations

98 https://www.miscarriageassociation.org.uk

99 https://www.tommys.org/miscourage

100 https://theillusionists.org

101 http://content.time.com/time/nation/article/0,8599,2025345,00.html

4. PARENTING

1 Huge thanks to Anna and Hannah, the midwives who got me through it. Absolutely superb support!

2 http://www.nhs.uk/Conditions/pregnancy-and-baby/Pages/Severe-vomiting-in-pregnancy-hyperemesis-gravidarum.aspx

3 https://ourworldindata.org/grapher/total-fertility-rate?tab=chart&country=DEU+GBR+USA

4 https://ourworldindata.org/grapher/total-fertility-rate?tab=chart

5 https://ourworldindata.org/child-mortality/

6 http://sowf.men-care.org/wp-content/uploads/sites/4/2015/06/State-of-the-Worlds-Fathers_23June2015-1.pdf (p. 17): 'State of the World's Fathers'

(a MenCare Advocacy Publication, 2015).

7 Interview with Daniele Fiandaca, 30/03/2016.

8 http://www.independent.co.uk/life-style/health-and-families/features/the-timeline-maternity-leave-2113236.html

9 http://www.legislation.gov.uk/uksi/2010/1055/regulation/3/made

10 http://www.legislation.gov.uk/ukpga/2014/6/part/7/enacted

11 http://www.dailymail.co.uk/news/article-2782950/Minister-hits-stay-home-mums-Swinson-claims-men-raise-children-women-career.html

12 http://visual.ons.gov.uk/what-is-the-gender-pay-gap/

13 http://gender.bitc.org.uk/system/files/research/project_28-40_the_report.pdf

14 http://ec.europa.eu/justice/gender-equality/files/documents/140502_gender_equality_work force_ssr5_en.pdf (p. 7): Shows that in UK couples, 58 per cent of men earn more, 14 per cent of women earn more, and the remainder are approximately equal.

15 http://www.cordeliafine.com/general-information.html

16 http://www.pnas.org/content/111/27/9792.full

17 http://www2.warwick.ac.uk/fac/arts/history/chm/outreach/hiding_in_the_pub/

18 https://www.theguardian.com/healthcare-network/2012/mar/28/fathers-bigger-role-pregnancy-childbirth

19 Interview with Simon Ragoonanan, 01/04/2016.

20 https://www.theguardian.com/lifeandstyle/2015/oct/10/dont-ask-me-if-ive-got-a-family

21 http://www.bbc.co.uk/news/uk-politics-24119088

22 http://www.thedrum.com/stuff/2014/09/01/telegraph-hot-water-referring-preferred-bbc-trust-chair-rona-fairhead-only-mother

23 Anecdote relayed by Tanni at a WOW committee meeting in 2015.

24 http://www.huffingtonpost.co.uk/entry/pregnant-women-bump-shamed-response_uk_577e3961e4b074297db29649

25 http://healthland.time.com/2012/12/07/is-kate-middleton-too-thin-to-be-pregnant/ and http://www.cosmopolitan.co.uk/body/news/a34613/pregnant-weather-presenter-reacts-to-body-shaming/ and http://www.ibtimes.com/pregnant-kim-kardashian-worst-dressed-met-gala-2013-fat-reality-star-wears-matching-dress-shoes

26 http://www.dailymail.co.uk/news/article-2861994/Put-baby-corner-Farage-tells-mothers-not-openly-ostentatious-breastfeeding-babies.html

27 http://www.bbc.co.uk/news/uk-england-london-30359606

28 https://twitter.com/r2ph/status/665965744136527872

29 http://www.bbc.co.uk/news/uk-england-york-north-yorkshire-16487188

30 http://www.mirror.co.uk/news/uk-news/breastfeeding-mum-asked-leave-restaurant-3773991

31 http://www.dailymail.co.uk/news/article-2385949/Mother-Tara-Powells-breastfeeding-called-disgusting-jobcentre-interview.html

32 http://www.express.co.uk/news/uk/579306/School-head-me-feel-dirty-breastfeeding-young-mother

33 http://www.dailymail.co.uk/news/article-2616220/Angry-mothers-

stage-mass-breastfeeding-protest-Sports-Direct-store-asked-woman-leave-against-company-policy.html

34 http://metro.co.uk/2015/07/03/young-mum-asked-to-leave-her-local-swimming-pool-for-breast-feeding-her-4-month-old-baby-5278277/

35 http://www.dailymail.co.uk/news/article-2014222/Breast-feeding-mother-told-leave-council-headquarters-multicultural-building.html

36 http://www.mirror.co.uk/news/uk-news/breastfeeding-mum-ordered-out-baby-2048569

37 https://www.ft.com/content/afc3f2e0-5cb0-11e6-bb77-a121aa8abd95

38 https://newrepublic.com/article/122734/paid-leave-week-marissa-mayers-bad-example-yahoo-workers?utm_content=buffer54837&utm_medium=social&utm_source=twitter.com&utm_campaign=buffer

39 https://twitter.com/kairyssdal/status/639459288365203457

40 http://www.cnet.com/uk/news/yahoos-marissa-mayer-defends-her-maternity-leave/

41 http://time.com/4136587/zuckerberg-baby-leave/

42 https://www.facebook.com/photo.php?fbid=10102521282381691&set=a.529237706231.2034669.4&type=3&theater

43 https://www.yahoo.com/news/could-a-powerful-woman-ever-post-a-baby-pic-like-201026662.html

44 https://www.tuc.org.uk/sites/default/files/Pay_and_Parenthood_Touchstone_Extra_2016_LR.pdf

45 http://www.economist.com/news/international/21659763-people-rich-countries-can-be-coaxed-having-more-children-lazy-husbands-and?fsrc=scn/tw/te/pe/ed/BreakingTheBabyStrike

46 http://mentalfloss.com/article/33485/5-creative-ways-countries-tried-their-birth-rates

47 https://www.gov.uk/government/uploads/system/uploads/attachment_data/file/323290/bis-14-903-costs-and-benefits-to-business-of-adopting-work-life-balance-working-practices-a-literature-review.pdf

48 https://www.familyandchildcaretrust.org/childcare-survey-2017

49 https://www.gov.uk/government/uploads/system/uploads/attachment_data/file/394623/bis-15-32-shared-parenting-leave-public-attitudes.pdf (Q7 and Q12)

50 http://www.ngomedia.org.uk/landing/mencandoit/

51 http://www.fatherhoodinstitute.org/2014/fi-research-summary-paternity-leave/

52 http://www.bps.org.uk/news/dads-can-boost-daughters-aspirations

53 https://www.ft.com/content/b10dc87a-fb43-11e5-8f41-df5bda8beb40

54 Interview with Tara Kaufmann, 24/08/2016.

55 https://www.rcm.org.uk/news-views-and-analysis/analysis/fathers-at-birth-and-beyond

5. WORK

1 https://www.gov.uk/government/uploads/system/uploads/attachment_data/file/477360/UKCES_Gender_Effects.pdf

2 http://www.kingsfund.org.uk/time-to-think-differently/

trends/professional-attitudes-
and-workforce/medical-
workforce#medical

3 http://www.uhce.ox.ac.uk/ukmcrg/
publications.php

4 https://www.ncbi.nlm.nih.gov/
pmc/articles/PMC4228926/

5 http://careers.bmj.com/careers/
advice/Why_do_female_doctors_
earn_less_money_for_doing_the_
same_job%3F

6 http://www.lawsociety.org.uk/
law-careers/becoming-a-solicitor/
entry-trends/

7 http://www.chambersstudent.
co.uk/where-to-start/newsletter/
2014-gender-in-the-law-survey

8 http://www.chambersstudent.
co.uk/where-to-start/newsletter/
women-at-the-bar

9 http://www.lawgazette.co.uk/
practice/three-solicitors-among-
107-new-qcs/5052951.fullarticle

10 https://www.girlguiding.org.uk/
globalassets/docs-and-resources/
research-and-campaigns/girls-
attitudes-survey-2016.pdf (p. 3)

11 https://royalsociety.org/~/media/
Royal_Society_Content/policy/
projects/leading-way-diversity/
picture-uk-scientific-workforce/
070314-diversity-report.pdf (p. 17)

12 https://royalsociety.org/~/media/
Royal_Society_Content/policy/
projects/leading-way-diversity/
picture-uk-scientific-workforce/
070314-diversity-report.pdf (p. 38
table, and graphs on pp. 39 and
40)

13 http://www.pnas.org/content/109/
41/16474.abstract#

14 https://blogs.scientificamerican.
com/unofficial-prognosis/study-
shows-gender-bias-in-science-is-
real-heres-why-it-matters/

15 https://royalsociety.org/~/media/
Royal_Society_Content/policy/

projects/leading-way-diversity/
picture-uk-scientific-workforce/
070314-diversity-report.pdf

16 https://blogs.scientificamerican.
com/guest-blog/engineering-is-
a-mane28099s-field-changing-
a-stereotype-with-a-lesson-from-
india/

17 https://qz.com/435820/more-
women-need-to-become-
engineers-and-that-means-letting-
girls-know-its-possible/

18 https://www.cliffordchance.com/
content/dam/cliffordchance/
CR2013/CRR2013.pdf (p. 12)

19 https://www.cliffordchance.com/
about_us/who_we_are_and_how_
we_work/how-we-manage-our-
firm.html – as of 3 September
2017: Matthew Layton, Chris
Perrin, Laura King, Patrick Glydon,
Caroline Firstbrook, Rob Lee,
Guy Norman, Jeremy Sandelson,
Evan Cohen, Geraint Hughes,
Yves Wehrli, Peter Dieners, David
Bickerton.

20 https://www.cliffordchance.com/
content/dam/cliffordchance/
About_us/SRA-Diversity-Data%20
June-2017.pdf

21 https://www.cliffordchance.
com/news/news/2017/04/
clifford-chance-appoints-24-
new-partners-.html and https://
www.cliffordchance.com/news/
news/2016/04/clifford-chance-
appoints-24-new-partners.html
and https://www.cliffordchance.
com/news/news/2015/04/
clifford-chance-appoints-25-new-
partners.html and https://www.
cliffordchance.com/news/news/
2014/04/clifford-chance-appoints-
21-new-partners.html and https:/
/www.cliffordchance.com/news/
news/2013/04/clifford_chance_
appoints20newpartners.html

22 https://www.slaughterandmay.
com/media/2428458/diversity-
and-inclusion-uk-statistics-2017.
pdf

23 http://www.linklaters.com/pdfs/cr/
Diversity_Statistics_2016.pdf

24 http://www.allenovery.com/
corporate-responsibility/diversity-
inclusion/Pages/statistics.aspx

25 https://view.pagetiger.com/
Responsible-business/rb19

26 https://gender.bitc.org.uk/all-
resources/factsheets/women-and-
work-facts

27 http://gender.bitc.org.uk/system/
files/research/project_28-40_the_
report.pdf (p. 9)

28 http://www.pwc.co.uk/economic-
services/assets/PwC-Women-in-
Work-2016-FINAL-3.pdf (p. 2)

29 https://www.furtherandmore.com/
job-share-blog/welcome-to-job-
sharing

30 https://www.eveningtelegraph.
co.uk/2013/10/18/howking-
holiday-how-tattie-pickers-helped-
feed-britain/

31 https://scotlandonscreen.org.uk/
browse-films/007-000-002-153-c

32 http://www.history.com/this-day-
in-history/ford-factory-workers-
get-40-hour-week

33 http://www.ford.co.uk/
experience-ford/Heritage/
EvolutionOfMassProduction

34 http://www.ons.gov.uk/
employmentandlabourmarket/
peopleinwork/employment
andemployeetypes/bulletins/
workingandworklesshouseholds/
2015-10-06

35 http://digiday.com/agencies/
agency-culture-long-hours-real-
problem/

36 https://digest.bps.org.uk/2014/
09/25/how-do-male-scientists-
balance-the-demands-of-work-
and-family/

37 http://dadbloguk.com/its-official-
stay-at-home-dads-do-not-exist/

38 http://www.dailymail.co.uk/news/
article-2976536/Decline-stay-
home-mother-Just-one-woman-
ten-time-mum.html

39 https://www.equalityhumanrights.
com/en/our-work/news/powerto
thebump-unites-young-mothers-
fight-against-pregnancy-and-
maternity

40 https://www.equalityhumanrights.
com/en/file/16631/
download?token=J-AbGZjd

41 http://www.enar-eu.org/IMG/pdf/
factsheet8-uk_lr.pdf

42 https://hbr.org/2016/03/why-so-
many-thirtysomething-women-
are-leaving-your-company

43 https://www.washingtonpost.com/
news/powerpost/wp/2016/09/13/
white-house-women-are-now-in-
the-room-where-it-happens/

44 http://www.bimplus.co.uk/news/
bim-comm3unity-re3acts-sexist-
att4itudes/

45 http://www.justpractising.com/
events/sexism-in-construction-
awards-not-just-a-joke/

46 http://www.justpractising.com/
events/sexism-at-construction-
awards-a-follow-up/

47 http://leanin.org/education/what-
works-for-women-at-work-part-1-
prove-it-again/

48 http://research.wpcarey.asu.edu/
management-entrepreneurship/
unfair-to-the-fairer-sex-female-
ceos-face-more-shareholder-
activism/

49 https://www.fastcompany.com/
3048342/the-future-of-work/the-
business-case-for-women-in-the-c-
suite

50 http://psychology.exeter.ac.uk/
research/glasscliff/

51 https://hbr.org/2014/08/why-
women-dont-apply-for-jobs-
unless-theyre-100-qualified

52 https://www.sussex.ac.uk/
webteam/gateway/file.

php?name=gendered-wording-in-job-adverts.pdf&site=7

53 http://asq.sagepub.com/content/56/4/622.short

54 http://www2.warwick.ac.uk/fac/soc/economics/news/2016/9/new_study_suggests_women_do_ask_for_pay_rises_but_dont_get_them

55 https://www.forbes.com/sites/kimelsesser/2016/09/07/research-stating-women-ask-for-pay-raises-as-much-as-men-is-just-wrong/#7b9fd40c3983

56 http://www.womendontask.com/stats.html

57 http://qz.com/624346/america-loves-women-like-hillary-clinton-as-long-as-theyre-not-asking-for-a-promotion/

58 http://nymag.com/thecut/2012/12/hillary-clinton-catch-22.html

59 http://time.com/4357406/hillary-clinton-sexist-donald-trump/

60 https://www.tuc.org.uk/sites/default/files/SexualHarassmentreport2016.pdf

61 http://gender.bitc.org.uk/all-resources/research-articles/project-28-40-report

62 https://www.tuc.org.uk/sites/default/files/SexualHarassmentreport2016.pdf

63 http://gender.bitc.org.uk/all-resources/research-articles/project-28-40-report

64 http://www.nytimes.com/2016/10/08/us/donald-trump-tape-transcript.html

65 Quoted in http://gender.bitc.org.uk/all-resources/research-articles/project-28-40-report

66 http://www.nber.org/papers/w19276.pdf?new_window=1

67 http://www.parliament.uk/about/living-heritage/transformingsociety/private-

68 http://www.ons.gov.uk/employmentandlabourmarket/peopleinwork/earningsandworkinghours/bulletins/annualsurveyofhoursandearnings/2016provisionalresults#gender-pay-differences

69 http://www.legislation.gov.uk/ukpga/1970/41/section/9/enacted

70 https://www.theguardian.com/money/2014/aug/12/gender-pay-gap-coalition-scheme

71 http://radix.org.uk/wp-content/uploads/2016/09/Radix-Working-Late-Report.pdf (p. 13)

72 https://www.tuc.org.uk/sites/default/files/UnequalTrappedControlled.pdf

73 https://www.theinformation.com/introducing-the-informations-future-list

74 https://techcrunch.com/2016/04/19/the-first-comprehensive-study-on-women-in-venture-capital/

75 https://techcrunch.com/2015/10/06/s23p-racial-gender-diversity-venture/

76 https://hbr.org/2016/07/research-the-gender-gap-in-startup-success-disappears-when-women-fund-women?utm_campaign=HBR&utm_source=linkedin&utm_medium=social

77 http://www.pnas.org/content/111/12/4427.full.pdf

78 https://30percentclub.org/assets/uploads/30__Club_Investors_Statement_of_Intent.pdf

79 https://www.theguardian.com/business/2014/jun/26/glencore-male-board-patrice-merrin-woman

80 http://www.ons.gov.uk/people populationandcommunity/

populationandmigration/
populationestimates/bulletins/
2011censuspopulationestimates
fortheunitedkingdom/2012-12-17

81 https://hbr.org/2010/09/why-
men-still-get-more-promotions-
than-women

82 http://www.theatlantic.com/
entertainment/archive/2015/03/
how-to-get-more-women-on-tv/
386378/

6. CULTURE

1 https://www.youtube.com/
playlist?list=PLbyvawx
ScNbuGmgshrhbBrBxKwJLmM7i8

2 http://news.bbc.co.uk/onthisday/
hi/dates/stories/may/18/
newsid_2380000/2380649.stm

3 http://www.independent.
co.uk/voices/were-all-proud-
tim-peake-but-we-shouldnt-
have-to-denigrate-a-womans-
achievements-at-the-same-time-
a6775546.html

4 http://www.anorak.co.uk/390317/
news/the-guardian-erases-helen-
sharman-from-history-in-the-race-
to-praise-tim-peake-the-first-brit-
in-space.html/

5 http://womeninjournalism.co.uk/
wp-content/uploads/2012/10/
Seen_but_not_heard.pdf

6 http://www.city.ac.uk/news/2015/
november/research-reveals-
success-of-campaign-to-increase-
proportion-of-women-experts-in-
news

7 https://www.strudel.org.uk/
panelshows/

8 https://twitter.com/
chicagotribune/status/
762401317050605568

9 https://www.thecut.com/2016/08/
olympic-swimmer-world-record-
husband.html

10 https://www.theguardian.com/
news/datablog/2012/dec/10/
women-in-theatre-research-full-
results#data

11 http://gap.hks.harvard.edu/
orchestrating-impartiality-impact-
%E2%80%9Cblind%E2%80%9D-
auditions-female-musicians

12 http://www.fawcettsociety.org.
uk/blog/east-london-fawcett-arts-
campaign/

13 http://www.nytimes.com/2016/09/
15/movies/geena-davis-inclusion-
quotient-research.html?_r=1

14 http://seejane.org/wp-content/
uploads/gdiq-reel-truth-women-
arent-seen-or-heard-automated-
analysis.pdf

15 https://www.washingtonpost.
com/news/wonk/wp/2016/01/
25/researchers-have-discovered-
a-major-problem-with-the-little-
mermaid-and-other-disney-
movies/

16 https://stephenfollows.com/
gender-of-film-crews/

17 http://www.hollywoodreporter.
com/news/geena-davis-two-easy-
steps-664573

18 http://seejane.org/wp-content/
uploads/gdiq-reel-truth-women-
arent-seen-or-heard-automated-
analysis.pdf page 6

19 http://www.thedailybeast.
com/articles/2016/08/24/the-
hacking-of-leslie-jones-exposes-
misogynoir-at-its-worst.html

20 http://www.bbc.co.uk/news/
world-us-canada-36842710

21 http://www.independent.co.uk/
news/people/leslie-jones-website-
suffers-massive-hack-with-
personal-photos-and-information-
leaked-a7208121.html

22 http://therepresentationproject.
org/film/miss-representation/

23 http://www.huffingtonpost.
co.uk/2015/03/14/jo-swinson-
sexism_n_6869688.html

24 https://twitter.com/joswinson/
status/719531889011331072

25 http://www.dnaindia.com/
lifestyle/books-and-more-write-
like-a-man-can-women-write-as-
well-as-men-2050875

26 http://www.stylist.co.uk/books/
my-novel-wasn-t-the-problem-it-
was-me-catherine-authors-male-
pseudonym-experiment-reveals-
gender-bias-in-publishing

27 http://blog.english-heritage.
org.uk/women-written-history-
interview-bettany-hughes/

28 http://invisiblewomen.org.uk/
vitalstatistics

29 http://invisiblewomen.org.uk/
timesletters

30 http://www.bjr.org.uk/archive
+why_do_the_best_jobs_go
_to_men and http://womenin
journalism.co.uk/why-is-british-
public-life-dominated-by-men/

31 http://www.endviolenceagainst
women.org.uk/data/files/
resources/43/EVAW-Coalition-
Submission-to-the-Leveson-
Inquiry-FINAL-Jan-2012.doc

32 Editions looked at: 05/03/2016,
02/04/2016, 18/06/2016,
27/08/2016, 03/09/2016 and
26/12/2015.

33 http://findingada.com/about/who-
was-ada/

34 http://www.telegraph.co.uk/
history/world-war-two/11323312/
Bletchley-the-womens-story.html

35 https://www.theguardian.com/
lifeandstyle/2014/oct/13/ada-
lovelace-day-women-computing-
60s

36 http://www.npr.org/sections/
money/2014/10/21/357629765/
when-women-stopped-coding

37 https://www.theguardian.com/
technology/2015/oct/18/martha-
lane-fox-technology-women-
computing

38 https://doteveryone.org.uk/about-
us/

39 https://www.theguardian.com/
technology/2016/apr/12/the-dark-
side-of-guardian-comments

40 http://www.ece.umd.edu/News/
news_story.php?id=1788

41 http://www.telegraph.co.uk/
news/2016/06/04/nigel-farage-
migrants-could-pose-sex-attack-
threat-to-britain/

42 http://www.reclaimtheinternet.
com/

43 http://www.un.org/en/universal-
declaration-human-rights/index.
html

44 http://www.xojane.com/issues/
why-im-masquerading-as-a-
bearded-white-hipster-guy-on-
twitter

45 https://hbr.org/2009/06/new-
twitter-research-men-follo

46 https://medium.com/the-web-we-
make/the-year-i-didnt-retweet-
men-79403a7eade1#.vtql7xh70

47 https://www.asa.org.uk/Rulings/
Adjudications/2013/7/Wynndel-
Property-Management-Ltd/SHP_
ADJ_231484.aspx#.V-UMD1QrLIU

48 https://www.theguardian.com/
media/2014/jun/06/twitter-trolls-
abuse-olympic-swimmer-rebecca-
adlington

49 http://www.telegraph.co.uk/
women/womens-life/10589168/
Vile-Twitter-abuse-Beth-Tweddle-
Women-its-time-to-shout-back-at-
trolls.html

50 http://www.bbc.co.uk/news/uk-
23214821

51 http://seejane.org/wp-content/
uploads/gender-bias-without-
borders-executive-summary.pdf

52 http://uk.businessinsider.com/donald-trump-carly-fiorina-face-insult-2015-9?op=1?r=US&IR=T

53 http://time.com/4037757/donald-trump-carly-fiorina-republican-debate/

54 https://www.fastcompany.com/3026265/work-smart/always-wear-the-same-suit-obamas-presidential-productivity-secrets

55 http://www.telegraph.co.uk/news/bbc/12195121/Louise-Minchin-complains-about-decision-to-hand-Dan-Walker-plum-position-on-BBC-Breakfast-sofa.html

56 https://www.theguardian.com/commentisfree/2016/mar/17/misogyny-bbc-breakfast-sofa-seating-women-sexism

57 https://www.theguardian.com/film/2015/may/21/maggie-gyllenhaal-too-old-hollywood

58 http://adage.com/article/global-news/advertising-u-k-ad-group-slaps-olay-doctored-pic/141121/

59 http://www.bbc.co.uk/news/health-35501487

60 http://www.which.co.uk/news/2006/01/cosmetic-surgery-increase-58720

61 http://www.independent.co.uk/news/uk/home-news/think-lauren-bacall-not-marilyn-monroe-the-clifford-chance-guide-to-women-speaking-in-public-8905075.html

62 http://news.bbc.co.uk/1/hi/england/south_yorkshire/3130654.stm

63 http://www.forbes.com/sites/raquellaneri/2010/09/24/appearances-do-matter-hillary-clintons-hair-clip-controversy/#139bc0a91a22

64 https://www.theguardian.com/fashion/2014/jun/10/hillary-clinton-scrunchie-hairstyle-accessory

65 http://www.thewrap.com/robin-thicke-says-miley-cyrus-vmas-controversy-video/

66 https://www.theguardian.com/music/2013/oct/03/sinead-o-connor-open-letter-miley-cyrus

67 http://mashable.com/2013/10/03/miley-cyrus-letter-sinead-oconnor/#Z5de.Doqnaqj

68 http://spicegirls.wikia.com/wiki/1997_BRIT_Awards and http://www.telegraph.co.uk/music/what-to-listen-to/brit-awards-most-controversial-moments-in-pictures/the-spice-girls-and-geris-union-jack-dress-1997---ginger-spice-g/

69 http://www.dailymail.co.uk/home/you/article-492706/The-dark-secret-raunchy-pop-sensation-Rihannas-past.html

70 http://fashion.telegraph.co.uk/article/TMG8876913/Dakota-Fannings-Oh-Lola-advert-for-Marc-Jacobs-is-banned.html

71 http://www.mediaed.org/discussion-guides/Killing-Us-Softly-4-Discussion-Guide.pdf

72 http://www.adweek.com/brand-marketing/men-appear-in-ads-4-times-more-than-women-according-to-research-revealed-at-cannes/

73 https://www.asa.org.uk/asset/2DF6E028-9C47-4944-850D00DAC5ECB45B.C3A4D948-B739-4AE4-9F17CA2110264347/

74 http://www.womenactionmedia.org/2013/07/03/update-on-fbrape-campaign-progress/

75 http://www.thedrum.com/news/2013/06/07/fbrape-campaign-what-does-it-mean-facebook-and-what-can-brands-take-backlash

76 http://www.womenactionmedia.org/examples-of-gender-based-hate-speech-on-facebook/

Endnotes

77 http://www.huffingtonpost.com/
soraya-chemaly/freethenipple-
facebook-changes_b_5473467.
html
78 http://mashable.com/2015/
09/30/do-i-have-boobs-now/
#.AJpZXYBskqP
79 https://www.theguardian.com/
technology/2015/nov/03/
facebook-instagram-do-i-have-
boobs-now
80 https://twitter.com/CourtDemone/
status/720778555840278528
81 http://qz.com/777855/norway-
facebook-censorship-norway-is-
furious-with-facebook-and-its-
algorithms-for-censoring-the-
pulitzer-prize-winning-war-photo-
of-a-young-girl-fleeing-a-napalm-
attack-the-terror-of-war/
82 http://fortune.com/2014/08/29/
how-tech-companies-compare-in-
employee-diversity/
83 http://alisonbechdel.blogspot.
co.uk/2005/08/rule.html
84 http://bechdeltest.com/
85 http://imgur.com/a/612eD#0
86 http://kevinbolk.deviantart.
com/art/Avengers-Booty-Ass-
emble-270937785
87 https://www.gov.uk/government/
uploads/system/uploads/
attachment_data/file/372128/
Drink_Drive_IPA_Paper_2012.pdf
88 http://www.independent.co.uk/
life-style/when-anna-and-beth-
kissed-margaret-anna-friel-plays-
brooksides-lesbian-pin-up-
monique-roffey-met-her-1440368.
html
89 http://www.cinemaofchange.com/
films-that-changed-the-world-
philadelphia-1993/
90 http://www.huffingtonpost.
com/kortney-ryan-ziegler-phd/
orange-is-the-new-black-trans-
women_b_3636402.html

91 http://www.bbc.co.uk/news/
blogs-ouch-24988596
92 http://www.bbc.co.uk/blogs/
thearchers/entries/69bbde62-
1f79-4b2d-9430-31ecf5941725
93 http://womeninjournalism.
co.uk/why-is-british-public-life-
dominated-by-men/
94 http://www.dailydot.com/irl/troll-
busters-online-harassment/

7. SPORT

1 http://horsetalk.co.nz/2014/10/
06/sidesaddles-suffragettes-fight-
ride-vote/#axzz40FUBqqlw
2 http://www.annielondonderry.
com/womenWheels.html
3 http://www.tejvan.co.uk/
marathons/first_woman_
marathon/
4 https://deadspin.com/why-it-took-
90-years-for-womens-ski-jumping-
to-make-the-1520520342
5 http://www.theguardian.com/
sport/2014/aug/08/nicola-adams-
boxing-was-my-path
6 http://www.independent.co.uk/
news/pmt-makes-women-unfit-to-
box-1144391.html
7 http://www.letourentier.com/
8 http://www.letourentier.com/new-
page-1/
9 http://www.theguardian.com/
sport/2013/apr/15/sir-stirling-
moss-women-f1
10 http://www.telegraph.co.uk/
culture/chess/11548840/Nigel-
Short-Girls-just-dont-have-the-
brains-to-play-chess.html
11 http://scienceblogs.com/
notrocketscience/2008/12/23/
why-are-there-so-few-female-
chess-grandmasters/
12 http://www.telegraph.co.uk/news/
uknews/11690553/Nigel-Short-
shrill-feminists-have-turned-me-

into-the-pantomine-villain-of-chess.html

13 http://www.theguardian.com/world/2015/apr/20/nigel-short-uk-grandmaster-men-hardwired-better-chess-players-women

14 http://kathrineswitzer.com/about-kathrine/1967-boston-marathon-the-real-story/

15 http://kathrineswitzer.com/about-kathrine/kathrines-full-bio/

16 http://www.nytimes.com/2014/02/12/sports/olympics/ski-jumping-for-joy-and-for-medals.html?_r=0

17 http://edition.cnn.com/2012/08/30/world/europe/judit-polgar/index.html

18 https://www.standard.co.uk/sport/football/arsenal-drop-ladies-reference-from-womens-team-in-statement-of-unity-a3598981.html

19 Interview, 19/2/2016.

20 http://www.ey.com/Publication/vwLUAssets/EY-where-will-you-find-your-next-leader/$FILE/where-will-you-find-your-next-leader-report-from-EY-and-espnw.pdf

21 https://www.womeninsport.org/resources/changing-the-game-for-girls-policy-report/ (p. 30)

22 https://www.gov.uk/government/uploads/system/uploads/attachment_data/file/447730/Taking_Part_2014_15_Child_Report_Repaired_.pdf (p. 34)

23 http://www.bbc.co.uk/sport/get-inspired/35281556

24 https://www.womeninsport.org/wp-content/uploads/2015/04/Changing-the-Game-for-Girls-Policy-Report.pdf (p. 6)

25 http://www.bbc.co.uk/sport/get-inspired/35281556

26 http://www.thisgirlcan.co.uk/activities/

27 https://www.youthsporttrust.org/resource-library

28 https://www.womeninsport.org/resources/changing-the-game-for-girls-teachers-toolkit/

29 http://www.theguardian.com/sport/2013/jan/14/nicole-cooke-retirement-statement

30 http://gritandrock.net/

31 http://www.bbc.co.uk/sport/formula1/35311058

32 Interview, 24/2/2016.

33 http://www.bbc.co.uk/news/blogs-trending-33411415

34 http://www.theguardian.com/lifeandstyle/womens-blog/2014/mar/13/womens-sport-newspaper-coverage-birmingham-university

35 http://www.pressgazette.co.uk/martin-samuel-named-top-uk-sports-journalist-press-gazette-top-50-poll

36 https://www.womeninsport.org/wp-content/uploads/2015/04/Media-Stats-Pack-June-2015.pdf?938151

37 http://www.mirror.co.uk/news/uk-news/bbc-to-review-spoty-shortlisting-after-279817

38 16/6/2016, 12/3/2015, 10/4/2014, 10/2/2013, 12/5/2012.

39 https://www.theguardian.com/tv-and-radio/2017/mar/05/bbc-sport-barbara-slater-transformation-in-womens-coverage

40 http://www.telegraph.co.uk/comment/columnists/borisjohnson/9437340/Heres-20-jolly-good-reasons-to-feel-cheerful-about-the-Games.html

41 https://www.theguardian.com/sport/2016/aug/17/caster-semenya-800m-heat-gender-controversy-rio-olympics

42 http://www.telegraph.co.uk/sport/
cricket/12080309/Chris-Gayle-
accused-of-sexism-after-asking-
female-cricket-presenter-out-on-a-
date.html

43 http://www.dailymail.co.uk/sport/
sportsnews/article-3449237/
This-women-stay-kitchen-mouths-
shut-BT-Sport-football-presenter-
reveals-shocking-misogynistic-
abuse-received-Twitter.html

44 http://time.com/3677729/
eugenie-bouchard-ian-cohen-
twirl-australian-open/

45 http://www.mirror.co.uk/sport/
cricket/more-people-watched-
womens-cricket-10868351

46 http://blogs.lse.ac.uk/lsereview
ofbooks/2014/12/22/book-review-
female-football-fans-community-
identity-and-sexism-by/

47 'Prime Time', Women in Sport,
2009.

48 http://www.independent.co.uk/
sport/football/womens-football-
england-commercial-landscape-
and-why-its-in-better-shape-ever-
a7875181.html

49 http://www.totalsportek.com/
tennis/grand-slam-titles-winners-
mens-women/

50 http://www.forbes.com/athletes/
#/tab:overall

51 https://www.forbes.com/sites/
kurtbadenhausen/2015/08/12/
the-worlds-highest-paid-female-
athletes-2015/#2ca244016746

52 http://www.buzzfeed.com/
lindseyadler/52-nba-players-
who-make-more-than-the-entire-
wnba#.cygdEJJkO

53 http://www.standard.co.uk/sport/
football/sports-minister-helen-
grant-calls-for-prize-money-
equality-in-men-and-womens-
sport-9823303.html

54 http://www.wimbledon.com/
en_GB/tickets/tickets_what_you_
need_to_know.html

55 http://espn.go.com/espnw/news-
commentary/article/8116142/
tandon-women-players-make-less-
male-counterparts

56 http://www.independent.co.uk/
life-style/wimbledon-2017-sexist-
women-three-sets-tennis-players-
championship-men-five-williams-
murray-a7825086.html

57 http://qz.com/224794/if-you-care-
about-equality-for-women-watch-
tennis/

58 http://www.nytimes.com/2006/
04/26/arts/television/the-legacy-
of-billie-jean-king-an-athlete-who-
demanded.html

59 http://www.economist.com/blogs/
economist-explains/2014/07/
economist-explains-19

60 'Trophy Women', Women in Sport,
2015.

61 http://www.telegraph.co.uk/
finance/comment/11515528/
Helena-Morrissey-Tide-turns-in-
favour-of-boat-race-women.html

62 http://www.womenssporttrust.
com/powerful-impact-of-womens-
sport-recognised-at-inaugural-
beagamechanger-awards/

63 http://olympics.time.com/2012/
08/09/olympic-homophobia-
why-are-there-so-few-openly-gay-
athletes/

8. VIOLENCE

1 https://www.gov.uk/government/
publications/revenge-porn

2 https://www.nspcc.org.uk/
fighting-for-childhood/news-
opinion/40-percent-teenage-girls-
pressured-into-sex/

3 http://new.girlguiding.org.uk/
girls-attitudes-survey-2014

4 https://www.gov.uk/government/
news/schools-to-teach-21st-
century-relationships-and-sex-
education

5 http://thetab.com/uk/warwick/
2015/10/14/dont-need-consent-
lessons-9925

6 http://www.nus.org.uk/en/news/
nus-research-reveals-one-in-
four-students-suffer-unwelcome-
sexual-advances/

7 http://www.nus.org.uk/Global/
Campaigns/That's%20what%20
she%20said%20full%20report%20
Final%20web.pdf

8 http://www.theguardian.com/
education/2015/sep/06/
government-inquiry-violence-
against-women-at-universities

9 https://www.nus.org.uk/PageFiles/
12238/Thats%20What%20She%
20Said%20-%20Full%20Report
%20(1).pdf (pp. 44 and 48)

10 http://www(.ucl.ac.uk/news/news-
articles/1113/26112013-Results-
from-third-National-Survey-of-
Sexual-Attitudes-and-Lifestyles

11 https://medium.com/human-
development-project/a-letter-to-
the-man-who-tried-to-rape-me-
3a18c17d8eb9

12 https://counterproductiverubbish.
wordpress.com/2015/04/28/28-
05-2015/

13 https://www.thesun.co.uk/
archives/news/154589/ban-
whistling-and-youll-have-to-stop-
girls-ogling-poldark-actor-and-
beckham/

14 https://www.sundaypost.com/
news/poppy-be-smart-and-
quietly-savour-cheeky-flattery-
while-you-can/

15 http://www.express.co.uk/news/
uk/573312/Police-blasted-
investigating-builders-wolf-
whistled-woman

16 http://www.express.co.uk/news/
uk/573759/Wolf-whistle-builder-
was-jailed-for-train-attack

17 http://fra.europa.eu/sites/default/
files/fra-2014-vaw-survey-main-
results-apr14_en.pdf

18 http://www.stopstreetharassment.
org/2014/01/lavernecox/

19 http://www.theatlantic.com/
politics/archive/2014/07/black-
women-street-harassment-even-if-
you-dont-like-it-youre-supposed-
to-appear-that-you-do/375175/

20 http://www.curvemag.com/
News/Why-Do-Hundreds-of-Men-
Want-to-Rape-and-Kill-Coralie-
Alison-630/

21 https://twitter.com/coraliealison/
status/625960427210407938

22 http://www.bbc.co.uk/news/uk-
25886026

23 https://twitter.com/jessphillips/
status/659881405669732352/
photo/1?ref_src=twsrc%5Etfw

24 https://www.theguardian.com/
commentisfree/2017/feb/14/
racism-misogyny-politics-online-
abuse-minorities

25 https://www.amnesty.org.uk/
online-violence-women-mps

26 http://www.nytimes.com/
packages/pdf/nyregion/
city_room/20070726_
hiddeninplainsight.pdf

27 http://www.independent.co.uk/
life-style/men-penis-pictures-
airdrop-public-transport-bus-train-
trend-bluetooth-sexual-images-
a7892136.html

28 http://www.france24.com/
en/20150416-france-women-
harassment-metro-transport-rights

29 http://www.citylab.com/commute/
2012/02/why-women-only-transit-
options-have-caught/1171/

30 http://www.mirror.co.uk/news/
uk-news/mind-gender-gap-whats-
wrong-6323340

31 http://india.blogs.nytimes.com/
2012/12/18/outrage-in-delhi-
after-latest-gang-rape-case/

32 http://www.thehindu.com/
news/national/delhi-gang-
rape-chronology-of-events/
article11862316.ece

33 http://www.theguardian.com/
world/2013/dec/10/delhi-rape-
one-year-anything-changed-india-
women

34 http://indianexpress.com/article/
india/crime/nothing-in-india-has-
changed-since-december-16-
2012-nirbhayas-father/

35 http://www.bbc.co.uk/news/
magazine-31698154

36 http://messymatters.com/rape/

37 http://www.bbc.co.uk/blogs/
thereporters/markeaston/2008/
07/rape_a_complex_crime.html

38 http://www.cps.gov.uk/legal/
a_to_c/controlling_or_coercive_
behaviour/

39 http://www.cps.gov.uk/
publications/docs/cps_vawg_
report_2016.pdf

40 http://foi.west-midlands.police.
uk/wp-content/uploads/2016/
05/4641_attachment_01.pdf and
https://www.avonandsomerset.
police.uk/about-us/freedom-of-
information/previous-foi-requests/
controlling-or-coercive-behaviour/
controllingcoercive-behaviour-
statistics/

41 http://www.ons.gov.uk/ons/rel/
crime-stats/crime-statistics/focus-
on-violent-crime-and-sexual-
offences--2013-14/rpt-chapter-2.
html#tab-Victims-aged-16-years-
and-over

42 http://www.heraldscotland.
com/news/13079970.Stranger_
murder_myth_dispelled/

43 http://apps.who.int/iris/bitstream/
10665/85239/1/9789241564625_
eng.pdf

44 http://www.who.int/mediacentre/
news/releases/2013/violence_
against_women_20130620/en/

45 http://www.refuge.org.uk/get-
help-now/what-is-domestic-
violence/domestic-violence-the-
facts/

46 http://www.womensaid.org.uk/
core/core_picker/download.
asp?id=1763

47 http://www.mwnhelpline.co.uk/
issuesstep2.php?id=14

48 http://www.bbc.co.uk/news/uk-
33424644

49 https://www.gov.uk/government/
uploads/system/uploads/
attachment_data/file/597869/
Forced_Marriage_Unit_
statistics-_2016.pdf

50 http://www.voanews.com/content/
in-africa-criminalizing-marital-
rape-remains-controversial/
1786061.html

51 http://edition.cnn.com/2015/03/
05/asia/marital-rape-india/ and
http://www.aware.org.sg/2012/
12/the-right-to-protection-from-
marital-rape/

52 http://www.plan-uk.org/because-
i-am-a-girl/early-and-forced-
marriage/

53 http://www.plan-uk.org/resources/
documents/320014/

54 *Desert Flower* by Waris Dirie
(Virago, 1999)

55 http://www.unfpa.org/sites/
default/files/resource-pdf/67th_
UNGA-Resolution_adopted_on_
FGM_0.pdf

56 http://eige.europa.eu/sites/
default/files/documents/eige-
report-fgm-in-the-eu-and-croatia.
pdf

57 https://www.theguardian.com/
global-development/2013/mar/
06/uk-funds-female-genital-
mutilation-generation

58 http://www.ohchr.org/
en/newsevents/pages/
rapeweaponwar.aspx

59 http://news.bbc.co.uk/1/hi/world/
africa/3426273.stm

60 https://www.oxfam.org/sites/www.
oxfam.org/files/file_attachments/
DRC-sexual-violence-2010-04_2.
pdf (p. 30)

61 http://www.womensmediacenter.
com/women-under-siege/witness/
bosnia

62 http://www.womensmediacenter.
com/women-under-siege/witness/
burma

63 https://www.washingtonpost.com/
news/worldviews/wp/2015/08/
20/the-islamic-states-horrifying-
practice-of-sex-slavery-explained/

64 http://www.nytimes.com/2015/
08/14/world/middleeast/isis-
enshrines-a-theology-of-rape.
html?_r=1

65 http://www.
womenundersiegeproject.org/
witness/colombia

66 http://www.ilo.org/wcmsp5/
groups/public/---ed_norm/
---declaration/documents/
publication/wcms_243391.pdf
(p. 13)

67 http://www.stopthetraffik.org/the-
scale-of-human-traffiking

68 http://www.ilo.org/global/
about-the-ilo/newsroom/news/
WCMS_181961/lang--en/index.
htm

69 http://www.marieclaire.com/
politics/news/a3618/diary-
escaped-sex-slave/

70 http://www.theguardian.com/
law/2015/jan/18/i-was-sold-into-
sexual-slavery

71 https://www.unodc.org/unodc/en/
frontpage/2012/October/nigeria-
launches-anti-human-trafficking-
campaign-appoints-goodwill-
ambassadors.html

72 https://www.gov.uk/government/
uploads/system/uploads/
attachment_data/file/412667/
FMU_Stats_2014.pdf

73 http://kareningalasmith.com/
2013/04/29/this-thing-about-
male-victims/

74 http://www.nr-foundation.org.uk/
downloads/Who-Does-What-to-
Whom.pdf

75 http://www.endvawnow.org/en/
articles/300-causes-protective-
and-risk-factors-.html?next=301

76 https://www.disrespectnobody.
co.uk/

77 http://www.huffingtonpost.
com/good-men-project/this-
is-how-you-teach-kids-about-
consent_b_10360296.html

78 hhttps://www.womensaid.org.
uk/the-survivors-handbook/im-
worried-about-someone-else/

79 http://www.ihollaback.org/wp-
content/uploads/2010/09/Final-
Bystanders-Draft.png

80 http://www.actiononviolence.org.
uk/projects/asc

81 http://www.stopthetraffik.org/
campaign/taxis

82 http://www.stopthetraffik.org/
campaign/travel/what-you-can-
do/26

83 https://www.girlguiding.org.uk/
globalassets/docs-and-resources/
research-and-campaigns/girls-
attitudes-survey-2014.pdf (p. 5)

84 http://www.ihollaback.org/
resources/

85 https://www.pshe-
association.org.uk/content.
aspx?CategoryID=1161

86 https://www.gov.uk/government/
publications/female-genital-
mutilation-resource-pack/female-
genital-mutilation-resource-pack

87 https://www.gov.uk/government/
uploads/system/uploads/
attachment_data/file/322310/
HMG_Statutory_Guidance_
publication_180614_Final.pdf

88 https://www.equalityhumanrights.
com/en/advice-and-guidance/
domestic-abuse-workplace-
policies-and-managing-and-
supporting-employees

89 http://www.acas.org.uk/index.
aspx?articleid=1814

90 http://issuu.com/jaecamer/
docs/final_employer_manual_
may_2013

91 http://www.womensaid.org.
uk/domestic-violence-articles.
asp?section=000100010022
00290002&itemid=1423

92 https://www.fawcettsociety.
org.uk/Handlers/Download.
ashx?IDMF=fbf75b5f-aee4-4624-
8df4-833ffcc1a2d7 p.10

93 http://respect.uk.net/highlights-
mirabal-research-findings-respect-
accredited-domestic-violence-
perpetrator-programmes-work/

9. MEN

1 https://www.theguardian.com/
media/gallery/2010/aug/20/
loaded-magazine-covers

2 http://www.standard.co.uk/
lifestyle/esmagazine/are-men-the-
new-women-how-martin-daubney-
went-from-lads-mag-editor-to-
stayathome-dad-a3367261.html

3 http://www.ippr.org/files/
publications/attachments/
youngpeoplesexrelationships.jpg

4 https://www.offa.org.uk/
universities-and-colleges/

guidance/topic-briefings/topic-
briefing-white-british-students/
#evidence

5 http://www.hepi.ac.uk/wp-
content/uploads/2016/05/Boys-
to-Men.pdf (p. 1)

6 https://www.gov.uk/government/
uploads/system/uploads/
attachment_data/file/533618/
SFR21_2016_MainText.pdf

7 http://www.firstdiscoverers.co.uk/
men-in-childcare-implications-
gender-bias/

8 http://press.hse.gov.uk/2016/
annual-workplace-fatality-
statistics-published/

9 Agriculture has a rate of 9 deaths
per 100,000: http://www.hse.
gov.uk/statistics/tables/index.
htm#riddor

10 https://www.ons.gov.uk/
file?uri=/peoplepopulationand
community/crimeandjustice/
datasets/appendixtables
focusonviolentcrimeandsexual
offences/yearendingmarch2015/
02appendixtablesviolentcrime
andsexualoffences201415
tcm774327773.xls (Table 4.28)

11 https://www.ons.gov.uk/
peoplepopulationandcommunity/
crimeandjustice/compendium/
focusonviolentcrimeandsexual
offences/yearendingmarch2016/
domesticabusesexualassaultand
stalking

12 http://www.nr-foundation.org.uk/
downloads/Who-Does-What-to-
Whom.pdf

13 https://www.ons.gov.uk/people
populationandcommunity/crime
andjustice/compendium/focuson
violentcrimeandsexualoffences/
yearendingmarch2015/chapter2
homicide#relationship-between-
victim-and-principal-suspect
(Figure 2.4)

14 http://www.cancerresearchuk.
org/health-professional/cancer-
statistics/mortality/all-cancers-
combined#heading-Zero

15 https://www.menshealthforum.
org.uk/key-data-cancer-and-
circulatory-diseases

16 https://www.ons.gov.uk/people
populationandcommunity/births
deathsandmarriages/deaths/
bulletins/suicidesintheunited
kingdom/2015registrations

17 https://storify.com/cbccommunity/
six-year-old-girl-writes-to-hasbro-
about-gender-im/elements/
50abb472a58047d66845c0c5

18 https://www.theguardian.com/
lifeandstyle/the-womens-blog-
with-jane-martinson/2012/nov/19/
so-few-men-gender-studies

19 http://www.andrewoswald.com/
docs/daughtersrestat08.pdf

20 https://hbr.org/2015/11/ceos-
with-daughters-run-more-
socially-responsible-firms?utm_
campaign=Socialflow&utm_
source=Socialflow&utm_
medium=Tweet

21 https://hansard.parliament.uk/
commons/2017-03-02/debates/
42672B78-03C7-44B0-9C5C-
7582EDEFECDF/International
Women%E2%80%99SDay

22 https://hansard.parliament.
uk/Commons/2016-10-27/
debates/E8D1B241-E24B-
4B01-85F9-ABCEAE678B9A/
InternationalMenSDay

23 http://gizmodo.com/exclusive-
heres-the-full-10-page-anti-
diversity-screed-1797564320

24 https://medium.com/@
yonatanzunger/so-about-
this-googlers-manifesto-
1e3773ed1788

25 http://www.breitbart.com/video/
2016/02/19/would-you-rather-
your-child-had-feminism-or-
cancer/

26 http://www.washingtontimes.com/
news/2017/jan/23/piers-morgan-
slams-man-hating-feminazis-at-
womens-/

27 http://www.telegraph.co.uk/
news/2016/06/04/nigel-farage-
migrants-could-pose-sex-attack-
threat-to-britain/

28 Such as replies to this, 'It's a
Muslim problem' https://twitter.
com/RidgeOnSunday/status/
739385585408708609

29 https://rapecrisis.org.uk/
mythsvsrealities.php

30 https://twitter.com/Surtrson/
status/755012392279543808
(see opposite)

31 https://www.collinsdictionary.
com/dictionary/english/feminism

32 https://www.theguardian.com/
politics/2013/oct/02/david-
cameron-i-am-feminist

CONCLUSION

1 https://www.vox.com/2016/11/9/
13570328/hillary-clinton-
concession-speech-full-transcript-
2016-presidential-election

2 https://www.theguardian.com/
world/2017/oct/20/women-
worldwide-use-hashtag-metoo-
against-sexual-harassment

3 https://www.thetimes.co.uk/
article/a-couple-of-misplaced-
kisses-could-end-my-career-
plwzh6n3l

4 Transcribed from event at WOW
2016

5 Quoted by Jess Phillips MP in
Hansard, 2 Mar 2017

Jossur Surtrson @Surtrson · 18 Jul 2016

Homophobic, misogynistic, racist abuse, & intimidation online is freedom of speech in practice.

> Jo Swinson ● @joswinson
>
> Homophobic, misogynistic & racist abuse & intimidation online curtail freedom of speech - so as a liberal, I support #ReclaimtheInternet

♡ 1   ↻ 1   ♡   ✉

Jossur Surtrson @Surtrson · 18 Jul 2016

@joswinson You simply hate free speech when it doesn't work in your favor. Attempting to silence it, in any form, is tyranny.

♡ 1   ↻   ♡   ✉

Jo Swinson ● @joswinson · 18 Jul 2016

so promoting respectful debate is tyranny but intimidation is free speech?

♡ 3   ↻   ♡   ᐧᶦᶦ

Jossur Surtrson @Surtrson · 18 Jul 2016

Promoting respect by wishing to shut down all free speech, despite its content, is tyranny.

♡ 1   ↻   ♡   ✉